SEX LIVES
OF THE
U.S. PRESIDENTS

SEX LIVES
OF THE
U.S. PRESIDENTS

An irreverent exposé of the Chief Executive
from George Washington to the present day

Nigel Cawthorne

First published in Great Britain in 1996
This revised edition published 2004 by

Prion
an imprint of the
Carlton Publishing Group
20 Mortimer Street
London W1T 3JW

A catalogue record for this book is available from the British
Library

ISBN 1 85375 547 8

Printed in Great Britain
by Mackays

CONTENTS

INTRODUCTION

America began its life in sexual confusion. The North American continent was discovered in 1497 by John Cabot. He was a Genoan like Christopher Columbus but Cabot sailed for England, not for Spain. Cabot wanted to name the ship built for the voyage *Matea*, after his wife, but the good shipwrights of Bristol could not spell it. So they gave it a man's name, *Matthew*, instead.

The first English colony in the Americas was Virginia, named for the 'Virgin Queen' Elizabeth I. It was established by Sir Walter Raleigh, who knew she was no virgin. He was one of Elizabeth's lovers, until he seduced Elizabeth Throckmorton, a lady of the bedchamber. Unmarried, Elizabeth I may have been, but the Virgin Queen's other lovers included Sir William Pickering; Sir Christopher Hatton; Thomas Heneage; Edward Vere, Earl of Oxford; the Duke of Alençon; Robert Dudley, Earl of Leicester and Dudley's son Robert Devereux, Earl of Essex. Virginia, indeed!

In the early eighteenth century, the governor-general of New York was Lord Cornbury. Cornbury was a veteran of the British parliament and the cousin of Queen Anne. He was also an outrageous transvestite. In 1702, he opened the New York Assembly in a gown with a hooped skirt and an ornate headdress. The kinky colonist explained that, as he was there to represent Queen Anne, he wanted to represent her as accurately as he could. Maybe he should have worn trousers – Queen Anne herself was a lesbian. She caused a scandal at the time when she rejected her aristocratic lover, Sarah Churchill, for Abigail Hill, a 'dirty chambermaid'.

Throughout the eighteenth century, the strain between the vigorous young colonies and the old country grew. Although the New England colonies were dominated by Puritans who had quit England after the failure of Cromwell's revolution, they were deeply influenced by the sexually liberated ethos of the times. America, after all, was a young country, much in need of an expanding population. The colonists' birth rate soared, while that in Britain declined.

The Pilgrim Fathers who had landed at Plymouth Rock in 1620 were, of course, above reproach; and the Founding Fathers have always been made out to be paragons of virtue. There has been mud-slinging but, by and large, the president has been revered and presidential peccadillos overlooked. When President Kennedy was smuggling air hostesses in and out of the White House, those who knew about it stayed quiet. Lyndon Johnson, another accomplished womanizer, was savaged for his prosecution of the Vietnam war, not for his singlehanded assault on the female sex.

It was only when presidential hopeful Gary Hart challenged the press to catch him out that the unholy alliance between politicians and the press fell apart, and catch him they did. His affair with jeans model Donna Rice appeared on every front page in America and blew his candidacy out of the water.

Since then George Bush has managed to parry suggestions that he had a long-term affair with an aide with a single 'No comment!' Bill Clinton got away with what can essentially be considered normal male behaviour – for a presidential candidate at least – with the support of a loyal and politically motivated wife making goo-goo eyes at him on TV. But he is not out of the woods yet. Charges of sexual harassment are pending.

A random survey of Chief Executives around the world reveals that those with the ambition to achieve high political office tend to be a highly sexed lot. The French have always got away with it. President Mitterrand openly maintained a long-term mistress. An earlier president attended orgies with his wife. French presidents would have no respect from the French people if they behaved otherwise. One French president said that if he had to form a government out of those who did not have mistresses, he would be left with a cabinet comprising only homosexuals and women.

It is only in Britain, the home of the yellow press, that government ministers are regularly savaged and forced to resign simply because they crave a more exciting sexual fare than is on offer at home. Slowly the British ethos is infecting the American press but, surely, in the land of the free, even the Chief Executive should be allowed to have his freedom. Powerful men will always want what they want – and find a way to get it. Who cares if the White House is rocking with hookers and orgies all night long, just as long as the orgiast in chief can run the country. America came through the Depression and World War II with a Martini-swigging fornicator at its helm and his wife and her lesbian lover in residence at 1600 Pennsylvania Avenue – just as Britain survived its war with a drunk in charge.

Do the American people really want their country run by automata like H. Ross Perot? I doubt it. Wouldn't you rather vote for a Yeltsin with his drunken pratfalls, a Mitterrand or a Papandreou? If not, bring back King George III or – worse – Jimmy Carter.

Surely it is better to have a man with human failings in power. At least, he can understand the rest of us, only he must not write his sexual proclivities into his manifesto. In public, as in private, life there is a premium on discretion.

1

STEPFATHER TO THE NATION

'The love of my country will be the ruling influence of my conduct,' wrote George Washington. But his love of women was stronger and it is amazing that he found the time to fight the British or found a nation.

Washington's interest in sex began on a trip to survey the Shenandoah Valley when he was sixteen years old. He was already infatuated with Frances Alexander of Fredericksburg, to whom he addressed some rather embarrassing adolescent love poetry. He bemoaned his 'poor restless heart, wounded by Cupid's dart', but he could not bring himself to tell her of his feelings. 'Ah, woe is me, that I should love and conceal; Long have I wished and never dare reveal,' he wrote excruciatingly.

However in Shenandoah, he took up with another 'Low Land Beauty' with rather more success. There is speculation that she was a Miss Grimes, who later married a man named Henry Lee. Her son, General Henry Lee – known during the War of Independence as Light Horse Harry – was a favourite of Washington's.

That December, after returning from Shenandoah, Washington met the love of his life. She was the wife of his best friend George William Fairfax, whose father, Lord

Fairfax, was Washington's patron. George Fairfax had been brought up in England where his family had made his life miserable by spreading rumours that he was a mulatto. When he came out to the colonies, a marriage was arranged with Sarah 'Sally' Cary, the eighteen-year-old daughter of a planter. Fairfax found her an acceptable wife. Washington found her unutterably lovely.

Washington would often visit Belvoir, the Fairfax's estate. He was sixteen at the time and, as Lord Fairfax observed, was 'beginning to feel the sap rising'.

At first, when he stayed at Belvoir with the Fairfaxes, Washington tried not to think about sex. He wrote to a friend 'was my heart disengaged [I might] pass my time very pleasantly, as there's a very agreeable young lady lives in the same house . . . but as that's only adding fuel to the fire, it makes me the more uneasy for, by often and unavoidably being in the company with her, revives my former passion for your Low Land Beauty, whereas was I to live more retired from young women, I might in some measure alleviate my sorrows by burying that chaste and troublesome passion in the grave of oblivion or eternal forgetfulness.'

Actually, the 'agreeable young lady' Washington mentions here was Mary Cary, Sally Fairfax's sister, but it was Sally who eventually stole his heart.

Sally was two years older than Washington, attractive, vivacious and the most fascinating woman he ever met. He was totally smitten by her and throughout his life he could not think of her without being choked with emotion.

He found relief from his infatuation in fox-hunting, English-style. Thomas Jefferson said later that he was 'the best horseman of his age and the most graceful figure that could be seen on horseback'.

Washington also took time out to compose his famous '110 Rules of Civility and Decent Behavior'. These included: 'When in company, put not your hands to any part of the body not usually discovered' and 'Put not off your clothes in the presence of others, nor go out of your chamber half dressed.' He was against spitting in the fire, killing fleas, lice and ticks in the presence of others, picking your teeth and talking with your mouth full. But the most important rules were: 'Let your recreations be manful not sinful' and 'Labour to keep alive in your breast that little spark of celestial fire called conscience'.

A tall, impressive man, Washington had light, grey-blue eyes, auburn hair and – according to several contemporaries – the largest hands and feet they had seen. It is popularly thought that the size of a man's hands and feet reflect the size of his member, so we can suppose that Washington was well endowed. Two local women would have been able to confirm this. In the summer of 1751, Washington went swimming in the Rappahannock near his mother's home, when the two women stole his clothes. The women were arrested and one of them turned state's evidence. The other, Mary McDaniel, was convicted of 'robbing the clothes of Mr George Washington when he was washing in the river' and received fifteen lashes on her bare back.

Washington was not there to see the punishment carried out. He had sailed for Barbados in September 1751, possibly to escape from an affair with the wife of a neighbour, Captain John Posey, who was heavily in debt to Washington. Mrs Posey's first son was, like Washington, inordinately tall and he rose through the ranks of the Revolutionary Army with extraordinary speed.

In 1752, Washington courted fifteen-year-old Betsy Fauntleroy, the daughter of a wealthy Richmond planter. Her father did not think that Washington was rich enough to maintain her in the manner to which she had become accustomed and she turned him down. Washington wrote to her begging her to 'revoke ... [her] cruel sentence', but she married a prosperous planter's son and died a wealthy woman. Washington consoled himself with one of the less sophisticated women in the valley. Nevertheless his infatuation with Sally Fairfax continued.

In 1753, Washington indulged his lifelong passion for uniforms and joined the Virginia militia. Sally was there to see him march off with General Braddock on a campaign to retake Fort Duquesne, in what is now Pittsburgh, from the French. She was a terrible coquette and could not resist flirting with Braddock.

Within twenty-four hours of leaving, Washington had fired off a letter to Sally. Two more letters followed in the next six weeks. When Sally failed to reply, Washington wrote to her brother and sister, asking them to persuade her to write, but it was George Fairfax's sister, having found out what was going on, who wrote to Washington, reproaching him. Washington was not to be put off.

When Braddock sent him on an errand to Williamsburg, he stopped off at Belvoir to see Sally. She rebuked him and told him to stop writing to her. He did not. If she would only send him a letter, he begged in his next missive, it would 'make me happier than the day is long'.

As it happens, his thoughts were not solely on Sally during the expedition. Encamped at Wills' Creek, the soldiers came across some Delaware Indians. Their young squaws liked the British – as Washington then was – and hung around Braddock's camp. They had small hands and feet, and soft voices. One particular squaw caught Washington's attention – Bright Lightning, the daughter of Chief White Thunder.

'The squaws bring in money aplenty,' the secretary of the expedition wrote to Governor Morris, 'the officers are scandalously fond of them.'

Eventually, the Delaware warriors got jealous and Bright Lightning and the other squaws had to be banned from the British camp for the sake of peace.

As Braddock progressed towards Fort Duquesne, his mission turned into a disaster. The column was ambushed by hostile Indians and Braddock died in the ensuing battle. Washington discharged himself bravely. Two horses were shot out from under him and four bullets tore through his clothes, miraculously, without hurting him. Already a full colonel, the twenty-three-year-old Washington assumed command of all Virginia's troops. He returned home to Mount Vernon a hero and found a letter from Sally waiting for him there. In it, Sally expressed her joy that he had returned home safely and she begged him to come to Belvoir the next day, if he was fit. If he was not, she and two other ladies would come to Mount Vernon.

Washington could hardly contain himself. The next day, he rode to the Fairfax mansion. Suddenly, Washington found that his feelings for Sally were, to some extent, reciprocated and he and Sally began an intense correspondence – though Sally repeatedly urged him to observe certain proprieties. She insisted, for example, that he did not write to her directly, rather he should communicate via a third party. The ardent young Washington took no notice and, though Sally chided him, she continued to write to him. In a brief note to her from Fort Cumberland, he wrote of his joy 'at the happy occasion of renewing a correspondence which I feared was disrelished on your part'. She even began performing womanly tasks for him, like having his shirts made.

Washington gradually began to accept the fact that he could never possess his true love, so he was constantly looking around for other women. On a visit to New York in 1756, he met Mary Eliza Philipse, who was known as 'the agreeable Miss Polly'. This was not least because of her social connections and the size of her inheritance. She was statuesque with a full, sensuous mouth and she was very wealthy. Her father owned 51,000 acres of prime New York real estate. Washington took her dancing and to a mechanical exhibition called 'The Microcosm, or World in Miniature'. Passion flared in his breast.

However, the main purpose of the trip to New York was not love, but military matters. The *Virginia Gazette* had accused Washington and his officers of 'all manner of debauchery, vice and idleness'. This was unfair. Washington was a stern disciplinarian, if anything he was rather too fond of the lash. He meted out brutal floggings of up to five hundred strokes.

In New York, Governor Shirley grilled Washington for several days on the conditions on the frontier and Polly grew impatient. Her affections turned elsewhere. Eventually she married Captain Roger Morris, who had been with Washington on the Braddock expedition.

During the War of Independence, Morris remained loyal to the British crown. Washington confiscated his house to use as his headquarters. He met Polly there again and there are indications that they had an affair.

After his trip to New York, Washington returned to Virginia and, during the winter of 1757–58 he fell ill. The doctor put him on a diet of 'jellies and such kinds of foods', but among the fourteen slaves he had inherited and the six – including a woman and her child – he had bought, there was no one at Mount Vernon capable of preparing such things, he complained. Sally came to his rescue.

Following the death of his father, George Fairfax had gone to England to sort out the estate. Sally had been left behind, alone, at Belvoir and she rode over to see Washington frequently. She prepared jellies for him, hyson tea and a special wine that was mixed with gum arabic. When

Washington rose from his sickbed, he was more in love with her than ever.

Their letters of that period are full of veiled suggestions and innuendo, but their conduct was always restrained and discreet. Even among their small circle of friends there was not a whiff of scandal.

Undoubtedly this was the high point of their affair. Soon after Washington was well again, George Fairfax returned from England and Washington set about finding himself a wife in earnest. As his heart was already taken, he decided to marry for money and started wooing Martha Custis, a widow and the richest woman in Virginia.

Martha Custis had been born Martha Dandridge on 2 June 1731 on a plantation near Williamsburg. The oldest daughter of John and Frances Dandridge, her education was limited to social and domestic skills. She displayed a natural ability as a horsewoman and as a young woman had horrified her aunt and stepmother when she rode her horse Fatima up and down the stairs of her uncle's house.

At the age of eighteen, she married wealthy planter Daniel Parke Custis, twenty years her senior, and took up residence in the Custis family home, which was called, ironically, the White House. She had four children by him, two of whom died in infancy. Her husband died in 1757, after seven years of marriage. The following year, the twenty-six-year-old Washington paid his first visit to her. He was eight months her junior. They sat in the parlour and talked. He stayed the night. A little more than a week later, he visited her again. This time he promised to marry her. She was not Sally Fairfax. Martha was plump, dowdy and rather shy. She once described herself as 'an old-fashioned housekeeper'. But Washington was sincere; after all, she was loaded. He ordered from London 'as much of the best superfine blue cotton velvet as will make a coat, a waistcoat and breeches for a tall man, with a fine silk button to suit it ... six pairs of the very latest shoes ... [and] six pairs of gloves'. At the same time, Martha sent out to have her nightgown dyed a more fashionable colour.

When Sally got wind of Washington's impending engagement, she wrote congratulating him. Although he was pleased to hear from her, he had hoped that she would have taken this last opportunity to spell out her feelings towards him. He felt he had nothing to lose and wrote back declaring his love for her – but also his resolve to go ahead with his marriage if she did not reciprocate.

'If you allow that any honour can be derived from my opposition to our present system of management, you destroy the merit of it entirely in me by attributing my anxiety to the animated prospect of possessing Mrs Custis,' he wrote. 'When – I need not name it – guess yourself. Should not my own honour and country's welfare be the excitement? 'Tis true, I profess myself a votary of love. I acknowledge that a lady is in the case, and further I confess that this lady is known to you. Yes, Madam, as well as she is to one who is too sensible of her charms to deny the power whose influence he feels and must ever submit to. I feel the force of her amiable beauties in recollection of a thousand tender passages that I could wish to obliterate. You have drawn me, dear Madam, or rather I have drawn myself, into an honest confession of a simple fact. Misconstrue not my meaning; doubt it not, nor expose it. The world has no business to know the object of my love, declared in this manner to you, when I want to conceal it. One thing, above all things in this world I wish to know, and only one person of your acquaintance can solve that, or guess my meaning. But adieu to this, till happier times, if I ever shall see them.' By comparison, Washington's letters to Martha are pedestrian.

Sally's reply has never been found. She did respond because, on 25 September 1758, Washington wrote again, still desperate for some declaration of love from Sally: 'Dear Madam, Do we still misunderstand the true meaning of each other's letters? I think it must appear so, though I would feign hope the contrary as I cannot speak plainer with. But I'll say no more and leave you to guess the rest ... '

In this letter, Washington also alluded to the play *Cato* by Joseph Addison and says that he would be 'doubly happy in being the Juba to such a Marcia as you must make'. In the play, Juba asks Marcia what he must do to win her love. She replies that he must make 'any woman but Marcia happy' for 'while Cato lives, his daughter has no right to love or hate but as his choice directs'.

Washington set about trying to make Martha happy. He sent to Philadelphia for a ring and at 1 p.m. on 6 January 1759, after what would have been considered a whirlwind romance, they married in front of forty guests. The ceremony was brief; the reception formal.

They honeymooned at the White House, while renovations were being completed at Mount Vernon. When they were completed, Washington moved his ready-made family there. Martha was a popular addition to the household. Later a slave at Mount Vernon would say: 'The General was only a man, but Mrs Washington was perfect.'

Within a year, Washington was writing to a friend: 'I am now I believe fixed at this seat with an agreeable consort for life and hope to find more happiness in retirement than I ever experienced amidst the wide and bustling world.'

In later life, he compared unfavourably 'the giddy round of promiscuous pleasure' he enjoyed in his youth with the 'domestic felicity' he found in marriage. He summed up his attitude to marriage in a letter to his stepdaughter. He advised her not to 'look for perfect felicity before you consent to wed. Nor conceived, from the fine tales the poets and lovers of old have told us of the transports of mutual love, that heaven has taken its abode on earth. Nor do not deceive yourself in supposing that the only means by which these are to be obtained is to drink deep of the cup and revel in an ocean of love. Love is a mighty pretty thing, but, like all other delicious things, it is cloying; and when the first transports of the passion begin to subside, which it assuredly will do, and yield, oftentimes too late, to more sober reflections, it serves to evince that love is too dainty a food to live on alone, and ought not to be considered further than as a necessary ingredient for that matrimonial happiness which results from a combination of causes: none of which are of greater importance than that the object on whom it is placed should possess good sense, a good disposition, and the means of supporting you in the way you have been brought up. Such qualifications cannot fail to attract (after marriage) your esteem and regard into which or into disgust, sooner or later love naturally resolves itself . . . Be assured, and experience will convince you that there is no truth more certain than that all our enjoyments fall short of our expectations, and to none does it apply with more force than to the gratification of the passions.'

Later still he wrote to his granddaughter telling her that 'men and women feel the same inclinations to each other now that they always have done' and warned: 'In the composition of the human frame there is a good deal of inflammable matter, however dormant it may lie. When the torch is put to it, that which is within you may burst into a blaze.'

But in marriage, he said, 'the madness ceases and all is quiet again. Why? not because there is any diminution in the charms of the lady, but because there is an end of hope.'

For Washington, though, this was not the whole story. The inflammable material would burst back into a blaze with the war, but for those first years of marriage the madness had ceased and for the moment, he devoted himself to the management of their joint estate and the rearing of Martha's children.

Martha had brought to the marriage livestock and goods worth almost £20,000, along with three hundred slaves. Washington was as brutal to the slaves as he was to his troops. Men were forced to work even when ill. Runaways were hunted down and severely flogged. Children were left without clothes or blankets. One died of the mange. He was no better with the female slaves. In his diaries, Washington refers quite dispassionately to this or that slave woman as 'a wench of mine'. He often had the women flogged too.

During his presidency, one female slave ran away from Washington's house in Philadelphia. He wanted her hunted down and punished for her 'ingratitude'. Such things may be quite all right in Virginia, he was told, but in Pennsylvania – a free state – the result would be a riot.

Washington was particularly harsh on 'nightwalking' – that is carousing in the slave quarters – because, he complained, it left his servants and field hands 'unfit for the duties of the day'. He knew what was going on because there is every indication that, like many Virginia planters, he visited women in the slave quarters at night himself.

After Washington's marriage, he still saw Sally. In fact, Sally and George Fairfax were regular visitors at Mount Vernon. Mrs Fairfax even attended Mrs Washington on her sickbed when Martha had the measles. Behind the backs of their respective spouses, Sally and Washington kept up a clandestine correspondence.

Then in September 1774, Sally Fairfax fell ill. The medical attention she required could only be found in Europe, so she and her husband sailed for England. Washington was heartbroken to see his love go. To console himself he bought £169-worth of her possessions, including the bolster and pillows from her bed. The Fairfaxes were stranded in England by the War of Independence and never returned.

Even though they slept together, George and Martha Washington never had children of their own. There has been a great deal of speculation about the reason for this. Martha had given birth to four children in her previous marriage, so she was certainly fertile. Author James T. Flexner concludes that Washington was sterile. Certainly, there is nothing in his behaviour to suggest that he was impotent. He was fond of women, enjoyed their company and had a passion for dancing. He and Matha shared a bedroom at Mount Vernon. However, he shared the eighteenth-century fear of bathing so, presumably, smelt a lot, especially in the hot Virginia summers.

A proud man and a natural athlete, Washington never reconciled himself to the fact that he may not have children. In his later years, he came to believe that, if Martha died and he were to remarry a 'girl', he might yet father an heir. Plainly, he was sexually potent.

Washington tried to be a good father to Martha's children. Her son Jack was a constant worry to him. Washington engaged a live-in tutor and kept a constant eye on the boy's studies. When that did not work out, Jack was sent to a school run by the Reverend Jonathan Boucher. Soon his schoolmasters were complaining of Jack's laziness and Boucher wrote that never had he known a lad 'so exceedingly indolent, or so surprisingly voluptuous'.

Boucher also complained that Jack had 'a propensity to the female sex, which I am at a loss how to judge, much more how to describe. One would suppose nature had intended him for some Asiatic prince.'

Jack quit school without his parents' permission and enrolled at King's College, which later became Columbia University. There, without even consulting his parents, he got engaged to Nelly Calvert, the daughter of an illegitimate son of the fifth Lord Baltimore.

Washington intervened. He wrote to Mr Calvert saying that Jack must finish his education before he got married, and hurried the boy off to New York. There he cut a swathe, living up to the reputation of an 'Asiatic prince'. He finally married, not to Nelly, at nineteen and was known generally as a wealthy idler. However, when the War of Independence came, he served as an aide to his stepfather. He died of 'camp fever' shortly after in the battle of Yorktown. Otherwise he would probably have turned out like Washington's brother who married five times.

In his book *The Making of the President 1789*, author Marvin Kitman claims that Washington himself became an accomplished womanizer, who spent little time with his wife. Kitman comes up with an 'A' list of women he thinks Washington slept with. These include Kitty Greene; leading Federalist Lucy Flucker Knox; the wife of the foragemaster-general of the army, Mrs Clement Biddle; the wife of another of his generals, Elizabeth Gates, who often appeared dressed in men's clothes; the wife of Aaron Burr, Theodosia Prevost Burr; socialite Lady Kitty Alexander Duer; the daughter of a tavern keeper, Phoebe Fraunces; Eliza Powel; Mrs William Bingham and lady poetess Mrs Perez Morton.

Kitman's 'B' list includes the two daughters of Mrs Watkings of Paramus, New Jersey, where Washington stayed one night; Benjamin Franklin's goddaughter, Mrs Bache, who danced the night away with Washington at his twentieth wedding anniversary ball; a Mary Gibbons who

Washington met during the war and was supposed to have 'maintained genteelly in Hoboken, New Jersey,' afterwards; and an unemployed seamstress named Betsy Ross.

The Continental Congresses in Philadelphia and the War of Independence certainly gave Washington the opportunity to spend a lot of time away from Martha. His predilection for young women led to a scandal known as the 'Washerwoman Kate Affair'.

It seems that a Congressman Harrison acted as Washington's procurer in Philadelphia while Washington was at the front. In a letter to Washington, Harrison wrote: 'As I was in the pleasing task of writing to you a little noise occasioned to turn my head around, and who should appear but pretty little Kate, the washerwoman's daughter, over the way, clean, trim, and rosy as the morning. I snatched the golden glorious opportunity, and but for that cursed antidote to love, Sukey [his wife, Mrs Harrison], I had fitted her for my General against his return. We were obliged to part, but not till we had contrived to meet again; if she keeps the appointment I shall relish a week's longer stay – I give you now and then some of these adventures to amuse you and unbend your mind from the cares of war.'

The letter was intercepted, found its way into the hands of the *Boston Weekly News-Letter* and was picked up by the *Gentlemen's Magazine* in London. The story then became the nub of a play which opened on Broadway with the rather unwieldy title of *The Battle of Brooklyn: A Farce of Two Acts: As It Was Performed on Long Island, on Tuesday the 27th day of 1776, by the Representatives of Americans, Assembled at Philadelphia.*

Throughout the War of Independence, the British used sexual propaganda against Washington. Rumours were spread that he had mistresses – both black and white

– throughout the colonies. It was also said that he was a woman dressed in men's clothing which explained why he had fathered no children by Martha.

In fact, the British propaganda was not wholly without foundation. During the war, Washington billetted himself at various well-appointed mansions and enjoyed the attentions of the pretty daughters of the house. He would get them to sing for him and he would enjoy watching his aides flirt with them.

He also enjoyed the flirtatious banter of women himself. During one absence, Annie Boudinot Stockton, a handsome widow, sent him a poem with a request for him to give her absolution for writing poetry. Washington wrote back, saying if she would dine with him 'and go through the proper course of penitence, which shall be prescribed, I will strive hard to assist you in expiating these poetical trespasses on this side of purgatory'.

Then he got downright fresh. 'You see, Madam,' he wrote, 'when once the woman has tempted us and we have tasted the forbidden fruit, there is no such thing as checking our appetites, whatever the consequences may be.'

Washington was not above a more direct approach – even with the wife of a brother officer. At a dinner party given by Colonel Clement Biddle, the Revolutionary Army's foragemaster general, the ladies withdrew to leave the men to their wine. George Olney, a civilian commissary, made it plain that he did not approve of the soldiers' drinking, so Washington and his cohorts attempted to get him drunk. He fled to be with the ladies and Washington led the assault on the drawing room to get him back.

The officers advanced 'with great formality to the adjoining room, and sent in a summons which the ladies refused. Such a scuffle then ensued as any good-natured person might suppose.'

The good-natured confrontation suddenly turned nasty when Mrs Olney shouted at Washington 'in a violent rage'. If he did not let go of her hand, she said, 'I will tear out your eyes and the hair from your head.' She also told Washington that he thought he was a general, but he was just a man.

The wife of General Greene rallied to Washington's defence. Twenty-two-year-old Kitty Greene was beautiful, slim and flirtatious – a younger version of Sally Fairfax, some said. In March 1779, General Greene remarked in a letter to a friend that Washington had danced with his wife non-stop for three hours. This was a gross breach of etiquette, but then Kitty Greene had no reputation to speak of.

The French General Lafayette had slept with Kitty and even wrote to his wife, telling her how fond of Kitty he was. Kitty herself said right out that she was 'sleeping with the Marquis' in a letter to Colonel Wadsworth. She had affairs with General 'Mad' Anthony Wayne, Colonel Kósciuscko and her husband's business partner. She was particularly mad about soldiers and seems to have built up an impressive score by the end of the war; so much so that it seems out of character for her not to have seized some opportunity to sleep with the Commander of the Continental Army, Washington himself. There were also rumours that Washington slept with Kitty's mother, Lady Stirling, a leading socialite who also liked to dance with the General.

Even at Valley Forge, the Revolutionary forces did not go without sex. General Charles Lee was caught smuggling local girls into the camp.

On one occasion, Washington had trouble with the beautiful actress Margaret 'Peggy' Shippen, wife of Benedict Arnold. She began running about his headquarters practically naked, shouting that there was 'a hot iron on her head, and no one but General Washington could take it off'. When Washington went to comfort her in a bedroom, the distraught woman pulled back the bedclothes, 'revealing her charms'.

Washington did not hide his amorous intentions from his wife. A French officer at Morristown observed that Washington 'admires pretty women ... notices their gowns and how their hair is dressed. He does it quite openly, and before his wife, who does not seem to mind at all.' According to a neighbour, Mrs Martha Bland, Martha Washington was 'in perfect felicity, while she is by the side of her "Old Man"'.

The wife of a Virginia colonel wrote to a female confidante: 'Now let me speak of our noble and agreeable commander, for he commands both sexes, one by his excellent skill in military matters, the other by his ability, politeness and attention ... from dinner till night he is free for all company. His worthy lady seems to be in perfect felicity when she is by the side of her Old Man as she calls him. We often make parties on horseback.'

But when Martha was not around, the woman notes, Washington 'throws off the hero and takes on the chatty, agreeable companion. He can be downright impudent sometimes – such impudence, Fanny, as you and I like.'

Washington tried to keep Martha at home, but when the British marched into Virginia and threatened Mount Vernon, it was the perfect excuse for her to join him permanently. She spent the war tending wounded soldiers, mending clothes, knitting socks and doing what she could to boost morale. 'Whilst our husbands and brothers are examples of patriotism,' she told American women, 'we must be patterns of industry.'

At the end of the war, Washington and Martha returned to Mount Vernon. In 1789, when he became the United States's first President, Martha reluctantly followed her husband first to New York, then to Philadelphia as the first First Lady, a role she hated.

'I cannot blame him for having acted according to his ideas of duty in obeying the voice of his country,' she wrote. But she took little satisfaction in the formal functions and ceremonies that aimed to put the revolutionary court on a par with those in Europe.

Washington himself greatly enjoyed being president. He had always revelled in the admiration of women. He must have thought he was in heaven on 21 April 1789 when he passed through Trenton, New Jersey – the site of his first victory during the War of Independence – on his way to New York for his inauguration. The people there had built an archway with thirteen pillars, one for each of the states. On it was the inscription: 'The defender of the mothers will be the protector of the daughters.' Thirteen young women, dressed in simple white gowns, scattered flowers in his path. They sang:

> *Welcome, mighty Chief! Once more*
> *Welcome to this grateful shore!*
> *Now no mercenary foe*
> *Aims again the fatal blow –*
> *Aims at thee the fatal blow.*
>
> *Virgins fair, and matrons grave,*
> *Those thy conquering arms did save,*
> *Build for thee triumphal blowers,*
> *Strew our hero's way with flowers.*

Then the ladies of the town gave him a reception. The following morning one of Washington's aides sent a note to James F. Armstrong, governor of New Jersey. It read: 'General Washington cannot leave this place without expressing his acknowledgements to the matrons and young ladies who received him in so novel and grateful a manner at the triumphal arch in Trenton, for the exquisite sensation he experienced in that affecting moment.'

Martha hated such occasions and found herself increasingly trapped. 'I think I am more like a state prisoner than anything else, there is certain bounds set for me which I must not depart,' she wrote. The position of First Lady, she conceded, would suit 'many younger and gayer women'. Washington may have thought so too. As it was, he seized every opportunity to meet ladies at the afternoon tea parties the First Lady gave.

In April 1791, Washington made a tour of the southern states. He was much impressed with the 'belles' he saw there, recording in his diary that there were 'about seventy' in Newbern, 'sixty-two' in Wilmington and in Charleston 'at least four hundred ladies, the number and appearance of which exceeded anything of the kind I have ever seen'. He later sent his 'grateful respect' to the 'fair compatriots' of Charleston who had so 'flattered' him.

During his presidency, Washington had a close relationship with a number of women, one of whom was the handsome Henrietta Liston, the Scottish-born wife of Robert Liston, the British minister to the United States. She was considerably younger than both her husband and Washington. With her, he opened up as he did with few others.

Another was Elizabeth Willing Powel, the wife of Samuel Powel, the last pre-revolutionary mayor of Philadelphia. They met when he attended the First Continental Congress in 1774. He wrote to her throughout the war and visited her regularly, even though she and her husband were widely suspected of harbouring pro-British sympathies.

She was a striking brunette, buxom, attractive, playful and coquettish – a quality Washington loved in women. She fulfilled his craving for approval. He loved to be looked up to by attractive women. She even persuaded him to run for a second term of office, when he had decided to quit. In his letters to her, he implies that he would be unconcerned at being caught in adultery. What would worry him more, he says, would be having 'betrayed the confidence of a lady'.

When an epidemic of yellow fever hit Philadelphia in August 1793, Washington urged Eliza Powel and her husband to flee with him to Mount Vernon. When they refused, Washington abandoned his plan and stayed behind too. Sadly, Samuel Powel came down with the disease and died.

When Washington finally stepped down in 1797 after two terms as President, he left Philadelphia after a flurry of deeply sincere and affectionate letters to Eliza Powel. She addressed him as 'My very dear sir', while he signed himself 'your sincere affectionate friend'.

On moving back to his small house at Mount Vernon, Washington and Martha found themselves with too much furniture. Some of it was put up for sale and Eliza Powel bought a desk. In a drawer, she found a large bundle of what she described as 'love letters to a lady' – though she claimed not to have read them. When she returned them to Washington, he denied that they were letters professing 'enamoured love'. If they had been, he said, they would have been consigned to the flames.

The Washingtons quit public life and 'fairly settled down to the pleasant duties' at Mount Vernon where Martha found herself as 'steady as a clock, busy as a bee, and cheerful as a cricket'. A local landowner asked the retired President: 'What would you have been, if you hadn't married the widow Custis?'

In 1798, a year and a half before his death and twenty-five years after they last met, George Washington wrote to his enduring love Sally Fairfax. Neither the War of Independence nor his Presidency seemed to have done anything to quench his ardour. 'None of these events, however, nor all of them together, have been able to eradicate

24

from my mind, the recollection of those happy moments, the happiest in my life, which I have enjoyed in your company,' he wrote. He begged her to return to Virginia now that she was a widow.

Meanwhile, he continued his correspondence with Eliza Powel. Eighteen months after retiring, Washington left Martha at Mount Vernon and returned to Philadelphia for a month-long visit. During that period Eliza Powel did not entertain any of her other friends. She took long walks with Washington, including one on a chilly, rainy Sunday. He visited her house on several afternoons and, she let slip in a letter, he breakfasted with her at her house one morning.

Six months later, in 1799, Washington died of a chill. The official story is that he caught cold riding his horse while it was snowing. According to Harvard historian Karal Ann Marling, Washington actually caught his chill jumping out of a back window with his trousers in his hand 'after an assignation with an overseer's wife in the Mount Vernon gardens on a cold afternoon'. While distinguished British historian Arnold Toynbee said Washington contracted his chill 'visiting a black beauty in his slave quarters'.

Washington was buried at Mount Vernon. Martha had the bedroom that they had shared closed off. Then she burnt his letters, including those from Sally Fairfax and Kitty Greene, and prepared to follow him to the grave. But her country had one more sacrifice to ask of her. In the new Capitol building, a crypt had been constructed where the body of George Washington was to be laid. At the request of Congress, Martha agreed to let his body be moved there, noting: 'I cannot say what a sacrifice of individual feeling I make of a sense of public duty.'

However, before he could be shifted, Martha died of a 'severe fever' on 22 May, 1802 and the executors of Washington's will refused to let the body be moved. So the crypt in the Capitol lies empty and George and Martha lie side by side at their beloved Mount Vernon.

Although Martha did a thorough job destroying Washington's letters, some emerged in the nineteenth century. According to author Dixon Wechter, the secretary-librarian to the financier J.P. Morgan came across a number of 'smutty' letters written by Washington, which he burnt, denying future generations a clear insight into the erotic nature of the founder of the nation.

2

ADAMS AND EVES

Washington was a hard act to follow. His successor was his Vice-President John Adams, who was one of the signatories to the Declaration of Independence and largely responsible for the framing of the Constitution. He was a serious man about love.

His first romance was with one Hannah Quincy. When she broke it off, he was relieved, believing that he had been saved from a marriage that 'might have depressed me to absolute poverty and obscurity to the end of my life'.

Instead he found himself admiring the 'wit' of seventeen-year-old Mary and fourteen-year-old Abigail Smith, the daughters of the Reverend William Smith of Weymouth. Soon he was writing to 'Miss Adorable' – Abigail – complaining that, for the two or three million kisses that he had given her, he had received only one in return.

'Of consequence, the account between us is immensely in favour of yours,' he wrote, and called for her to settle up. Still, he teased that 'Miss Aurora' – Abigail's sister Mary – was a 'sweet girl' whose 'breath is wholesome as the sweetly blowing spices of Arabia'. How did he know?

Nevertheless, marriage plans were soon under way and Adams's ardour reached fever-pitch. 'Itches, aches, agues and repentance might be the consequence of a contact at present,' Adams warned Abigail. Then he turned up on her doorstep with a letter demanding that she give the bearer 'as many kisses and as many hours of your company after nine o'clock as he shall please to demand and charge them to my account'.

They married in 1764 and they remained passionately in love throughout their lives, though they were frequently parted by affairs of state. During their long separations they wrote uninhibited letters to each other. Early in their relationship they addressed each other in their correspondence as 'Lysander' and 'Diana'. Lysander was a Spartan military leader, while Diana was the goddess of fertility. Later she became 'Portia', after the Roman matron renowned for her virtue and the learned female jurist in *The Merchant of Venice*. This probably suited her better. Although 'Diana' bore five children between 1765 and 1772, the Continental Congresses became her birth control and her fecundity declined the more he was away.

This is in no way to suggest that Adams was a sensualist. At the Constitutional Convention in Philadelphia in 1776, Adams suggested as symbol for the Great Seal of the new nation a favourite classical image of his – Hercules choosing between the 'rugged mountain' of virtue and the 'flowery path' of pleasure. Hercules – and Adams – naturally chose the rugged mountain.

It must be said that Abigail Adams was not much of a looker. Her face was very masculine and commanding, but then he was no great catch either. He was short and fat – commonly called 'His Rotundity' during his period as president – and judging by dull state papers and turgid treatises, he was a bit of a bore.

Posted to Paris as assistant to Benjamin Franklin, Adams took little advantage of the opportunities for pleasure that France offered. He was greatly shocked by the behaviour of French women. The first day he arrived in France, he noted, 'one of the most elegant ladies at table, young and handsome, though married to a gentleman of the company, was pleased to address her discourse to me.

She said: 'Mr Adams, by your name I conclude you are descended from the first man and woman, and probably in your family may be preserved the tradition which may resolve a difficulty which I could never explain. I never could understand how the first couple found out about the art of lying together?'

Adams was taken aback. He blushed, but was determined not to be disconcerted. 'I thought it would be as well for one to set a brazen face against a brazen face and answer a fool according to her folly,' he wrote in his autobiography.

Adams went on to explain to the woman that 'the subject is fully understood by us, whether by tradition I could not tell: I rather thought it was by instinct, for there is a physical quality in us resembling the power of electricity.' The lady said she knew nothing of electricity, except that sex 'is a very happy shock'.

'This is a decent story in comparison with many I heard in Bordeaux, in the short time I remained there, concerning married ladies of fashion and reputation,' Adams lamented.

In a letter to his wife, he warns his countrymen against the 'plague of Europe' – sexual promiscuity – but slowly he was seduced by Paris.

'To tell you the truth, I admire the ladies here,' he wrote to his 'dearest friend' – Abigail, his wife. 'Don't be jealous. They are handsome and very well educated. Their accomplishments are exceedingly brilliant. And their knowledge of letters and arts exceeds that of the English ladies much, I believe.' Nevertheless, he still claimed to be scandalized by the 'profligate females' he saw there.

He also had 'as great a terror of learned ladies, as you have. I have such a consciousness of inferiority, as mortifies and humiliates my self-love, to such a degree that I can scarcely speak in their presence. Very few of these ladies have ever had the condescension to allow me to talk. And when it has so happened, I have always come off mortified at the discovery of my inferiority.'

Adams's behaviour was in stark contrast to that of Benjamin Franklin. Franklin cut a dash by appearing in the French court dressed in the plain garb of the American farmer. His straight, unpowdered hair, round hat and brown cloth coat stood out against the laced and embroidered coats and powdered and perfumed heads of the courtiers of Versailles. It also turned the heads of French women. His reputation as the most skilled of natural philosophers, his patriotism and his fame as an apostle of liberty all added to the effect. Elegant entertainments were laid on in his honour. At one, the most beautiful woman was picked out of the three hundred present to place a crown of laurels upon his head and kiss him twice upon each cheek. Afterwards the other women smothered him with kisses too.

'My venerable colleague enjoys a privilege here that is much to be envied,' Adams wrote. 'Being seventy years of age, the ladies not only allow him to embrace them as often as he pleases, but they are perpetually embracing him.'

However, Adams complained, jealously perhaps: 'The life of Dr Franklin's ... is a scene of continual dissipation.'

Adams griped that he could never see Franklin before breakfast, to read over the diplomatic letters and papers with him. The rest of Franklin's morning was taken up with visitors 'some philosophers, academics, economists, but by far the greater part were women'. Then, in the afternoon, 'Madam Helvétius, Madam Chaumont, Madam Le Roy etc., and others I never knew and never enquired for . . . who were complaisant enough to depart from the custom of France as to . . . make tea for him'.

The evenings too, Adams complained, were spent 'in hearing the ladies sing and play upon their piano fortes'. Franklin actually spent most evenings in the company of the Brillon family, who lived near by. Monsieur Brillon, 'a rough kind of country squire', was usually accompanied by his lover, who lived with the family and posed as a companion of Madam Brillon. Madam Brillon had a lover of her own – apart from Franklin – who also attended these dinners. Adams was deeply shocked by such behaviour.

'I was astonished that these people could live together in such apparent friendship and indeed without cutting each other's throats,' he wrote. 'But I do not know the world. I soon saw and heard so much of these things in other families and among almost all the great people of the kingdom that I found it was the natural course of things. It was universally understood and nobody lost any reputation by it.'

Adams was also shocked by Franklin's behaviour at the Auteuil household, where Franklin simultaneously tried to seduce the lady of the house and her two daughters. Then there was Madam Le Roy, the tiny wife of one of Franklin's scientific collaborators, who Franklin called his 'pocket wife'. A Madame Filleul would have him picked up by her carriage and sent notes saying how she 'looked forward to kissing him'.

Adams tried not to criticize his colleague and elder statesman too harshly in his autobiography, noting simply: 'Mr Franklin, who at the age of seventy odd, has neither lost his love of beauty nor his taste for it.' He mentions that Mademoiselle de Passy, the beautiful young daughter of the noble lord of the village outside Paris where Franklin lived, was 'his favourite and his flame and his love and his mistress, which flattered the family and did not displease the young lady.'

During Adams's time in France, his wife reproached him for neglecting her. She wrote that 'the tears have flowed faster than ink' and that she might 'assume the signature of Penelope' – the faithful wife who rejected other suitors while her husband Odysseus was away having fun. But, as Adams reminded his wife, 'my voyages and journeys are not for my private information, instruction, improvement, entertainment or pleasure, but laborious and hazardous enterprises of business'.

When in 1784 Abigail Adams joined her husband in France, she too was shocked by the behaviour of French women – especially Franklin's lover Madame Helvétius.

'This lady I dined with at Dr Franklin's,' she wrote, 'she entered the room with a careless, jaunty air; upon seeing ladies who were strangers to her, she bawled out, "Ah! mon Dieu, where is Franklin? Why did you not tell me there were ladies here?" You must suppose her speaking all this in French. "How I look!" she said, taking hold of a chemise made of tiffany, which she had on over a blue lutestring. She was once a handsome woman; her hair was frizzled; over it, she had a small straw hat, with a dirty gauze half-handkerchief round it, and a bit of dirtier gauze, that ever my maids wore, was bowed on behind. She had a black gauze scarf thrown over her shoulders. She ran out of the room; when she returned, the Doctor entered at one door, she at the other; upon which she ran forward to him, caught him by the hand, "Hélas Franklin"; then she gave him a double kiss, one upon each cheek, and another upon his forehead. When we went into the room to dine, she was placed between the Doctor

and Mr Adams. During dinner, she frequently locking her hand into the Doctor's ... sometimes spreading her arms upon the backs of both gentlemen's chairs, then throwing her arm carelessly upon the Doctor's neck.

'I should have been greatly astonished at this conduct, if the good Doctor had not told me that in this lady I should see a genuine Frenchwoman, wholly free from affectation of stiffness of behaviour, and one of the best women in the world. For this I must take the Doctor's word; but I should have set her down for a very bad one, although sixty years of age, and a widow. I own I was highly disgusted, and never wish for an acquaintance with any ladies of this cast. After dinner she threw herself upon a settee, where she showed more than her feet. She had a little lap-dog, who was, next to the Doctor, her favourite. This she kissed, and when he wet the floor, she wiped it up with her chemise. This is one of the Doctor's most intimate friends, with whom he dines once every week, and she with him.'

Adams's daughter Abby wrote of the same event in her journal: 'Dined at Dr Franklin's invitation, a number of gentlemen, and Mme Helvétius, a French lady, sixty years of age. Odious indeed do our sex appear when divested of those ornaments, with which modesty and delicacy adorn them.'

Although she was no longer a great beauty, Madame Helvétius was still sexually attractive, and a witty, liberated woman. Seeing her in a daringly low-cut dress, the writer Fontenelle, then in his nineties, sighed: 'Oh, to be seventy again.'

Franklin used to say that the purest and most useful friend a man could possibly procure was a Frenchwoman of a certain age. 'They are,' he said, 'so ready to do you a service and, from their knowledge of the world, know so well how to serve you wisely.' And Frenchwomen of a

certain age or otherwise were seemingly always ready to render him a service.

After Paris, John and Abigail Adams were posted to London, where he became the first U.S. Minister to the Court of St James. After that, they returned to America where Adams became Washington's Vice-President.

Abigail Adams, an educated woman, had a huge influence on the early presidency. Unlike Martha Washington, who had never travelled overseas, she had observed European courts first-hand and, both as the wife of the first Vice-President and as First Lady, she helped bring European style to state occasions. Mrs President, as she was often called, was the first First Lady to entertain in the new Presidential Mansion in Washington, DC, which was built during Adams's term of office. She held state dinners and receptions despite the primitive conditions she found there.

'We had not the least fence, yard or other conveniences without,' Abigail wrote, 'and the great unfinished audience room, I made a drying room of.'

The Adamses only had to suffer the privations of Washington for three months, though. John Adams was voted out of office after one term. Abigail was disappointed, but took consolation in the fact that for the next seventeen years, living in retirement in Quincy, Massachusetts, they were rarely separated.

Their sexual passion for each other continued into later life. In one of her letters, the long-suffering Abigail wrote: 'No man, even if he is sixty, ought to live more than three months at a time away from his family.' He replied irately: 'How dare you hint or lisp a word about "sixty years of age". If I were near, I would soon convince you that I am not above forty.'

At other times, Adams bemoaned the fact that his 'sauciness' continued into later life. He wrote 'when a man's vivacity increases with years it becomes frenzy at

last'. Towards the end of his life he complains in his notebooks of being 'coaxed by a fascinating woman into a subscription' for a book he did not really want.

When Abigail came down with typhoid fever in 1818, Adams wrote to Jefferson: 'The dear partner of my life for fifty-four years and for many years more as a lover, now lies *in extremis*, forbidden to speak or be spoken to.' When she died the following week, Adams stood next to her bed and said simply: 'I wish I could lay down beside her and die too.'

Adams's daughter-in-law Louise Catherine replaced his wife in his affections. They began a long and intimate correspondence. Even in old age his spark had not left him. At eighty-nine, he greeted a lady he had known in his youth with the line: 'Madam, shall we not go walk in Cupid's Grove together?'

She was mortified by this remark, but after an embarrassed pause, she admitted: 'It would not be the first time we walked together.'

3

MAD TOM AND HIS MULATTOS

'Mad Tom' Jefferson was the author of the Declaration of Independence and probably the most intelligent man ever to be president. When President Kennedy held a reception in the White House honouring a number of Nobel laureates in 1962, he remarked that they comprised 'the most extraordinary collection of talent, of human knowledge, that has ever been gathered at the White House, with the possible exception of when Thomas Jefferson dined alone.'

As a young man, Thomas Jefferson had a close friendship with Dabney Carr, the son of a wealthy Virginia planter. On one of their long rambles in the hills around Shadwell, Jefferson's birthplace, they came across a huge oak tree which Jefferson named Monticello. Later he built a house there. Romantically, the two young men swore to be buried there. In 1773, shortly after Jefferson's marriage, Carr died and Jefferson interred him there in a small private plot. Over half a century later, Jefferson joined him.

As a youth, Jefferson liked to keep company with his own sex. He believed in the strict segregation of men and women. Even when he was 73, he was warning that the promiscuous mixing of men and women would produce 'deprivation of morals and ambiguity of issue' – that is, bastards.

However, at nineteen, Jefferson briefly courted a girl he called 'Belinda', the sixteen-year-old Rebecca Burwell. Usually he fought shy of virgins. As a young man, he courted a married woman and, later, married a widow.

The married woman was Betsy Walker the wife of John Walker, one of his classmates at William and Mary College. In 1769, while Walker was away, he wrote notes to her suggesting that there was no harm in a little promiscuity among friends. Apparently, he tried to slip these notes into Betsy's dress. Betsy complained that Jefferson laid siege to her for over ten years – longer than the siege of Troy. Even in 1779, seven years after Jefferson married, he was still to be seen prowling near to her bedroom with amorous intent. On one occasion, she said he entered her bedroom with the intention of taking her by force, but she fought him off with a pair of scissors.

Jefferson met Martha Wayles Skelton – the woman who was to become his wife – when he was twenty-nine. She was twenty-two, but she was already a widow and the mother of a son who died in early childhood. With hazel eyes and auburn hair, she was a famous beauty. They were brought together by a love of music. The first thing that Jefferson bought for her at the home he was building at Monticello was a piano.

They married on 1 January, 1772 at her plantation home, then travelled to Monticello. On the way, they were caught in a snow storm and had to abandon their carriage and proceed on horseback. They arrived at Monticello late at night to find the house dark and deserted, but Jefferson managed to find half a bottle of wine on a shelf behind some books to celebrate their homecoming.

Martha bore him six children. Only two – Martha, known as 'Patsy', and Mary, known as 'Polly' – survived infancy. Her own health was further weakened when she narrowly escaped capture twice as British forces overran Virginia. In 1781, she became pregnant again and Jefferson retired briefly from public life to nurse her. She gave birth in May 1782, but never regained her strength. As she lay dying, he promised her that he would never marry again.

Jefferson devoted himself to his daughters, taking Patsy with him to Paris when he was sent there as ambassador. He sent for Polly later. Jefferson eventually gave up his post in Paris, fearful that his daughters would marry louche Europeans. He was outraged by the 'depravity' he saw there, claiming that fidelity between lovers never lasted more than a year. However, Jefferson's own loose behaviour in Paris led to a scandal after he became President in 1801.

The man who broke the story was Scots journalist James Callender. He had first come to Jefferson's attention with the publication of *The Political Progress of Britain*, which predicted the imminent downfall of the British Empire. The two men met and Jefferson, by then Vice-President in the Adams administration, promised his help with Callender's next publication. This was *The History of the United States for 1796*, which exposed Secretary of the Treasury and Jefferson's political rival Alexander Hamilton's illicit affair with Mrs James Reynolds – an affair that Hamilton was forced to admit publicly. In response, Alexander Hamilton accused Jefferson of being a 'concealed voluptuary ... in the plain garb of Quaker simplicity'.

Although a man of high morals, Jefferson overlooked the fact that Callender was a scruffy drunk, who stooped to the lowest form of journalism and scandalmongering. Callender accused George Washington of profiting from the privations of his troops at Valley Forge, John Jay of being a traitor and John Adams of being a British spy. But he took care to espouse all of Jefferson's political ideas – to the point where he was accused of being a 'hireling'. Indeed, Jefferson was Callender's patron, but claimed the money he gave Callender was 'charity'.

Callender's outrageous accusations led to his conviction under the Sedition Act. He was sent to prison for nine months and fined $200. When Jefferson became President in 1801, he pardoned Callender and ordered that the fine imposed on him be reimbursed. However, the local marshal in Richmond, where Callender had been sentenced, claimed that the fine could not legally be refunded and Callender thought that Jefferson was trying to hold out on him.

To prove his good faith, Jefferson had a fund established to refund the money and donated $50 himself. Callender accepted this as 'hush-money', but warned that he could not be bought off so cheaply.

Jefferson braced himself for the onslaught. He thought that Callender would accuse him of aiding in the publication of the tracts that had later been judged libellous in Federal Court. Instead, Callender wrote an article for the *Richmond Recorder*, a Federalist and rabidly anti-Jeffersonian paper, that accused Jefferson of scandalous behaviour with women. He regurgitated the story of Betsy Walker and Betsy's husband demanded a public apology from the President. Privately, Jefferson admitted that 'when young and single I offered to love a handsome lady. I acknowledge its incorrectness'. John Walker accepted this and the scandal ebbed away.

A second allegation proved much more damaging. Callender said that Jefferson had seduced a young slave girl named Sally Hemings who bore him several mulatto children who were kept as slaves at Monticello. Callender painted the picture of Jefferson, under the agonized gaze of his innocent daughters, sending out to the kitchen 'or perhaps to the pigsty, for his mahogany-coloured charmer'. Callender said that Jefferson regularly enjoyed the favours of his 'black Venus' and could be seen frolicking with his 'black wench and her mulatto litter'.

Callender went on to warn that if the eighty thousand white men in Virginia followed their President's example, there would soon be four hundred thousand additional slaves in the Commonwealth and the race war which Jefferson so earnestly sought to avoid would be inevitable.

As the story of Jefferson and his slave girl seized the American public's imagination, Callender upped the ante and accused Jefferson of maintaining a 'Congo harem' in the Executive Mansion itself. Then he claimed to have identified a slave named 'Yellow Tom', a light-skinned man at Monticello who bore a striking resemblance to the President.

Mrs Francis Trollope – mother of novelist Anthony – picked up the theme in her 1832-bestseller *The Democratic Manners of the Americans*. She said that Jefferson was the progenitor of 'unnumbered generations of slaves'. She also said that Jefferson had forced Harriet Hemings, Sally's sister, into a life of prostitution in Baltimore.

Federalist poet William Cullen Bryant wrote:

> *Go wretch, resign the presidential chair,*
> *Go scan, Philosophist, thy Sally's charms,*
> *And sink supinely in her sable arms,*
> *But quit to abler hands the helm of state.*

Even John Quincy Adams – the son of John Adams, who went on to become the sixth President of the United States – was moved to versify, anonymously, bewailing Jefferson's platitudes about freedom as he enjoyed the favours of his slave concubines. The English poet Tom Moore wrote:

The patriot, fresh from freedom's council come,
Now pleas'd, retires to lash his slaves at home;
Or woo some black Aspasia's charms
And dreams of freedom in his bondsmaid's arms.

Aspasia was a courtesan who became the mistress, then wife, of the Greek statesman Pericles.

Although still leader of the Federalist Party, Alexander Hamilton was in no position to take advantage of the situation, given his own peccadillo. Nevertheless Tom Paine leapt to Jefferson's defence, only to be accused of seducing the 'African Venus' himself and cuckolding his friend.

The controversy surrounding Jefferson's affair with a slave woman continues to this day. Many historians still deny that it happened. The truth is that 'Dusky Sally' was probably not black at all. She was a quadroon and her quarter-part African heritage barely showed. Her mother was Betty Hemings, the daughter of a full-black African slave and an English sea captain.

Betty Hemings and her children came into Jefferson's possession in 1773, when Jefferson's father-in-law, wealthy Virginia planter John Wayles, died. The children's father was probably Wayles himself. He had been a long-time widower and exercised the traditional slave-owners' *droit de seigneur* over the slave women in his possession. It was certainly not unusual for slave-owners in eighteenth-century Virginia to take their slave women as concubines.

Sadly, few slave-owners acknowledged their offspring from these illicit unions, but they were so common that many slaves were practically white. The Comte de Volney, who visited Monticello in 1796, remarked that there were a number of slaves, 'who, neither in point of colour nor features, showed the least trace of their original descent'.

41

So Sally Hemings was probably Jefferson's wife's half-sister and she and her family were accorded special treatment at Monticello. They were not put to work in the fields, but given household jobs or taught spinning or carpentry. At that time, Jefferson's racial attitudes – especially towards people of mixed race – underwent a profound change. Until then, he had believed that miscegenation – the mixing of the races – was one of the reasons that the institution of slavery must be preserved, at least until all those of African descent could be returned to Africa. The privileges given to the Hemings family were soon extended to other light-skinned slaves born at Monticello. There were a lot of them. Peter and Samuel Carr, sons of Jefferson's childhood friend Dabney Carr, certainly made free with the slave women. Ellen Randolph Coolidge, Jefferson's granddaughter, called Samuel Carr 'the most notorious good-natured Turk that ever was master of a black seraglio kept at other men's expense'.

After the Hemingses arrived at Monticello, the workload of mixed-race slaves was lightened and they were not sold or hired out. The only child of Betty Hemings to be sold was Thenia, who became the property of James Monroe, fifth President of the United States.

Betty Hemings and her young daughter Sally helped in Mrs Jefferson's sick-room during her final illness. Sally remained at Monticello doing light housework until 1787 when she was picked to accompany Jefferson's daughter Mary to Paris. Her brother James Hemings was already in Paris with Jefferson. He had been taken there to learn to cook.

Jefferson was not expecting Sally. He had written instructing that Mary be accompanied by a gentleman and 'a careful negro woman, Isabel, for instance, if she has had the smallpox'. However, fourteen-year-old Sally was despatched instead.

When Mary Jefferson arrived in England *en route* to Paris, Abigail Adams took charge and wrote to Jefferson that Sally was much too young and inexperienced for the job, needing 'more care than the child' – Mary herself.

When Mary and the teenage Sally arrived in Paris, Jefferson was already coming round to the French way of doing things. Initially, he had been shocked by the sexual mores of the French. In the manner of the time, he was required to pay court to women, but he tried to avoid sexual encounters. Those who received his attentions were largely young enough to be his daughter, or old enough to be his mother. But then he was introduced to Maria Cosway, the wife of a celebrated English miniaturist, and he was electrified.

Born in Italy, she was an artist in her own right. She was intelligent, beautiful and surrounded by a court of admirers. In London, it was said that the Prince of Wales had a tunnel dug between his house and hers.

Maria's husband, Richard Cosway, was much older than her and she plainly did not love him. She had only married out of financial necessity, having even considered entering a nunnery to escape poverty before her marriage. Cosway had settled £2,800 on her and supported her penniless mother.

Maria confided to Jefferson that she despised her husband. His only use for women was as models – she was his favourite. He used his models to pose for the erotic scenes he painted on pornographic snuff-boxes which he produced as a lucrative sideline. Maria believed that her husband was habitually unfaithful to her, probably with young men. He kept her with him because her beauty attracted profitable commissions.

Maria quickly turned Jefferson from a stuffy puritan into a man about town, and he admitted that, for the first time since the death of his wife, he was happy. At the time, his thoughts were certainly on sexual love. He raved over the nude statue of *Venus Pudique* he found in the niche of an English garden, which was 'turned half round as if inviting you with her into the recess'. Maria, he recorded, provoked in him a 'generous spasm of the heart'. In an adolescent attempt to show off in front of her, he leapt over a fence and broke his wrist.

Then suddenly in 1786, Maria Cosway and her husband left Paris. In what must be one of the most eloquent love letters of all time, Jefferson poured out his feelings in what he called *A Dialogue Between Head and Heart*. The head spoke for reason, the heart for emotion. His heart claimed to be 'the most wretched of all earthly beings' and 'overwhelmed with grief' at her departure. He was, he said, 'overwhelmed with more and greater misfortunes than have befallen a descendant of Adam for three thousand years . . . and perhaps, after excepting Job, since the creation of the world'.

'When heaven has taken some object of our love,' he wrote, 'how sweet is it to have a bosom whereon to recline our heads, and into which we may pour the torrent of our tears.'

Later, he wrote to Maria again, begging for her love. Her letters too became passionate. He wanted to know when she was coming back to him, promised to have breakfast with her everyday and 'forget that we are ever to part again'.

In August 1787, she returned to Paris, without her husband, and threw herself into Jefferson's arms. In December, though, she had to return to London. She skipped their farewell breakfast, writing later that she could not bear this second parting. In response, he said that the affair had left him 'more dead than alive'.

This seems a little disingenuous as the affair seems to have rekindled his amorous instincts. Later that month, he took up with Mrs Angelica Schuyler Church, Alexander Hamilton's sister-in-law. When she left Paris a few months later, she left her daughter in his care. The letters between Angelica and Jefferson became steamy. 'I esteem you infinitely,' she wrote. 'I am with you always in spirit; be you with me sometimes?'

Maria Cosway knew Angelica Church and got wind of the relationship. 'If I did not love her so much I would fear her rivalry,' Maria wrote to Jefferson, 'but no I give you free permission to love her with all your heart, and I shall feel happy if I think you keep me in a little corner of it, when you admit her even to reigning Queen.' Later Maria upbraided Jefferson for not writing to her as frequently as he had done before.

In 1789, Jefferson suggested that Maria join him and Angelica at Le Havre and travel with them to the United States. Maria declined this offer sharply. She wanted to be alone with him, not the third corner of a bizarre *ménage à trois*.

The affair with Angelica Church did not last either. Much later, Jefferson wrote to Maria Cosway from Monticello, saying that he feared he was destined to lose everything he loved. But Maria had long realized that no one could truly take the place of his dead wife Martha in Jefferson's heart. In February 1787, she asked him bluntly: 'Are you to be painted in future ages sitting solitary and sad, on the beautiful Monticello, tormented by the shadow of a woman?'

Plainly, he wasn't. Behind the scenes Jefferson had taken up with Sally Hemings, but sleeping with a slave woman was not something an upright Virginian could admit to openly, even in the relaxed atmosphere of Paris. However, it was noted that Sally would frequently accompany her master on shopping trips and return with expensive clothes.

In 1790, when he returned to Virginia, she went with him. Back at Monticello, Sally became, officially, his chambermaid. As his mistress, she bore him five children.

Two of them were allowed to leave Monticello. Harriet was given $50 and put on the stage-coach for Philadelphia and her brother Beverly was allowed to 'run away' to Pennsylvania, a free state. Both were light enough to pass for Caucasian, married white people and passed into the white community.

The remaining members of the Hemings family were freed by Jefferson in his will. Their son, Eston Hemings, married a white woman and passed into the white community. Madison Hemings, who was said to resemble Jefferson, claimed he was named by Dolley Madison, wife of James Madison, the fourth President of the United States, during a visit to Monticello. He married a black woman and moved to Pike County, Ohio.

Sally herself was freed by Jefferson's daughter Martha and spent her last years living with Madison. She died in 1835. In 1873, Madison told the editor of the Pike County *Republican* that, before she had died, his mother had told him that he, his brothers and his sisters were indeed the children of Thomas Jefferson. She had said that her first child had been conceived in 1789, while Jefferson was still Minister to France. When he was recalled to America, she decided to return with him rather than stay in France with her brother James and be free, because she was pregnant. That child had died in infancy, but Sally had continued to be Jefferson's lover at Monticello on the condition that her children would eventually be set free.

The political scandal surrounding the Sally Hemings affair did little damage to Jefferson in the long run. He made the Louisiana Purchase, founded the University of Virginia and was elected for a second term of office.

4

THE STRAITLACE
UNRAVELS

Thomas Jefferson was followed into the White House by
James Madison, who along with John Adams was largely
responsible for framing the Constitution. He was a straitlaced puritan and a confirmed bachelor when, at the age
of forty-three, he met a vivacious young widow, Dolley
Payne Todd.

Not only did Dolley transform the life of the dour
Madison, she presided over the role of First Lady for
nearly fifty years. 'Queen Dolley' was described as the
'leader of everything fashionable in Washington' – quite
an achievement for a woman who spent the first twenty-
four years of her life as a Quaker.

Born in May 1768 in Piedmont, North Carolina, Dolley
Payne was the daughter of two settlers from Virginia. She
was brought up in the strict discipline of the Society of
Friends, but her maternal grandmother was an Anglican
who taught her about fine food and fabrics. She secretly
wore her grandmother's gold brooch beneath her plain
Quaker dress and later spoke of her grandmother as the
greatest influence in her life.

In 1783, the family moved to Philadelphia, where her
father went into business. Dolley married a young lawyer,

John Todd Jr, in 1790, but he died in the epidemic of yellow fever that hit Philadelphia three years later, leaving Dolley with a young son.

By this time, the Payne family had fallen on hard times. Dolley's father's business had failed and he had been disowned by the Quakers for falling into debt. Dolley's mother opened a boarding house, catering for delegates to the Continental Congress. There the beautiful young widow attracted the amorous attentions of the accomplished womanizer Aaron Burr. When she rejected his advances because he was married, he introduced her to the forty-three-year-old delegate from Virginia, James Madison.

Dolley wrote to a friend: 'Thou must come to me. Aaron Burr says that the great little Madison has asked to be brought to see me this evening.' Determined to impress, Madison wore his new 'round beaver', a hat bought from Quaker merchant Isaac Parrish.

Seventeen years her senior, Madison was such a confirmed bachelor that the mothers of Philadelphia had decided he held no prospect for their daughters. But as soon as he met Dolley, he was smitten. He bombarded her with a series of rather dull love letters and implored her to marry him. Dolley was sceptical but her sister Anna, half in love with Madison herself, forced the pace. She suggested that Dolley spend the summer in Virginia where the heat would be even more intense than in Philadelphia. Madison rented a coach, absented himself from Congress and accompanied her.

Despite Madison's reputation for dullness, there was a wild man inside, trying to get out. As a young man, he wrote doggerel about drinking and brothels. Tradition has it that he met his first love, Mary Freneau, sister of the poet Philip Freneau, while he was a student at Princeton. Then at the age of twenty, he had fallen for a 'pretty Philadelphian' named Catherine 'Kitty' Floyd. She was just fifteen and boyish in appearance. There was great rivalry for her among the delegates to the Continental Congress. She accepted Madison's offer of his heart and his hand. He carried her picture, painted on ivory, in a heavy locket and she carried his. But at the end of his first term, instead of marrying him, she dropped him.

Instead of being the father of Kitty's children, Madison went on to become one of the father's of the Constitution. He was still trying to get it ratified by Congress when he absented himself with Dolley Payne. News of the affair spread quickly throughout Philadelphia. The difference in their ages caused much comment and people were scandalized that Dolley should be enjoying male company so soon after the death of her husband.

Madison and Dolley married in September 1794. The honeymoon was far from satisfactory as young John Payne, Dolley's son, slept with his mother and continued to do so. But Madison so relished the 'joys perpetual' of married life that he was soon talking of retiring from Congress.

Madison and Dolley produced no children of their own. They had separate bedrooms, but Dolley always kept the door between them open. Madison reconciled himself to being childless from early on. Why that was is a matter for speculation. Just eighteen months after the wedding, Aaron Burr remarked to James Monroe: 'Madison is still childless, and I fear likely to continue so.'

Dolley, disowned by the Quakers for marrying outside the faith, took the opportunity to put aside the Society's dull garb and to dress in the finest fashions. She championed the French style, created by Napoleon's Josephine, with its plunging necklines. Abigail Adams attacked Dolley's décolleté dress as 'an outrage upon all decency'.

'Most ladies wear their clothes too scant upon the body and too full upon the bosom for my fancy,' Abigail clucked. 'Not content with the show which nature bestows, they borrow from air, and literally look like nursing mothers.'

James Madison had become president in 1809; the fashion also reflected on him, Abigail maintained: 'Since Dolley Madison and her sisters adopted the new fashions and seemed in every way delighted with the French-influenced manners of Philadelphia society, we may assume ex-bachelor Madison enjoyed fully the "luxuriant" feminine displays for which the Republican Court of the 1790s was famous – or infamous.'

Dolley attended elegant balls and presided over fashionable dinner parties in Philadelphia and at Madison's plantation in Montpelier, Virginia. These chic gatherings made Dolley the country's leading hostess. Men flocked to her and vied for the right to escort her to dinner. Even Washington fell for her, declaring her to be 'the sprightliest partner I've ever had' – one assumes he means dancing partner. When Jefferson became president he invited Dolley to organize formal functions and, briefly, their names were coupled romantically. She also became a close friend of Andrew Jackson and Alexander Hamilton.

When the British set fire to the Presidential Mansion in 1812, Dolley saved what she could, including a famous portrait of George Washington. She returned to Washington, DC, before her husband, to the cheers of crowds lining the streets. While the marks of the British flames on the Presidential Mansion were being covered with a coat of white paint – making it the White House – she continued her elegant entertaining from the Octagon.

When Madison left office in 1817, Dolley simply moved the centre of fashionable society to Montpelier. When the Marquis de Lafayette visited in 1824, he wrote: 'Nowhere have I encountered a lady who is lovelier or more steadfast.'

Dolley acted as her husband's secretary and took down *My Advice to My Country* which Madison dictated shortly before his death in 1836. The following year Dolley returned to Washington where she played hostess to numerous presidents.

Martin Van Buren said: 'Mrs Madison is the most brilliant hostess in the country.' And Daniel Webster described her as the only permanent power in Washington.

However, her son John Payne Todd was a constant source of worry. He served briefly as Madison's secretary then, in 1813, was sent to Russia with the Peace Commission. In St Petersburg, as stepson of the U.S. President, he was treated as an American prince. He began drinking heavily. He fell in love with Countess Olga. They got engaged, but her father abducted her to prevent the marriage going ahead. She was never heard of again.

Todd then headed for Paris, where he was overwhelmed by the beauty of the women and began his dissipation in earnest. Back in America, his name was linked romantically with a series of ladies, before he became a 'puffed and reckless libertine' and though his stepfather tried to pay off his creditors he ended up in jail for debt on two occasions.

When her son's mismanagement and gambling debts forced Dolley to sell the Montpelier estate, Congress helped out by buying her husband's papers. At the age of eighty, she was still dispensing advice to Sarah Polk, when her husband became president. When Dolley Madison died in 1849, at the age of eighty-one, the then president, Zachary Taylor said: 'She will never be forgotten because she was truly our First Lady for a half-century.'

Madison's successor James Monroe – he of the Monroe Doctrine – was a bit more of a lad. During the War of

Independence he fell in love with Christine Wynkoop, the daughter of a Dutchman who had rallied to the American cause. But she was already engaged and turned him down when he proposed marriage.

Monroe was stationed in New Jersey where he enjoyed convivial evenings at the governor's mansion 'Liberty Hall'. He fell in love with Catherine, the daughter of Lord Stirling – or, at least, she fell in love with him. Complaining to Mrs Prevost, the future wife of Aaron Burr, he wrote: 'A young lady who either is, or pretends to be, in love, is, you know, my dear Mrs Prevost, the most unreasonable creature in existence. If she looks a smile or a frown, which does not immediately give or deprive you of happiness (at least to appearance), your company soon becomes very insipid. Each feature has its beauty, and each attitude the graces, or you have no judgment. But if you are so stupidly insensible of her charms as to deprive your tongue and eyes of every expression of admiration, and not only to be silent respecting her, but to devote them to an absent object, she cannot receive a higher insult; nor would she, if not restrained by politeness, refrain from open resentment.'

Catherine was exceedingly jealous and even resented Monroe's correspondence with Mrs Prevost. However, the relationship progressed almost to the point of a formal engagement. But when it became clear that the attachment was standing in the way of his political ambitions, he rather awkwardly broke it off.

Instead he married Elizabeth Kortright, a High Tory and, perhaps, a strange choice of wife for a Jeffersonian Republican. She was expected to have done better. However she soon found that she was the wife of a U.S. Senator, and went on to become the toast of Paris – when he was the U.S. Minister to France – before becoming First Lady.

Elizabeth was born in 1768 in New York City. Her father had made his fortune as a British privateer during the French and Indian War. He was hurt, financially, by the Revolution but with aristocratic hauteur his daughter Elizabeth was determined to get on under the new order.

Not yet eighteen, she married James Monroe in 1786, attracted perhaps by his political ambitions. She was known as 'the most beautiful woman in the United States', while he was considered a 'not very attractive Virginia congressman'. They had two daughters and a son who died in infancy.

The Monroes spent nearly ten years abroad. She disliked London, where the envoy from the United States was looked down on, but in Paris she was celebrated as 'la belle Américaine'. At the theatre, they would be cheered and the orchestra would strike up 'Yankee Doodle' in their honour.

In France, Elizabeth Monroe was celebrated as much for her courage as for her beauty. When Lafayette's wife was arrested by a Revolutionary tribunal and sentenced to death, Elizabeth visited her in prison and announced loudly that she would visit her again the following day, after the time she was supposed to have gone to the guillotine. Fearing diplomatic protests from America, the Revolutionary authorities thought better of executing her and released Madame Lafayette.

In 1811, Monroe was appointed Secretary of State and Elizabeth accompanied him to Washington. She became an accomplished hostess but, when Monroe became President in 1817, her health faltered. She did not have the strength to visit the wives of foreign ambassadors and other dignitaries all over Washington, struggling along unpaved streets as Dolley Madison had. She was considered cold and distant and her White House entertaining thought formal and European in style.

Elizabeth Monroe died on 4 July 1830, aged sixty-three, five years after her husband left the White House. John Quincy Adams gave the eulogy but it was clear that he knew as little about her as did the rest of Washington.

5

THE ADAMS FAMILY

John Quincy Adams was a dedicated puritan. He deliberately denied himself pleasure and welcomed adversity as a method of improving his character, but he was not the great Christian he thought himself to be. He held grudges and kept a neat list of his enemies. He also enjoyed nude swimming in the Potomac – his wife Louisa thought he swam too often.

While president, he was caught out skinny dipping by Anne Royall, a woman journalist to whom he had refused an interview. She had heard of his habit and followed him one morning. She watched from a safe distance while the President undressed. Then, when he had waded into the water, she sat down on his clothes. An embarrassed Adams said he would grant her an interview back at the White House, but Anne Royall would have none of it. She refused to move until the naked President had answered all her questions there and then.

John Quincy Adams maintained that there were three rules to live by – regularity, regularity, regularity. But in his youth he had enjoyed drinking, dancing and the company of ladies. On 21 January, 1788, he noted in his diaries that he 'danced with the oldest Miss Frazier, with

Miss Fletcher and with Miss Coates'. He noted Miss Fletcher's 'genteel shape'. Miss Coates was also 'agreeable'. She was an only child and 'her father has money'. But it was Miss Frazier he was interested in. They had met a week before at her home where they played 'pawns', a kissing game.

'Ah! What kissing!' John Quincy Adams wrote. ''Tis a profanation of one of the most endearing demonstrations of love.'

The problem was that Mary Frazier was only fourteen – not a marriageable age. His ardour thwarted, John Quincy Adams found himself in low spirits. 'Not even dissipation has been able to support me,' he wrote. He had trouble sleeping, and when he finally dozed off he was disturbed by 'extravagant dreams'.

He became ill, but found a cure in writing love poetry to Mary. Some of it was published in *Massachusetts Magazine* and other Boston journals. Gradually picnics and long walks with Mary restored his health and his ambition to possess her made him finish his law studies which had been flagging since his discovery of cider. He confided to a friend: 'All my hopes of future happiness in this life, centre on the possession of that girl.'

However, he could not get his law firm set up quickly enough to marry her. His family was poor and could not support them. His father was then existing on the meagre salary of vice-president. His older sister had married a man who was not prepared to work and had recently produced her third child by him.

His mother urged him to marry a rich woman, if he was to marry at all. Eventually, his parents forced him to give up his love, leaving him crushed. It was a blow he never fully got over. He stopped writing poetry and dedicated himself with puritanical zeal to duty.

Mary too was devastated. It was only years later, after she heard that John Quincy Adams had married someone else, that she married Daniel Sargent Jr, one of his friends. She died of consumption in 1804.

In 1864, a local paper, the *Newburyport Herald*, carried an account of the love affair. In it, John Quincy Adams was quoted at the age of seventy, recalling Mary's beauty, intellect and purity, rating her above any woman in Europe or America, and saying that he loved her then and loved her still.

However, his loss of Mary did not leave him quite as upset as it might. In 1791, on his way home from Philadelphia by boat, he spent several hours admiring 'the prettiest Quaker girl' he had ever seen. Back in Boston, he quickly returned to his life of drinking and dancing in Boston's inns. During the Revolution, his father said that bastards and legislators were born in the taverns of Boston.

Adams joined the 'Crackbrain Club', full of like-minded young men and danced until two. One night, he admitted, he made 'an intentionally offensive reply' to a young woman and found himself 'heavy and dissipated'. He began to visit prostitutes. His diaries recount meetings with unknown persons in strange places, late at night. Boston was teeming with prostitutes at the time. Benjamin Franklin, no stranger to the issue, noted women 'who by throwing their heads to the right or the left of everyone who passed by them, I concluded came out with no other design than to revive the spirit of love in disappointed bachelors and expose themselves to sale at the highest bidder'. Indeed, the innocently named Mount Vernon in Boston was then known as Mount Whoredom.

John Quincy Adams was freed from the grip of vice by a letter from George Washington appointing him U.S. Minister to the Netherlands. On the way there, he stopped in London where he noted: 'There is something so fascinating in the women I meet in this country that it

is not well for me. I am obliged immediately to leave it.'
However, after just two months in The Hague, John
Quincy Adams was ordered back to London where he
met Louisa Johnson.

Louisa Adams, as she became, was born in England and
never felt at home in her husband's country, especially
not in the White House. She thought of it as a prison. Her
father was born in Maryland, but had moved to England
in 1771. He married an Englishwoman and Louisa was
born in London in 1775. However, her father remained
loyal to his American origins and, during the War of
Independence, moved to France. After 1790, he became
a US consul.

At school, Louisa had a crush on her teacher, Miss
Young, who wore men's clothing. Louisa was extremely
pretty and, according to one observer, had 'the most
bewitching smile'. This could have been because she kept
her lips closed when she smiled. Her fondness for sweets
meant she began losing her teeth at an early age.

Nevertheless, she did not find any trouble in attracting
young beaux, especially in the countryside where she
could put away the wire stays and cork bustles that were all
the rage in the city. She fell in love repeatedly. One man
asked for her hand only to be 'lured to destruction' by the
wiles of married women during a trip to America, Louisa
noted. However, she mended her broken heart with a
round of other brief affairs.

In 1794, Louisa met the young, ambitious American
Minister to the Netherlands, John Quincy Adams. He had
just received a letter from his younger brother Charles
who was about to marry one Sarah Smith. Adams ex-
ploded when he heard the news. Charles had no pro-
fession, no income and was younger than John Quincy
Adams had been when he was forced to give up Mary
Frazier.

John Quincy Adams wrote to his parents remonstrating. They were unsympathetic. He decided that he must marry as a matter of urgency and get on with his life. He had only one requirement – that the woman be short. Otherwise he feared she would appear superior to him.

At first he wooed Nancy Johnson, Louisa's older sister, but Louisa seized his attention by issuing him a challenge. If he really was a poet, as he claimed, he would have to prove it by writing a poem to her. He did and handed it to her one evening over the dinner table. It was a love poem. Louisa took it and began to read it aloud, much to everyone's great embarrassment. The situation was saved by Louisa's governess who stopped her mid-flow with the admonition that it was rude to read at table. But the cat was out of the bag. Nancy went into a sulk and Louisa completed her conquest at her twenty-first birthday ball, by spending the night dancing with her sister's former beau.

Still, Louisa was not entirely sure that John Quincy Adams was really the man for her. 'An American minister was to me a very small personage,' she wrote.

Her parents were keen. He was the first man they ever allowed her to be alone with. He was the first man she kissed, and the first who ever held her in a passionate embrace. 'I can swear before the living God that I came pure and virtuous to his arms,' she wrote.

The engagement was a stormy one. They rowed constantly, usually over his sloppy manner of dressing. When John Quincy Adams's parents got wind of the affair, they wrote disapprovingly. They thought 'the siren' was too English – anti-British feelings were still running high in the U.S. His parents' disapproval made the match all the more appealing to John Quincy Adams.

The match made sense too. She was twenty-two; he was thirty. They had both been disappointed in early loves and were now at an age when they must marry. He concluded that marriage was better than celibacy. She compared it to hanging.

They married at All Hallows Church on Tower Hill in London in 1797. The custom of the time in England was for the wedding guests to carry the bride and groom to their wedding chamber, making lewd and suggestive comments on the way. Once they were alone, the bride was supposed to scramble into bed naked except for a pair of long white gloves. These her husband would symbolically remove before they proceeded to consummate the marriage.

But the wedding of John Quincy Adams and Louisa Johnson, typically, was an altogether more sober affair. Even on their honeymoon, a tour of England by carriage, the newly-weds were accompanied by chaperones. Within days of their marriage, her father was ruined by the loss of a ship in the Indian Ocean. Then it transpired that he had been swindled by his partner in Maryland. He could not pay the huge dowry he had promised and fled his creditors, who sought recompense from Adams. When Adams could not pay, he considered himself disgraced and Louisa carried the shame to her death. She wrote later that, at that moment, she had lost all her husband's esteem. It was an inauspicious beginning.

Worse was to come. John Quincy Adams and his penniless new wife were totally incompatible. She was a free spirit, used to the uninhibited ways of Europe. Much of her childhood had been spent in France. He was a hidebound New Englander. 'Though Boston is the land of learning,' she wrote later, 'I never found it the land of wit.'

Adams was appointed U.S. Minister to Prussia where they spent four years. While he went soberly about his business, Louisa became the belle of Berlin society, accompanied everywhere by his brother Thomas who many regarded as her surrogate husband. She had frequent arguments with the irascible Adams, usually over rouge. The Queen of Prussia had given her some, but he disapproved and forbade her to use it. Eventually, Louisa stood up to her husband and wore make-up when she chose to.

They must have managed to have some sex. In Berlin, she gave birth to a son and then had the first of many miscarriages. In the first thirteen years of their marriage, she was pregnant eleven times. Her twelfth and final pregnancy happened in 1817, when she was forty-two. She was terrified each time, but John Quincy Adams considered the pain and danger of pregnancy 'the pleasing punishment that women bear'.

Louisa was actually much more astute than her husband. While John Quincy Adams considered Prussia to be nothing more than a nation of soldiery and the King a model of propriety, Louisa had 'a peep behind the scenery' care of her friend Countess Neale, maid of honour to the Queen. Louisa's journal is full of stories of the beautiful Princess Lucia, who became pregnant by the King and was shipped off to a frontier town with her husband, and 'a very beautiful cousin ... who had twins supposed to be his majesty's and married off to an officer of the army who was promoted suddenly for the occasion'. Slow on the uptake, John Quincy Adams only gradually became aware of what he later condemned as this 'sea of dissipation'.

In 1801, Louisa made her first visit to America. She spent two months with her parents who then lived outside Washington, DC, before joining her husband in Quincy, Massachusetts. She disliked austere Massachusetts society and clashed with Abigail Adams. She got on well with John Adams though and learned to love him.

She was delighted when John Quincy Adams's election to the U.S. Senate meant she could leave Massachusetts for Washington, DC. In the summer recess, her husband would travel home alone, leaving her in the capital.

Voted out of office after just one term, John Quincy Adams was appointed U.S. Minister to Russia. Leaving her two oldest sons at school in Massachusetts, she travelled with her husband to St Petersburg. Life in the Tsar's court was exhausting and the winters intolerably cold. She bore a daughter there in 1811, but the child died the following year.

John Quincy Adams went to Belgium to negotiate the Treaty of Ghent in 1814, ending the war with the British. He sent word for Louisa to join him in Paris. The forty-day coach-trip across war-torn Europe in winter filled her with 'unspeakable terror'. Her reward was a two-year sojourn in London, where at least she felt at home.

Then in 1817, John Quincy Adams was appointed Secretary of State and Louisa returned to Washington with him. They received Joseph Bonaparte, Napoleon's brother the exiled king of Spain, when he visited the US. His wife refused to come with him so he kept his mistress Annette Savage at Bow Hill – renamed Beau Hill – in Trenton.

Around that time Louisa suffered from haemorrhoids – not a condition to have in the days before anaesthetics and sterile surgery. After an horrendous operation, during which she had to be strapped down, the haemorrhoids were wired and fell off. She made a complete recovery. The treatment cost $100.

Louisa went on to become a notable hostess and her drawing room became a hub of political and diplomatic activity in the run up to the presidential election of 1825. The move to the White House did not suit her though.

'There is something about the great unsocial house,' she wrote, 'which depresses my spirit beyond expression and makes it impossible for me to feel at home or to fancy that I have a home anywhere.'

However, life in the White House had its moments. Senator Mills dropped round for dinner one evening, where he 'found Mrs A and her two nieces, and had a supper of roast oysters in the shell, opening them, which of course was not a very pleasant or *cleanly* process; but with whiskey and water with supper and a little hot punch after it, we had quite a frolic'.

Louisa's health gradually suffered, though she managed to provide the elegant hospitality her position called for. However, her husband became increasingly unpopular and his 'English' wife was an easy target for his political opponents. When he was voted out of office, she was relieved, though she feared permanent retirement in Massachusetts.

Fortunately, in 1831, he began a new political career in the House of Representatives. After years of stormy marriage, they gradually grew together, campaigning together against slavery and for women's rights.

She took up the case of an Irish serving girl who had been seduced by her master. This was not an uncommon occurrence, even in the Adams family. The maid had lived in hope that he would marry her, but when the master of the house married a younger, prettier maid, she drank mercury and died in agony.

In Congress, John Quincy Adams championed the anti-slavery cause. Pro-slavery factions argued that the women's petitions Adams brought to the House came from 'mulattos and infamous prostitutes'.

John Quincy Adams answered: 'I am inclined to believe it is the case, that in the South there existed great resemblances between the progeny of the coloured people and the white men who claim possession of them. Thus, perhaps, the charge of infamous might be retorted to those who made it, as originating from themselves.' There was, the Congressional record shows, 'great agitation in the House'.

On another occasion in the House, he openly accused slave-owners of sexual misconduct. The life of a slave-owner, he said, 'is but one of unbridled lust, of filthy amalgamation.'

However, although he opposed slavery and thought that miscegenation was the only solution to America's race problem, he was 'disgusted' by Desdemona pursuing a 'nigger' in Shakespeare's *Othello*.

The Quincy Adams children did not turn out too well. One son, Charles, visited prostitutes and kept a mistress while he was a student. Widespread knowledge of his liaison caused problems when he tried to marry nineteen-year-old socialite Abigail Brooks.

Another son, George, was turned down by a number of eligible young ladies in Boston. He took to the bottle and his law office became known as a centre for drunkenness and fornication. He committed suicide by jumping off a boat and drowned somewhere off Long Island.

Their third son Thomas, who became an alcoholic, married a woman everyone considered beneath him.

6

HICKORY, DICKORY

Andrew Jackson was the first president to be born in a log cabin and the first to come from west of the Appalachians. He was also the first to be elected by a truly popular vote and he could not have been more different from the eastern aristocrats who had preceded him.

He was feisty and troublesome from an early age. A slave woman from a nearby plantation recalled years later that the young Jackson was the 'most mischievous of the youngsters thereabouts'. Part of the problem may have been a skin disease called the 'bit itch' he suffered from throughout his life which would have made him irritable.

Jackson's father died before he was born and the rest of his family were wiped out during the War of Independence. One grandfather left him nearly £400 when Jackson was fifteen and he headed off to Charleston where he spent it on clothes and gambling. There he sowed his wild oats and lived a life of almost complete dissipation.

At eighteen, he moved to Salisbury, North Carolina, where he was renowned as 'the most roaring, rollicking, game-cocking, horse-racing, card-playing, mischievous fellow, that ever lived in Salisbury ... the head of the rowdies hereabouts'.

'Why he was such a rake that my husband would not let him in the house,' one village matron recalled.

He cut quite a swathe with the young ladies and there were rumours of mulatto mistresses. While still a poor man with no income and very few resources, he found $300 to buy a 'negro woman named Nancy, about eighteen or twenty years of age'. It is hard to imagine what real need he had of a domestic servant.

'We all knew he was wild and was by no means a Christian man,' said one young female admirer. 'Still his ways and manners were most captivating.'

He was tall and athletic with red hair, steel blue eyes and a marked Northern Irish accent. He was 'quite a beau in town' and was often away on 'parties of pleasure'. He wooed and won a number of young ladies in the vicinity, but their parents objected to marriage because they 'thought he would get killed before he was many years older'.

One Christmas, Jackson succeeded in outraging the whole town by sending invitations to the Christmas ball to the town's two most notorious prostitutes, Molly Wood and her fun-loving daughter. It was just 'a piece of fun' Jackson maintained. The respected pillars of the community did not see it that way, and when Molly and her daughter turned up in their finery, they were escorted from the ballroom.

Jackson went on to become a famous Indian fighter. It is said that he fought the Creek with such fervour, and conspicuous lack of mercy, because he suspected that they indulged in 'infernal orgies'.

When Jackson moved to Nashville, he stayed at the boarding house of Mrs John Donelson and fell in love with her daughter Rachel. An extremely pious woman, Rachel had been married at seventeen to Kentucky landowner Lewis Robards, but his unreasoning jealousy sent her running back to her mother's boarding house.

When Robards heard rumours about a liaison between his wife and Jackson, he turned up at the boarding house and there was a fight. To protect Rachel from further damage, Jackson took her to Natchez, then in Spanish territory. There, she heard that Robards was filing for divorce on the grounds of her 'elopement' and, in 1791, she married Jackson.

Jackson, a lawyer by then, should have known better. Robards had only filed for divorce. It had not been granted, but Jackson did not check. Two years later he discovered that Robards still had not obtained a divorce. Rachel was a bigamist – a shock from which she never entirely recovered – and he himself was an adulterer. Robards eventually obtained a divorce on the grounds of adultery and, in 1794, the Jacksons got married again – this time legally.

Jackson tried to keep this honest mistake quiet and, throughout her lifetime, was quick to defend his wife's honour against any slight. He even fought a duel over it and only escaped with his life because the bullet lodged in the thick coat he was wearing. His opponent, who had accused Rachel of adultery, died in the exchange of fire.

In the bitter 1828 election, the old accusations came out again. One anti-Jackson pamphlet read: 'Anyone approving of Andrew Jackson must therefore declare in favor of the philosophy that any man wanting anyone else's pretty wife has nothing to do but take his pistol in one hand and a horsewhip in the other and possess her.'

Somehow Jackson managed to keep these accusations from his wife. But after he was elected, she came across some election literature defending her and realized that the whole world knew her secret. The White House no longer held attraction for her and she quite simply died of shame.

She was buried in the gown that she had bought for the inauguration on 24 December 1828. Her epitaph reads: 'A being so gentle and so virtuous slander might wound, but could not dishonor.'

They had no children.

Jackson took office, grieving for his wife. No one thought he would last his term and rivalries broke out in cabinet over who would be his successor. The two contenders were Vice-President James C. Calhoun from South Carolina and Secretary of State Martin Van Buren. The issue they fought over was Peggy O'Neal Eaton, the wife of the Secretary of War.

Peggy O'Neal was a green-eyed brunette, the daughter of a Washington tavern keeper, who was happy to bounce on customers' knees and dance with them. In fact, she was so free with the customers that soon she was the talk of Washington. However, when a young congressman from Tennessee, who had a lovely young wife at home, tried it on with her she hit him with the firetongs.

Peggy was keen on marriage. At the age of fifteen, she tried to elope with an army officer who was staying at the tavern, but her father caught them and ended the match. Later she married a purser in the U.S. Navy, John Bowie Timberlake. However, while he was at sea, she began an affair with Jackson's old friend and campaign manager Senator John Henry Eaton. When her husband died – some said he drank himself to death over the affair – Eaton turned to Jackson for advice.

'Sir, I want to marry Peggy O'Neal,' Eaton said. 'Do you think I should? You know what people are saying.'

Indeed Jackson did. He had been present one night when the politician Henry Clay had made a Shakespearean wisecrack at Peggy's expense. 'Age cannot wither nor custom stale her infinite virginity,' Clay had quipped.

However, Clay was a long-time political opponent and Jackson blamed the death of his wife on this sort of gossip.

He also knew Peggy and had stayed at her father's inn when he had first come to Washington.

Jackson advised Eaton to marry Peggy and the couple were wed. Other Washington wives snubbed her. Leading the anti-Peggy campaign was John Calhoun's wife Floride, who refused to invite her to dinner parties where other cabinet members and their wives would be present.

Jackson also learnt that Calhoun had secretly opposed his invasion of Florida and had taken up the issue of Peggy to crush Jackson.

Jackson publicly compared the treatment of Peggy Eaton to the slanders that had destroyed his wife Rachel and declared, in cabinet, that Peggy was as 'chaste as a virgin'. At a formal cabinet dinner, he seated her next to him. Peggy wore a gown with a plunging neckline which further outraged the Washington wives, who walked out when she took to the dance floor.

Martin Van Buren led the pro-Peggy faction. He threw a party in her honour and persuaded his bachelor friends to do the same. Cabinet members, congressmen, even foreign diplomats had to take sides in the 'petticoat war'. Soon the administration was a laughing stock over the Peggy Eaton affair. Van Buren proposed a solution. He and Eaton would resign. Then Jackson would ask for the resignation of Calhoun and the rest of the anti-Peggyites. The entire cabinet would be dissolved, leaving Jackson free to pick new men.

Van Buren was rewarded for this gesture by being picked as Jackson's running mate in 1832. Jackson even introduced the two-thirds rule in the nominating convention to give no other contender a chance. The two-thirds rule stayed in place until 1936.

Despite the heated sexual atmosphere surrounding the Peggy Eaton scandal, Jackson never looked at another woman after the loss of his wife. He had a miniature of her on a strong black cord around his neck. One night when his private secretary disturbed him on some pressing presidential business, he found Jackson holding his wife's prayer book. A larger miniature of her was propped against some books in front of him.

Jackson kept a large portrait of her in his bedroom, opposite his bed. Each morning he would kneel before it and thank God that he had been spared so that he could look once more on her face. When he did die, he died staring at her portrait on the wall opposite.

7

WOOING AT THE WHITE HOUSE

Hannah Hoes Van Buren was the First Lady who never was. Not only did she die eighteen years before her husband entered the White House, he omitted her from his autobiography on the grounds that a gentleman would not bandy the name of a lady in public.

Martin Van Buren and Hannah Hoes had been childhood sweethearts in the close-knit Dutch-American community in Kinderhook, New York. They married in 1807 and had five sons, one of whom died in childhood.

The Van Burens spoke Dutch at home and Martin called his wife by her Dutch name Jannetje. In 1817, the family moved to Albany where Martin became state attorney. He built his reputation on a number of high-profile rape and murder cases.

The winter of 1818 was particularly severe and Hannah developed tuberculosis. She died on 5 February 1819 at the age of thirty-six.

Little is known of her beyond her obituary which described her as 'an ornament of the Christian faith'. Her niece Maria later recalled Hannah's 'perfect composure' on her deathbed. She also asked for her money to be given to the poor.

Van Buren's feelings about his wife are unknown. He rarely mentioned her in his correspondence. The inscription on her gravestone, which was presumably written by him, refers to her only as a 'tender mother and a most affectionate wife'.

Hannah's sister Christina stepped in to help bring up the children. Van Buren liked female company. He soon began escorting a number of eligible women to parties and was positively promiscuous in his correspondence with female friends.

Elected to the Senate, Van Buren would have had ample opportunity to misbehave as a single and powerful man in Washington. He was widely known for his polite flirtations with a variety of women. His close friend and political ally, Congressman Louis McLane of Delaware, suspected him of 'licentious' conduct and filled his letters home with stories of Van Buren's affairs. As both men were fond of good food and good wines and frequently ate together, McLane was in a position to know what Van Buren got up to.

New York politician De Witt Clinton, from Van Buren's home state, also said that Van Buren had several affairs. He certainly enjoyed the company of beautiful women, especially those of wit and intellect. He was positively gallant in the Peggy Eaton affair, though he used it to his political advantage.

Van Buren's name was linked with those of a series of eligible young ladies. Thomas Jefferson's granddaughter was often seen in his company. Once, at a ball, she asked the band to play 'The Yellow-haired Laddie'. Van Buren was known for his golden locks and tongues began to wag. When he went to Virginia, gossips had him married off to her or one of her sisters.

A 'Mrs O.L.' was also mentioned as a prospective wife for Van Buren by Washington insider Churchill C. Cambreleng. Van Buren's response to this assertion was to call

Cambreleng a rogue, while admitting that the rumour had put him in a 'peck of trouble'. When Jackson made Van Buren Secretary of State it was predicted by all that he would divide his time evenly between 'international law and the ladies'.

Washington grande dame Harriet Butler accused Van Buren of being promiscuous with his affections. While flirting in Washington, apparently, he was sending amorous messages to a woman in Albany, while allowing another to wear 'an emblematic color' for him. Mrs Butler also offered to tell a certain 'Elvira the Fair' that there was no chance for her. Van Buren's response to Harriet's interest in his love life was to flirt with her too. 'Nothing serves so well to season the perpetual dissipation of this Sodom as an occasional letter from a kind-hearted and sensible female friend,' he said.

To another woman he wrote: 'Your letter has been to me a green shoot in the midst of a desert of political cares.' To a third he said he hoped he deserved 'half the compliments' that she had given him. To Lucy Evans, wife of political ally David E. Evans, he sent a small present – a twig from a cedar growing next to Washington's tomb at Mount Vernon.

Some husbands objected. His friend Louis McLane eventually got jealous of the steady stream of letters between his wife and Van Buren and accused Van Buren of being 'morally licentious'. His correspondence with a Mrs Taylor ended when 'her little husband interdicted it'. But usually Van Buren managed to smooth things over with the husbands and carried right on writing.

Maybe the husbands did not really have anything to worry about. Van Buren himself admitted that he merely liked 'to hear the gossip of the female world . . . for those concerns [are] among the real comforts of life'. Within weeks of arriving in Washington, he had moved out of the downtown Strother's Hotel on Pennsylvania Avenue,

73

which was inhabited by the other New York congressmen, and into Peck's Hotel in Georgetown where Senator Rufus King lived. Indeed, they were so close that it was rumoured that Van Buren was 'wedded to Mr King'.

Van Buren was extravagant in his praise of other men. Secretary of War John C. Calhoun was a 'fascinating man'. Congressman John Randolph was 'an extraordinary man' and they often went riding together. Van Buren liked to befriend young politicians new in town.

From the beginning of his political career, Van Buren had an extraordinary reputation for exuberant clothing. This is how journalist Henry B. Stanton described how Van Buren's 'exquisite personal appearance' dazzled the congregation at the First Presbyterian Church in Rochester, New York, one Sunday morning: 'His complexion was a bright blond and he dressed accordingly. On this occasion he wore an elegant snuff-coloured broadcloth coat, with velvet collar to match; his cravat was orange tinted silk with modest lace tips; his vest was of pearl hue; his trousers were white duck; his silk hose corresponded to his vest, his shoes were Morocco; his nicely fitting gloves were yellow kid; his hat, a long-furred beaver, with broad brim, was of Quaker colour.' And this was in the middle of a long political tour during a hot New York summer.

On another occasion Stanton described him wearing a 'snuff-coloured' coat with an orange cravat, white duck trouser and yellow gloves, flirting with married women and exchanging jokes with younger men. He was also known for his green dress coats, his white-topped boots and, always, his extravagant use of lace. He was vain enough to have his portrait painted twice while he was Secretary of State.

If one were of a mind, it is possible to conclude that Van Buren was, at least, a closet homosexual. This would explain why, when he had such ample opportunity with willing women, he did not marry again. Certainly having a woman around the house would have been invaluable to a busy politician bringing up four growing lads.

Maybe history cannot make up its mind about Martin Van Buren because his amorous adventures while in office were overshadowed by the scandal surrounding his Vice President, Richard Johnson. A Kentuckian, Johnson had taken as his mistress Julia Chinn, a black slave who he had inherited from his father. Although she had died before he stood for election, he still supported their mulatto children which outraged Southern states.

Once elected, Johnson took a defiant stand. He took a second black mistress, and when she ran off with an Indian, he took a third black mistress. He was not nominated for a second term.

Van Buren's successor William Henry Harrison hardly counts as a president. He rode to his inauguration on horseback through a rainstorm. Hatless and coatless, he was sworn in on the East Portico of the Capitol, then insisted on giving an 8,441-word speech which took an hour and forty minutes to read. After attending three inaugural balls, he took to his bed with a chill. This turned into full-blown pneumonia and he died a month to the day after taking office.

Ironically, his wife, who was too ill to accompany him to Washington for his inauguration, succeeded him by twenty-three years.

Harrison's sex life was similarly undistinguished. As a youth, he had joined the army and gained a considerable reputation as an Indian fighter. The only women he saw were the officers' wives who he escorted to remote posts and the Indian women who gleefully scalped dead soldiers and tortured the wounded to death.

One day in 1797, Harrison rode up to the Short mansion in Lexington were Anna Turthill Symmes was staying. The moment she saw the gallant young captain on horseback, she fell in love with him. Her father Judge Symmes, former chief justice of the New Jersey Supreme Court, disapproved of the rough Indian-fighter. When he asked how Harrison intended to support his daughter, Harrison replied: 'By my sword and by my right hand.'

This may not have impressed the judge, but it certainly impressed the romantic twenty-year-old Anna. She secretly married Harrison, her father grudgingly giving his approval four weeks later. The marriage produced ten children and Harrison seems to have been too busy slaughtering Indians to have got up to any extra-marital mischief.

When Harrison died, his Vice-President John Tyler succeeded him and brought fresh scandal to the White House. Two years before he succeeded unexpectedly to the presidency, his wife Letitia had been crippled by a stroke. She moved into the White House with her husband, but lived in seclusion on the second floor, attending only one public function there – the wedding of their daughter Elizabeth.

They had married in 1813 and, although his letters talk of love, their marriage was really a uniting of two sizeable fortunes. He was less than ardent. Three weeks before the wedding, Tyler confessed that he dare not even kiss her hand because she looked 'so perfectly reserved and modest'. Six days before the ceremony, Tyler wrote to a friend saying that he was approaching his nuptials like 'an old man'. However, by all accounts, Letitia was a great beauty. They remained happily married for twenty-nine years and had seven children.

Letitia Tyler was the first president's wife to die in the White House. She passed away peacefully on 10 September 1842, with a damask rose in her hand. Four months later, in January 1843, Tyler met twenty-two-year-old Julia Gardiner. She was introduced to him at the White House by Congressman Fernando Wood.

Julia was renowned as the 'Rose of Long Island'. She was raven-haired with a radiant complexion, an hour-glass waist and a full bust. President Tyler found her dark oval eyes animated and her full lips irresistible.

Julia was no stranger to love. During a European trip she had been courted by a Belgian nobleman and a War Office official in England. And she had already made a number of conquests in Washington.

In 1839, she had posed for an advertisement for a department store alongside an older man dressed as a dandy. The handbill caused something of a scandal. Then, a few months later, a poem by one 'Romeo Ring-dove' appeared on the front page of the Brooklyn *Daily News* singing the praises of the 'Rose of Long Island' with such immortal lines as:

> *When gallants buzz like bees around*
> *Who sweets from flowers suck,*
> *Where shall the man so vain be found*
> *As hopes this rose to pluck.*

For the nineteenth century, this was pretty racy stuff.

At the White House reception where they met, Tyler was immediately smitten. So effusive were the 'thousand compliments' that he paid her that those near by 'looked and listened in perfect amazement'. He had never been like this with his wife.

Julia was impressed too. She wrote: 'We could not help commenting, after we left the room, upon the silvery sweetness of his voice ... the incomparable grace of his bearing, and the elegant ease of his conversation.'

Her sister Margaret, who was also there, was less enthu-siastic and recalled later that the President was a rather jolly old man.

However, John Tyler had a rival for Julia's affections – his own son John Jr, who bombarded her with bad poetry. John Jr's unsuccessful attempts to divorce his wife Mattie Rochelle Tyler were common gossip around Washington. Margaret and Julia were also befriended by a second son, Robert Tyler, but found him 'not handsome'.

Meeting the President again at a whist drive at the White House, Julia was teased about her beaux. Tyler demanded to know how many she had 'in the name of the President of the United States'.

'He had quite a flirtation with Julia,' Margaret reported, 'and played several games of All Fours with her.'

Thomas Cooper, Robert Tyler's father-in-law, saw trouble coming. 'Do see the President playing old sledge with Miss Gardiner,' he said. 'It will be in the *Globe* tomorrow.'

Fortunately the papers did not pick up on it. Nor did they pick up on the fact that, after the party, Margaret and Julia went upstairs to the presidential apartments. When they made a move to leave 'what does he do but give me a kiss,' wrote Margaret excitedly. 'He proceeded to treat Julia in the same manner when she snatched away her hand and flew down the stairs with the President after her around the chairs and tables until at last he caught her. It was truly amusing.'

President Tyler and Julia conducted a whirlwind courtship amid a storm of salacious rumour and vicious gossip, especially as Tyler was still officially in mourning at the time. There was even some rivalry between Julia and her sister Margaret for the heart of the President.

'He was extremely affectionate,' Margaret recorded. 'Julia declared he was rather too tender, for he gave her three kisses while I received only two.'

Along with her sister and her father, Julia joined the President on the steam frigate *Princeton* for a cruise down the Potomac in February 1844. Tragedy struck when Julia's father was killed in a freak explosion. Tyler comforted her and they grew even closer.

Then at Washington's Birthday in the White House on 22 February 1843, Tyler spotted Julia dancing with a young naval officer and could control himself no longer. As the young man's Commander-in-Chief, he cut in and led Julia away. Then he asked Julia straight out to marry him.

'I said, "No, no, no," ' she recalled later, 'and shook my head with each word, which flung the tassel of my Greek cap into his face with every move. It was undignified, but it amused me very much to see his expression as he tried to make love to me and the tassel brushed his face.'

Tyler was not to be brushed off. He began writing love poems to Julia. He was so ardent that she was forced to inform her family of the President's proposal. They thought she should wait a few months to make sure of her feelings, especially as she was also being pursued by Judge John McLean. The fifty-seven-year-old McLean eventually stepped aside, telling a colleague that if he were twenty-five years younger he'd have cut the President out.

Tyler's son Robert was still writing flirtatious letters to Julia, while Tyler's own love letters were read aloud by the whole of the Gardiner family and sent to their lawyers 'for perusal'.

Eventually Tyler wrote to Julia's mother making a formal request for her hand and guaranteeing, after the recent death of Julia's father, that he would maintain her financial and social status.

In March 1843, Tyler and his young love had come to a 'definite understanding', though no formal engagement was announced. Julia's mother Juliana was still against the match – after all, she herself was nine years younger than her prospective son-in-law – but in the end, she had no alternative but to accept it.

Even Tyler's friends thought he was making a fool of himself. In March 1844, while riding in his carriage, Tyler told Henry A. Wise, a Virginia politician, that he intended to marry a much younger woman.

'Have you really won her?' Wise asked in amazement.

'Yes,' said the President. 'And why should I not?'

'You are far too advanced in life to be imprudent in a love-scrape,' his friend said.

'How imprudent?' said Tyler, pressing for an explanation.

'Easily,' said Wise. 'You are not only past middle age, but you are President of the United States, and that is a dazzling dignity which may charm a damsel more than the man she marries.'

'Pooh!' exclaimed the President. 'Why, my dear sir, I am just full in my prime!'

Wise was not convinced and told Tyler the story of a James River planter who had decided to marry a younger woman and asked his house slave, Toney, what he thought of the idea.

'Massa, you think you can stand that?' replied Toney.

'Yes, Toney, why not? I am yet strong and I can now, as well as ever I could, make her happy.'

'Yes, but Massa,' said Toney, 'you is now in your prime, that's true; but when she is in her prime, where then, Massa, will your prime be?'

Tyler laughed – but, at the age of fifty-four, he went ahead and married twenty-four-year-old Julia Gardiner.

The wedding took place on 26 June, 1844 in New York, just four months after the death of her father. The young bride wore a simple white dress of lisse 'with a gauze veil descending from a circlet of white flowers, wreathed in her hair'. Still in mourning, she wore no jewelry and was a picture of elegant simplicity.

The couple's age difference – some thirty years – attracted a great deal of public interest, but the newspapers were kind. Already known as 'Honest John', he now became 'Lucky Honest John'.

In fact, the news management of the story was brilliant. The story did not appear in the New York papers until the day after the marriage and it forced the sensational murder trial of Polly Bodine off the front pages for several days.

The New York *Herald* said: 'Miss Gardiner is an honour to her sex ... the President has concluded a treaty of immediate annexation, which will be ratified without the aid of the Senate of the United States ... Neither Polk nor Clay can bring to the White House such beauty, elegance, grace, and high accomplishments as does John Tyler, and meetings should be at once convened, committees appointed, and all proper measures taken to ensure the reign of so much loveliness for four years in the White House.'

But the Washington papers were taken completely by surprise. John Jones, the editor of the pro-Tyler *Madisonian*, had run a routine announcement the day before saying that the President had taken a temporary absence from his 'arduous duties' in the capital to take a few days 'repose'.

The *Herald* mocked: 'John don't know what's going on. We rather think that the President's "arduous duties" are only beginning. "Repose", indeed!'

The ladies of New York were shocked and 'will not recover in some weeks', the papers said. Many were offended at having been left off the guest list while Tyler's socially unacceptable political cronies had been included.

Tyler's daughters were upset too. They had known nothing of their father's intentions. Just weeks before the wedding he had written to them saying he had 'nothing

81

to write about which would be of interest to you'. When the deed was done, he wrote telling them that he had married 'the most beautiful woman of the age and at the same time the most accomplished' and begging for their understanding.

His oldest daughter Mary, who was five years older than his new bride, accepted the situation. But it was three months before his youngest daughter, twenty-one-year-old Elizabeth, could bring herself to write to 'My dear Mrs Tyler', explaining that 'even now it is with difficulty that I can convince myself that another fills the place which was once occupied by my beloved Mother'.

Tyler's second daughter Letitia never accepted Julia at all and the feud lasted for the rest of their years. His sons, though, accepted their new stepmother gladly.

The honeymoon turned into a triumphant procession. The wedding night was in Philadelphia. There was a brief stopover in Baltimore, then on to Washington. Julia was thrilled by the public's reaction.

'Wherever we stopped, wherever we went, crowds of people outstripping one another, came to gaze on the President's bride,' she said. 'The secrecy of the affair is on the tongue and admiration of everyone. Everyone says it was the best managed thing they ever heard of.'

On Friday 28 June, there was a formal reception in the Blue Room of the White House.

'I have commenced my auspicious reign,' she told her mother, 'and am in quiet possession of the Presidential Mansion.'

However, the happy couple soon fell out. Tyler complained that his wife had trouble getting out of bed in the morning and that she constantly demanded his attention rather than letting him get on with his work. Despite the triumph of his marriage, Tyler was still unpopular and had a difficult election to face.

Julia's sister Margaret even complained: 'You spend so much time kissing, things of more importance are left undone.' Julia's mother urged her: 'Let your husband work during all business hours. Business should take the precedence of caressing – reserve your caressing for private leisure and be sure you let no one see it unless you wish to be laughed at.'

Despite the forthcoming election, on 1 July, the newly-weds set off by boat to Old Point Comfort, where they stayed in what Julia described as a 'true love cottage'. Tyler had put Colonel Gustavus A. De Russy, commanding officer of Fort Monroe, in charge of bedroom arrangements. He provided 'a richly covered high post bedstead hung with white lace curtains looped up with blue ribbon, and the cover at the top of the bedstead lined also with blue – new matting which emitted its sweet fragrance, two handsome mahogany dressing tables, writing table and sofa'.

While the President should have been preparing himself for the 1844 election, instead, he stayed on at his honeymoon cottage, spending his time writing love poetry to his new wife. One of his poems – 'Sweet Lady, Awake! – A Serenade Dedicated to Miss Julia Gardiner' – was set to music by Julia herself. She was thrilled and completely happy.

'The P. bids me tell you the honeymoon is likely to last forever,' she told her mother, 'for he finds himself falling in love with me every day.'

Her mother was sceptical. 'You must not believe all the President says about the honeymoon lasting always,' she told her daughter. 'He has found out that you in common with the rest of Eve's daughters are fond of flattery.'

On 6 July, Tyler took her up to Sherwood Forest, the plantation he had bought as his retirement home. He assembled his sixty slaves to greet their new mistress. They, naturally, were embarrassed. So Tyler called out to one of the older men: 'Well, how do you like her looks?' He said: 'She is mighty handsome – just like a doll-baby.' Julia took this as 'the quintessence of a negro compliment'.

Back in the White House, the new Mrs Tyler greeted guests with ostrich plumes in her hair and surrounded herself with maids of honour dressed in white. But her reign was short – just eight months. When Tyler returned from his honeymoon, he decided that there was more to life than being President and stood aside in favour of James K. Polk.

Tyler and his wife attended Polk's inauguration, then they retired to Sherwood Forest and started having babies. After the birth of their first child, the papers began running stories of their separation and possible divorce. The problem was their May-to-December marriage, it was said. But the Tylers confounded their critics, stayed together and produced seven children.

When Tyler's old friend Henry A. Wise, who had counselled against marriage, returned to the U.S. in the autumn of 1847, after a spell as ambassador to Brazil, he bumped into the Tylers on a river boat. Among the ex-President's baggage, he spotted a double-seater wicker baby carriage.

'It has come to this, has it?' said Wise, shaking his head.

'You see how right I was,' said Tyler. 'It was not vain boast when I told you I was in my prime. I have a houseful of goodly babies budding around me.'

In Tyler's correspondence, there is no indication that he ever worried about the thirty-year age gap between him and his wife. Indeed, their seventh and last child was born when he was seventy. Nor did Julia worry about the long widowhood she knew she would face. Her love seemed only to deepen with the years. On his sixty-second birthday she wrote:

There may be those with courtier tongue
Who homage pay to me –
But deep the tribute love compels,
With which I bend to thee!
Let ruthless age then, mark thy brow –
It need not touch thy heart –
And what e'er changes time may bring
I'll love thee as thou art . . .

Then listen, dearest, to my strain –
And never doubt its truth –
Thy ripen'd charms are all to me,
Wit I prefer to youth!

Tyler and Julia were buried together at Hollywood Cemetery, Virginia. His first wife, Letitia, lies alongside her parents at Cedar Grove, where she was born.

After Julia Gardiner Tyler left the White House, the gloom descended again. Her successor as First Lady was the forbidding Sarah Childress Polk. She was an educated woman, a rare thing in the nineteenth century. Her wealthy father had sent her to the Moravians' women's academy at Salem, North Carolina.

James K. Polk – characterized by historian Carl R. Fish as 'the least conspicuous man who had ever been nominated for President' – had already begun his political career when they met and it is said that his political patron, Andrew Jackson, encouraged the romance. The couple married on 1 January, 1824. She was twenty; he was twenty-eight.

The marriage was childless and Sarah devoted herself to promoting his political career, helping him write speeches, dealing with his correspondence and giving him advice.

Sarah entertained with high style in the White House but, a devout woman, she prohibited dancing. Even at the inaugural ball, when the Polks arrived, the dancing ceased and resumed only after they had left. She would not go to the theatre or to horse races and discouraged visitors to the White House on a Sunday.

Polk died three months after leaving office, but Sarah survived another forty-two years, turning their home 'Polk Place' in Nashville into a shrine to her husband's memory.

It seems that Polk's successor, the thrusting Zachary Taylor, did not even marry his 'wife' Margaret Mackall Smith Taylor, the daughter of a well-to-do Maryland planter and a woman of genteel upbringing. Although a marriage licence was issued on 18, June 1810, there is no record of a ceremony being performed and no return was lodged with the Marriage Records of Jefferson County, Kentucky, where Taylor was stationed at the time. There are records, however, of their six children, all but one born in or around Louisville, Kentucky.

Old Rough and Ready, as Taylor was known in the army, was not much of a catch. At best, he was said to be 'an ordinary looking man'. Others paint him as downright ugly – dumpy, thick-necked with a large head. He had a big nose, thick lips puckered in a permanent scowl and his bow legs were so short that his orderly had to help him into the saddle of his favourite war horse, 'Old Whitey'.

A second lieutenant wrote home: 'Taylor is short and very heavy, with pronounced face lines and gray hair, wears an old oil cloth, a dusty green coat, a frightful pair of trousers and on horseback looks like a toad.'

During the Mexican war, Taylor commanded the Indiana Volunteers. They were about to leave for the war when one of them accidentally tore the shirt from the breast of a companion, revealing his comrade-in-arms to be a woman. She explained that she had a father in Texas but did not have the money to get there. Taylor's men had a whip round and paid her fare.

Taylor himself was less charitable. He opposed the marriage of his second daughter, Knox, to a young lieutenant under his command. The lieutenant's name was Jefferson Davis, who went on to lead the Confederacy to defeat. Shortly after their wedding, Davis took his young bride home to Mississippi where she caught malaria and died. Taylor never forgave him.

When Margaret Taylor heard that the Whigs intended to nominate her husband for president in 1848, she decried it as 'a plot to deprive her of his society and shorten his life by unnecessary care and responsibility'. She was right. He died in office.

During his time in the White House, she took no part in the formal social functions. It is said, she preferred to spend her time in her room smoking a corn-cob pipe. Her twenty-two-year-old daughter Betty Knox Bliss acted as the 'Lady of the White House'. She organized stately dinners and lively dances, and was said by a visitor to combine 'the artlessness of a rustic belle and the grace of a duchess'.

Margaret herself remained upstairs, venturing out solely to go to church. Following the sudden death of her husband, she left Washington directly after the funeral and never spoke of the White House again.

These days an affair between a pupil and schoolteacher would be frowned on, but the thirteenth President of the United States, Millard Fillmore, fell in love with his school-marm and married her.

Her name was Abigail Powers and she was born in Saratoga County, New York, in 1798. She was the daughter of a prominent Baptist preacher who died shortly after she was born. Her mother moved westwards, thinking that her scant funds would stretch further in a more remote region and she educated her son and daughter herself, using her late husband's library.

At the age of twenty-one, Abigail was teaching in New Hope, when nineteen-year-old Millard Fillmore joined her school as a pupil. He was the son of a dirt farmer, but his six foot of sturdy manhood aroused her admiration and his dignified bearing, she thought, promised a bright future. He, in turn, fell for her large, dark eyes and her long black hair that was drawn tightly back across her head. It was the first time he had been around female company and during the cold winter months of 1819 they fell in love.

Abigail helped Fillmore in his struggle to become a lawyer and they married in February 1826, three years after he had been admitted to the bar. They were still poor though, and Abigail continued working as a teacher.

By 1832, when Fillmore was first elected to the House of Representatives, they had moved into a six-room house in Buffalo. Though she preferred books and cultivating her flower garden, she made an effort to enter society as the wife of a politician.

As a congressman, he was considered competent, if colourless – an 'able and faithful public servant' John Quincy Adams said. Always faultlessly groomed, he neither smoked nor drank. He would seek out 'temperance hotels' to stay in when he was away from home. He also had a horror of gambling and suffered agonies of guilt because he had won a turkey in a raffle when he was fifteen.

'That was the beginning and the end of my gambling,' he said. 'I have never since gambled to the value of one cent.'

In the White House, Abigail presided over state dinners and receptions, but ill health dogged her and she asked her daughter Abby to take over her social duties.

With a grant from Congress, Abigail set about organizing a White House library in an upstairs room where Abby kept her piano, guitar and harp. There was not so much as a Bible in the White House when she arrived. She also installed the first bathtub in the Executive Mansion. The Fillmores always travelled in a splendid wine-coloured carriage, with blue silk seats and silver-mounted harnesses which had been presented to Abigail by the women of New York. The coach cost $2,000, the horses $1,000 each.

At the inauguration of her husband's successor Franklin Pierce, Abigail caught a severe chill and died a few weeks later in the Willard Hotel, probably of bronchial pneumonia. Congress adjourned as a mark of respect and her body was returned to Buffalo for burial.

When their daughter Abby died of cholera the following year, Fillmore took off on a trip to Europe. He met Pope Pius IX in Rome; and in England, Queen Victoria said that he was the most handsome man she had ever seen. He was frequently seen at the opera in the company of a number of beautiful American women.

Back in America, he married Mrs Caroline C. McIntosh, a wealthy widow. She was childless and had a tragic air about her which caused some to compare her to the Mona Lisa grown old. But the marriage brought him the largest mansion in Buffalo.

From an early age, Franklin Pierce believed that he was destined to go through life alone. Perhaps he should have. His marriage in 1834 to Jane Means Appleton, the shy, frail, tubercular daughter of his college principal was dogged with tragedy. Their first child, a son, died after three days. Their second, Frank, died of typhus at the age of four. Their third son, Benny, was healthy enough, but just two months before Pierce was sworn in as president, he was killed in a train crash near Andover, Massachusetts. His parents were on the train and escaped unscathed, but they watched the precious child die before their eyes. He was just eleven.

Mrs Pierce saw this tragedy as a sign from God and withdrew from public life. Pierce went on alone, gloomy and distracted. The loss of his son was a punishment for his own shortcomings, he thought. He refrained from taking the usual oath of office, simply affirming his loyalty to the Constitution instead.

Jane Pierce was too distraught to attend the inauguration and there was no inauguration ball. When Jane did arrive in Washington, the sombre mood deepened further with the death of Abigail Fillmore and, the following month, Vice-President Rufus King.

The loss of their precious third and final son pushed Jane Pierce over the brink of sanity and Franklin into heavy drinking. It seems unlikely that they had much of a sex life after that.

Never strong, Jane's health declined in the White House. For years after, the Pierces travelled to the West Indies and across Europe in the hope that a change of climate and scenery would restore her health. Everywhere she went she carried her son's Bible and a box of hair from her 'precious dead' – her sons, her mother and her little sister. Nothing could shake her morbid affliction and the Pierces returned to New Hampshire where Jane died in 1863. She is buried near the grave of her beloved Benny.

Pierce was, by all accounts, a good-looking and active man. But finding a new sexual partner seemed to be the last thing on his mind. He drank himself to death six years later.

8

MRS VICE-PRESIDENT

By 1857, it had almost become a tradition that the president had to be born in a log cabin. James Buchanan first saw the light of day in a cabin at Stony Batter near Mercersburg, Pennsylvania. From an early age he was determined to make something of himself.

As a youth he moved to Lancaster, Pennsylvania. After graduating, he quit the company of the footloose young men he used to drink with in the backroom of taverns to spend evenings in the parlours of fashionable homes. His ploy was to make himself agreeable to wealthy families in the hope of ensnaring an unmarried daughter. As a rising young lawyer, he was an extremely eligible bachelor.

He became attached to Anne Coleman, the daughter of the ironmaster Robert Coleman, one of America's first millionaires. They became engaged in 1819, but Anne's father did not approve. He was a trustee of Dickson College, where Buchanan had come within a whisker of being dismissed for disorderly conduct. Buchanan's student friends had been a wild bunch and Buchanan himself had lost three tracts of land in a bet.

That year saw a financial panic and, at its peak, the old Federalist Party – the party of George Washington and

91

John Adams – began falling apart. Buchanan was frantically busy trying to prevent the collapse of the Columbia Bridge Company and politicking for the party. He had little time for his fiancée and Lancaster society concluded that it was not Anne he was interested in but the Coleman fortune.

Returning from a business trip to Philadelphia, Buchanan dropped around to see Mrs William Jenkins. With her was staying the pretty and charming Miss Hubley. The gossip this visit inspired sent Anne into a fit of jealousy. She wrote to Buchanan breaking the engagement off and went to stay with her sister Margaret in Philadelphia. Before the couple could be reconciled, Anne had died in mysterious circumstances, possibly suicide.

Buchanan wrote a note to Anne's father expressing his deep love for Anne and asking to be allowed to attend the funeral. The letter was returned unopened, further fuelling speculation that Anne had committed suicide when she believed her love to be unrequited.

The truth of the matter, and what part it might have played in the death of Anne Coleman, will never be known. Papers which Buchanan intimated revealed all were lodged in a New York bank during the Civil War to protect them from Confederate troops, but when Buchanan died, the sealed papers were destroyed without being opened, as requested in his will.

It has often been said that this incident prompted Buchanan to remain a bachelor for the rest of his life. However, in 1837, Buchanan wrote to Mrs Francis Preston Blair, saying: 'I would gladly join your party to the Hermitage next year ... but long ere that time I expect to be married and have the cares of a family resting upon my shoulders.'

Senator William Rufus De Vane King of Alabama was also teasing Buchanan about suffering 'the anxieties of love' and neglecting his work. The woman in question was probably Mary Snyder, the young niece of Thomas Kittera. Kittera and his sister Ann brought up Mary after her mother died. They also raised Buchanan's niece Elizabeth Huston, after his sister Sarah died. So it is likely that a marriage of convenience was arranged to keep the money in the family. However, it is also possible that Buchanan intended to marry Ann Kittera, Thomas's sister, for the same reason. But subsequent wrangles over the inheritance scuppered his plans.

Later, Buchanan became seriously interested in Anna Payne, who lived with her famous aunt Dolley Madison in the grey house on Lafayette Square in Washington. At the time it was fashionable for young women to marry men old enough to be their grandfathers. The resulting unions were rarely satisfactory. Buchanan let his better judgment overrule his heart and explained his decision to his intended in verse.

> *In thee my chilled and blighted heart has found*
> *A green spot in the dreary waster around*
> *Oh! that my fate in youthful days had been*
> *T'have lived with such an one, unknown, unseen,*
> *Loving and lov'd, t'have passed away our days*
> *Sequestered from the world's malignant gaze!*

> *A match of age with youth can only bring*
> *The farce of 'winter dancing with spring'.*
> *Blooming nineteen can never well agree*
> *With the dull age of half a century.*
> *Thus reason speaks what rebel passion hates,*
> *Passion – which would control the very fates.*
> *Meantime, where e'er you go, what e'er your lot*
> *By me you'll never, never be forgot.*
> *May Heaven's rich blessings crown your future life!*
> *And may you be a happy, loving wife!*

Until the end of his life, Buchanan still fondly harboured the idea that he would one day be married.

'I feel that it is not good for a man to be alone,' he wrote to his old friend Mrs James J. Roosevelt, 'and should not be astonished to find myself married to some old maid who can nurse me when I am sick, provide good dinners for me when I am well, and not expect from me any very ardent romantic affection.'

In fact, he already had a woman to do just that. He employed Ester Parker – or Miss Hetty as she was known – in 1834, when she was twenty-eight, to be his house-keeper. She stayed with him until he died thirty-four years later.

Buchanan was sixty-five when he became president, but it seemed to give him a new lease of life. On a trip through the South, the newspapers reported him to be 'gay and frisky as a young buck'. His companion on the journey, Secretary of the Interior Jacob Thompson, said that Buchanan 'kissed hundreds of pretty girls which made his mouth water'.

Mrs Kate Thompson was his favourite among the wives of his cabinet ministers. She was an 'easy and free-hearted woman' who loved to flirt. Buchanan was captivated by her passion and impetuous nature and would drop by to visit her when her husband was out of town.

He then became enamoured of Mrs Bass, a married woman with three young children. It was noted by the ladies of Washington society that the President would dress up in his finest clothes when he was to see her. Buchanan took her on a vacation, which was marred when abolitionists ran off with her maid servant.

However, during Buchanan's lifetime, there were persistent rumours that he was a homosexual. He had a twenty-three-year friendship with William Rufus De Vane King of Alabama, who became Vice-President under Franklin Pierce. They were roommates in Washington and King's 'fastidious habits and conspicuous intimacy with bachelor Buchanan gave rise to some cruel jibes'.

Andrew Jackson called King 'Miss Nancy'. He was also known as Buchanan's 'better half' and 'Aunt Fancy'. James K. Polk's law partner, Tennessee Democrat Aaron Brown, made smirking references to 'Mr Buchanan and wife' and 'Mrs B'.

King himself penned long and intimate letters to Buchanan. When appointed minister to France, King wrote: 'I am selfish enough to hope you will not be able to procure an associate who will cause you to feel no regret at our separation.'

King was the United States' only unmarried vice-president, and Buchanan the only unmarried president.

9

THE GREAT EMANCIPATOR

The young Abraham Lincoln seems to have been awkward in the company of women. However, he used to tell a story that shows he was interested in the opposite sex from an early age. In later life, he related an erotic fantasy from his time in Indiana when he must have been between the ages of seven and nine.

'When I was a little codger,' he wrote, 'one day a wagon with a lady and two girls and a man broke down near us, and while they were fixing up, they cooked in our kitchen. The woman had books and read us stories, and they were the first I had ever heard. I took a great fancy to one of the girls; and when they were gone I thought of her a great deal, and one day, when I was sitting out in the sun by the house, I wrote a story in my mind. I thought I took my father's horse and followed the wagon, and finally found it, and they were surprised to see me. I talked with the girl and persuaded her to elope with me; and that night I put her on my horse, and we started off across the prairie. After several hours we came to a camp; and when we rode up we found it was the one we had left a few hours before, and we went in. The next night we tried again, and the same thing happened – the horse

96

came back to the same place. I stayed until I had persuaded her father to give her to me. I always meant to
write the story out and publish it, and I began once, but I
concluded that it was not much of a story. But I think it
was the beginning of love in me.'

Lincoln probably believed that he was, like his mother
Nancy, illegitimate. One traditional tale says that John C.
Calhoun was his father, after having a brief affair with his
mother when she was a tavern maid. But there are several
other versions and the truth has been lost in the mists of
time.

Lincoln would certainly have been familiar with the
physical side of love from an early age. He was brought up
in a one-room cabin. In 1818, when Lincoln was nine, his
mother died of milk sickness, a poisoning caused by white
snakeroot. When cows grazed on it, they passed its toxic
quality on in their milk. The family fell into total squalor
for almost a year until Thomas Lincoln returned to his
home town in Kentucky where he found a second wife,
Sarah Bush Johnson, a widow, and brought her and her
three children back to Indiana. Tradition has it that
Thomas Lincoln had wooed Sarah before he had married
Nancy. Learning that she was a widow when he was a
widower, he seized the opportunity the second time
around.

Lincoln doted on his stepmother, who he described as
his 'angel mother'. She encouraged him to read. His
newly extended family now meant he was surrounded by
girls. As well as his older sister Sarah, his stepmother
brought with her two step-sisters, Betsy and Mathilda. The
newly-weds, Lincoln and the girls were all crammed together in a single room and there can have been little
chance of privacy.

During his brief schooling, Lincoln became attached
to Katie Roby, but she married James Gentry, the son of

Lincoln's employer, because his prospects seemed so much brighter.

Seventeen-year-old Caroline Meeker, niece of the local squire, fancied Lincoln who she first saw defending himself in a Kentucky court-room. Her uncle was also impressed and invited Lincoln to the house. Caroline waylaid him in the orchard and invited him to a cornhusking the following week.

The local custom was that, at a cornhusking, any man who found a red ear was allowed to kiss the girl of his choice. Lincoln did not find a red husk, but Caroline did. She hid it under her apron and, surreptitiously, slipped it to him. Then, in front of everyone, he kissed her. Later, he walked her home, but the penniless young Lincoln had no chance to take the affair any further. The aristocratic Caroline married a local landowner, but she never forgot her gallant young beau.

When Lincoln was twenty-one, his family moved to Illinois. He acted quite flirtatiously with older married women, but in front of younger women he became shy and awkward. The matrons of New Salem took him under their wing and he formed close attachments to at least three married women.

Despite his shyness, Lincoln's name was linked with several young ladies who went on to marry other men. One of them was Polly Warnick, the daughter of Major Warnick who employed Lincoln as a rail-splitter. She saw him when he made his first political speech and was impressed. But his lack of money and prospects stood in the way of the courtship yet again, and Lincoln was soon seen escorting other girls.

It was around that time he met Ann Rutledge, the daughter of the inn-owner John Rutledge who was a founder of New Salem. Ann, it is said, was the love of Lincoln's life. She was 'a gentle, amiable maiden without any of the airs of your city belles, but winsome and comely withal, a blonde in complexion with golden hair, cherry red lips and bonny blue eyes'.

Unfortunately, Ann was already engaged to the richest man in New Salem, John McNeil, although that romance had run into difficulty. It seems that McNeil's name was really John McNamar and he was living under a false name because he had swindled his parents out of everything they owned. Soon after his engagement to Ann, he headed back east to sort out some financial problems and never returned. By the time Lincoln met Ann, McNamar had been gone two years and she waited every day for a letter. She had ceased to love him but had received no formal release from her engagement.

Lincoln proposed to her, but he was not the only one in the field. His friend, Sam Hill, had also asked for her hand. He was rich while Lincoln, as ever, was penniless. Ann preferred the tall, awkward Lincoln, but her family were in dire financial straits, so marriage to Lincoln was out of the question.

In the summer of 1835, typhoid and malaria swept through the Mid-West. Ann died of 'brain fever' and, it is said, Lincoln's heart was buried with her.

Lincoln too had the symptoms of malaria, but he threw himself into his work to mend both his body and his broken heart. Whether Ann Rutledge ever loved Lincoln, we cannot know. Many say that she really died of a broken heart over John McNamar.

One of Lincoln's married lady friends was Mrs Bennett Abell. When the unmarried Mary Owens came to stay in her house, the twenty-five-year-old Lincoln was called in to keep her company. Mary had 'fair skin, deep blue eyes, with dark curly hair; height, five feet five inches, weighing about one hundred and fifty pounds'. She was handsome and well-educated. He proposed, but she refused him after some ungentlemanly behaviour on his part. They had been out riding with a number of other couples when they came to a ford. The other men helped their ladies across, but Lincoln rode on ahead.

'You are a nice fellow,' she chided when she caught up with him. 'I suppose you did not care whether my neck was broken or not.'

He replied simply that she was 'plenty smart to take care of herself'. This was not taken as a compliment.

They were forced to separate when he was elected to the Illinois state legislature at Springfield in 1837. There, he became enamoured of Mrs Orille H. Browning, a colleague's wife, though he continued writing to Mary Owens.

Springfield was full of pretty women and as an up-and-coming young lawyer and politician, Lincoln was spoilt for choice. It was then that Lincoln 'began to discover the flaws' in Mary Owens's beauty. He decided that she was old and fat, and 'rather too willing to marry'. However, being a mortal, if not morbid, man, he continued to press his suit. She, to his surprise, rejected him once again. To his relief, she released him from any obligation and returned to Kentucky.

Free at last, Lincoln began to play the field. He was perfectly placed to do so. Mrs Browning had two handsome and unmarried sisters who, between them, knew every eligible young woman in Springfield, if not the whole of Illinois.

Mary Todd was not quite twenty-one when she met Lincoln. She was a celebrated beauty from Lexington, Kentucky, who had moved to Springfield after her mother died and her father married again. She was bright and vivacious. Her hair was chestnut, her eyes blue and her lips cherry-red and seductive. She was short and fiery – 'an alluring armful for a courageous man'.

They met at a ball given to mark the opening of the General Assembly of the sovereign State of Illinois. Every pretty girl in Springfield was there.

She wore a silk dress over seven or eight starched (or flounced) white petticoats but 'did not wear a great deal above her waist, for she knew she had an attractive neck and shoulders and she made the most of them'. That night, it was said, she dressed 'within an inch of her life. There was not a man there who did not turn and look after her, nor a woman who did not look after her without turning.'

Undoubtedly the belle of the ball, she spent most of the night dancing. But she noticed one tall man who did not dance with her. He stood around telling stories, so she commanded her cousin, Major John Todd Stuart, to bring him to her so they could be properly introduced. Lincoln was immediately captivated.

Lincoln was not alone in his passion. She had countless admirers but she chose him, she said later, because she knew he would be president – 'that was why I married him; for you know he is not handsome'.

They became engaged, but she soon began complaining that he did not visit her as often as he should. He explained that he had an election to fight. When he was re-elected that excuse no longer held true.

Lincoln became so exasperated by her demands on his time that he wrote her a letter breaking off the engagement, but a friend persuaded him to go and tell her in person. Mary wept copiously. It was ironic, she said, that she who had broken so many hearts was now being rejected. As he left, she demanded that he kiss her goodbye. The embrace was so warm and passionate, that Lincoln went home more engaged than ever.

At the same time, Mary Todd was flirting with another young politician, Stephen A. Douglas. They would go dancing whenever he was in town and the two of them were seen walking arm-in-arm in broad daylight. Worse, Lincoln did not reveal the slightest hint of jealousy.

At that time the young blonde Matilda Edwards, daughter of the governor of Illinois, had come to stay with Mary. The two girls shared the same bed – and the same beau. Next time Mary went dancing with Stephen A. Douglas, she saw, over his shoulder, Matilda deep in conversation with Lincoln.

Matilda's parents saw the dangers and lined up other eligible males for her. Joshua Fry Speed, Lincoln's roommate, proposed and was refused. Stephen A. Douglas then fell under Matilda's spell. He proposed and he too was rejected.

Mary became frantic. When she flirted wildly with other men, Lincoln took no notice. She herself grew increasingly jealous of the growing attachment of Matilda and Lincoln. Her discomfort was all the greater because she and Matilda were bedfellows.

Mary took the matter up with Lincoln, but he was unrepentant, even giving the impression that he loved Matilda more than he did Mary. Matilda, too, was brazen. If Mary could not keep hold of her lover, she said, she could not expect any help from other girls.

One night in bed Mary plucked up the courage to ask Matilda: 'Do you think Mr Lincoln really ever loved you?'

'Mercy, no!' said Matilda. 'He only thought he did.'

'Did he every propose to you?' asked Mary

Matilda laughed. 'Propose to me? He never even paid me a compliment.'

Matilda Edwards went on, reputedly, to break more hearts – both men's and women's – than anyone in the history of Springfield, before marrying a man from out of town.

Mary could not escape the idea that Lincoln may love another and on 1 January, 1841 she broke off the engagement. In some versions of the story, the wedding was planned for that day and Lincoln simply did not show up.

In others, Lincoln, half crazy with passion, openly declared his love for Matilda Edwards.

Whatever happened, Lincoln was so distraught that he had to spend several months away from Springfield, and he went to Louisville, Kentucky, with Joshua Fry Speed. As roomates Speed and Lincoln shared the same double bed and American gay activist groups have since claimed, on this evidence, that Lincoln was a homosexual.

However, even in his grief Lincoln did not shy away from other women. He had two tickets for *Babes in the Wood* and was determined not to let them go to waste. He took with him seventeen-year-old Sarah Richard, who he had known since she was twelve. He later proposed to her, but she turned him down because of the difference in their ages. He was thirty-three at the time. Nevertheless, their relationship was intimate and it lasted fifteen months.

During that time, Mary had taken up with a widower, twenty years her senior, but she was unwilling to take on his children and the relationship foundered.

Lincoln continued to be active in politics. He wrote an article for the *Sangamon Journal* ridiculing his political rival, Irishman James Shields. The article was signed 'Aunt Rebecca'. Mary Todd read it and liked it so much that she wrote a second article, continuing the satire and using the same pen-name.

Shields was annoyed by the first article and enraged by the second. He demanded to know who had written the two articles. To protect Mary, the editor of the *Journal* told him that Lincoln had written both of them. Shields challenged Lincoln to a duel which, happily, ended without bloodshed when mutual friends intervened.

Slowly the truth of the matter came out in public and the names of Lincoln and Mary Todd were once again linked. Several secret meetings were arranged and on 4 November, 1842, they were married. Recently unearthed evidence suggests that Mary was pregnant at the time and had trapped Lincoln into marriage.

The union was not a happy one. Mary Todd mixed extravagant flirtations with other men with jealous tantrums if he even so much as looked at another woman. Not looking was something of a problem for Lincoln. Lincoln's partner in his law practice, William H. Herndon, wrote: 'Lincoln had a strong, if not terrible, passion for women. He could hardly keep his hands off a woman; and yet, much to his credit, he lived a pure and virtuous life. His idea was that a woman has as much right to violate the marriage vow as a man – no more, no less. His sense of right, his sense of justice, his honor, forbade his violating his marriage vow. Judge Davis said to me in 1865, "Mr Lincoln's honor saved many a woman", and this is true to the spirit. I have seen Lincoln tempted, and have seen him reject the approach of women.'

In 1846, Lincoln was elected to the U.S. Congress and Mary greatly enjoyed being the belle of Washington. They even took a little time off for a romantic cruise on the Great Lakes. However, his radical anti-slavery views found disfavour with the Illinois electorate. He was not reelected and Mary found her social aspirations dashed.

She set up home in Springfield and employed a number of maids. Many quit because they found Mary's tantrums intolerable and some expressed sympathy for Lincoln. All of them testified to the passion of the woman and that Lincoln, slow as he was, loved to hold her hot body in his arms.

In 1858, Lincoln came to national prominence with a series of debates on slavery with Mary's former lover Stephen A. Douglas. Known as the 'Little Giant', Douglas was the Democratic incumbent in the Senate race. Lincoln was the candidate for the newly formed Republican party.

Lincoln lost the election, but his speeches were re-produced in newspapers across America. This was enough to win him the Republican nomination and then the presidency in 1861. As First Lady, Mary was in her element. She squandered money on fashionable clothes and her daring décolleté gowns were widely criticized.

'Mrs Lincoln had her bosom on exhibition,' wrote one visitor to the White House.

Her extravagance during the Civil War was a continual political embarrassment – particularly as she was a South-erner and from a slave-owning family – and her gowns were so expensive that Lincoln worried about re-election, simply to continue his presidential salary.

Mary became so unpopular that she was charged with treason. Lincoln appeared before a Congressional hear-ing to quash the charges. Mary's sympathies were indeed with the South and Union soldiers sang ribald songs linking her sexually to the Confederate's President, Jef-ferson Davis.

Confederate propaganda also spread lewd rumours about Mary and the men she was alleged to be planning to elope to a slave state with. These were, of course, without foundation. But it has to be said that, while in the White House, she continued to enjoy the attention of many men, particularly Charles Sumner who secured her a pension after the assassination of her husband.

During his time in office, Lincoln became an accom-plished flirt and his wife had to keep an eye on him constantly. He would tease her by listing the names of the women he fancied and those to whom he might talk. When Mary was out of town, Lincoln flirted with anyone he liked. He loved the racy dialogue of Shakespeare's comedies and would go to see dancing girls. One night at Ford's Theatre, he took a private box and carried on 'a hefty flirtation with the girls in the flies'. It was not unusual for Lincoln to receive pretty pictures or saucy notes from schoolgirls after the war. When he was shot, Laura Keene, star of *Our American Cousin*, cradled his head in her lap.

After Lincoln died, William H. Herndon went about the country proclaiming that Lincoln had never loved his wife and had only married her after being nagged into matrimony. The love of Lincoln's life was, Herndon said, Ann Rutledge.

Mary Lincoln spent much of her time abroad after the death of her husband. Travelling back from France in 1880, on board the *Amérique*, she became friendly with the notorious actress Sarah Bernhardt. Slowly, Mary became mentally unstable. She died in 1882. On her finger was a ring that Lincoln had given her. In it were inscribed the words: 'Love is Eternal.'

Abraham Lincoln was an impossible act to follow, and during his time in office Lincoln's successor Andrew Johnson got little credit for his lofty principles. He lacked the political skill to push through his conciliatory reconstruction plans and, for his pains, he was impeached.

Johnson was the only president never to have had a day's schooling in his life. He was born in an employee's shack at Casso's Inn, in Raleigh, North Carolina, where his father worked as an ostler and a janitor. He died of over-exertion when Johnson was three after rescuing two friends from drowning. Johnson's mother married again and, when they were old enough, bound Andrew and his elder brother as apprentices to James J. Selby, a local tailor. They were to be fed and clothed in return for their work until they were twenty-one.

At sixteen, Johnson got into trouble for throwing stones at a woman's house in Raleigh and teasing her daughters. He also had fun flashing in front of the granddaughter of local aristocrat John Dereaux, streaking naked down the path outside her house. Threatened with arrest, Johnson grabbed his tailor's tools and fled first to Carthage and then to Laurens, South Carolina, where he set up as a journeyman tailor.

There, he fell in love with a beautiful girl named Mary Wood. She was eager and yielding, but her parents opposed the match of a local belle to a penniless illiterate.

When he returned to Raleigh, he found that there was a $10 reward on his head. His family sold up, loaded their possessions on to a cart and set out westwards across the Smokies. After a month's journey on the Daniel Boone trail, they stopped at Greeneville, Tennessee, where Johnson set up a tailor's shop.

As they arrived in town driving a blind pony hitched to a small cart carrying pots and pans, Johnson was spotted by Eliza McCardle. A friend remarked that he would make a fine beau for a Greeneville girl, once he had washed his face. Eliza said that she intended to take him as her husband. Within a year they were married. He was just eighteen and she seventeen.

An attractive girl with soft, wavy brown hair, hazel eyes and fine features, Eliza had a good basic education and she set about teaching Johnson to read and write. While he set about politicking in the back room of his tailor's shop, she raised five kids.

During the Civil War, Andrew Johnson was appointed military governor in Nashville. Eliza stayed in Greeneville to attend to business. When Jefferson Davis imposed martial law on East Tennessee and gave Unionists thirty-six hours to leave, Eliza pleaded illness and was allowed to stay, but the Johnsons' property was impounded and she had to stay with relatives. Eventually she got permission to cross the lines and after an arduous journey joined her husband in Nashville. However, her health never recovered and she remained an invalid for the rest of her life.

She stayed in Nashville when her husband was sworn in as Vice-President and feared for his safety after Lincoln's assassination. When she moved into the White House, she found the place had been wrecked by souvenir hunters. Congress appropriated $30,000 for renovations, but it was not nearly enough.

Eliza retired to a second-floor room and only twice came downstairs to appear in public – once when Hawaii's Queen Emma visited and once to attend the first children's ball held at the White House. Otherwise her eldest daughter Martha, the wife of Senator David T. Patterson, acted as hostess. Eliza died six months after her husband in 1875.

Throughout his career Johnson had trouble with his sons, Robert and Charles. Both became alcoholics and a constant source of embarrassment to him. In 1863, Charles died after falling from a horse, presumably drunk. Robert went on to become his father's private secretary, but the responsibility did not improve his behaviour.

'There is too much whiskey in the White House,' complained Johnson's envoy to Berlin Norman Judd, 'and harlots go into the private secretary's office unannounced in broad daylight. Mrs C. did that ... while a friend of mine was waiting for an audience – and she came out leaning on the arm of the half-drunken son of the President.'

To add to his troubles, Johnson received letters from pardon-broker Jennie A. Perry, who attempted to blackmail him with tales about an illegitimate son, though apparently he never took her threats seriously.

Robert Johnson eventually committed suicide in 1869.

President Johnson himself liked a drink. When he was sworn in as Lincoln's Vice-President he was famously drunk and made a rambling incoherent speech. When the chief justice and Senator Foot went to tell him that Lincoln was dead and he was now the President, they found him 'half dressed, dirty, shabby, with matted hair as though from mud in the gutter, apparently trying to overcome a hangover'. After the oath of office had been administered, they went to inform Secretary of War Edwin Stanton. When they returned they found Johnson asleep again. So they dressed him as best they could and took him to the White House. There, they bathed him and called for a doctor, a barber and a tailor to fix him up. It was only in the late afternoon that they allowed visitors in to assure themselves that a new man had his hands firmly on the tiller of state.

Johnson and that other famous dipsomaniac General Ulysses S. Grant went on a whistlestop tour of the U.S. The crowds booed Johnson and demanded to see Grant. Sadly the great general was usually too inebriated to put in an appearance.

10

USELESS GRANT

Grant was undoubtedly a great general, but he was useless as a president. His administration was dogged by scandal and he admitted himself that accepting the presidency was the greatest mistake he made in his life.

In fact, apart from generalship, Grant was useless at just about everything he turned his hand to in life. With his over-fondness for whiskey, it would not be unfair to imagine that he was pretty useless as a lover too.

Born Hiram Ulysses Grant in 1822, he hated the idea of his name being abbreviated to HUG, so he abandoned the Hiram and added his mother's maiden name 'Simpson', making him U.S. – or Unconditional Surrender – Grant.

His wife Julia Dent Grant was one of the First Ladies who actually enjoyed her tenure of the White House. It was one of the few periods of her life that was not attended by deprivation and hardship.

Brought up on a plantation near St Louis, she first met Ulysses S. Grant when his roommate – Julia's brother – brought him home on vacation from West Point. She claimed the night before she met Grant that she had a dream in which she met, fell in love with and married an officer she did not know and had never seen.

When, on a pleasure trip, a party of them were fording the swollen Gravois river in a light rig, she clung to him in fear of the water. This, Grant said, inspired him to ask for her hand in marriage. They became engaged and Julia wore his West Point ring, but her father opposed the match, saying that Grant was too poor. Julia pointed out that as cash-starved slave-owners, they were no better off than he was.

The marriage was delayed until 1848 by Grant's service in the Mexican war. When he arrived back in his home town of Bethel, Ohio, after the war with an attractive young woman, his family immediately took her to be Julia, the fiancée they had heard so much about. She was not – just someone he had picked up on the stage coach.

After the war, Grant was stationed at Sackets Harbor, New York, where he eventually married Julia. Then the 4th Infantry was suddenly posted to Fort Vancouver in what would become Washington State. Unwilling to risk their lives on the dangerous journey across the Isthmus of Panama, he left his wife and new-born son behind in the East.

On the voyage, Grant struck up a friendship with Delia B. Sheffield. She claimed to be married but Grant did not believe her, saying she was too young. They reached the Isthmus of Panama on 13 July, 1852, in the middle of the rainy season, and went by railroad as far as the Chagres river. From there, they travelled in flat-bottomed boats poled by 'stark naked' black 'natives' who apparently fascinated both Grant and Mrs Sheffield.

The posting was boring and the separation from his young family unsettled Grant. He tried his hand unsuccessfully at several business ventures, then sought solace in the bottle. In April 1854, he was found drunk in public and resigned his commission rather than face court-martial. Grant was re-united with Julia and his son, but hardship followed as Grant's business and farming ventures failed. The Civil War brought separation again when he returned to arms. Julia tried to join her husband as often as his duties allowed, but when she was not around, he missed her a lot and his heavy drinking 'seemed in part sexual' a contemporary said.

During his presidential candidacy in 1868, it was alleged that Grant had sired a mixed-race child by an Indian in Vancouver. However, the alleged daughter was born less than nine months after Grant arrived there and her father was probably one Richard Grant. No one believed the allegation. Besides it was far more credible and defaming to believe that he was a drunk.

Once in the White House, more allegations of sexual impropriety were made against Grant. Typically, these came up as part of the notorious 'Whiskey Ring' scandal of 1875. Headed by General John McDonald, the ring skimmed millions of dollars of liquor taxes. Corruption was deep in the government. A telegram warning the ring of the investigation being conducted by the Internal Revenue Service was uncovered. It was signed 'Slyph'. One of the ring explained: ' "Slyph" was a lewd woman with whom the President of the United States had been in intimate association, and ... she had bothered and annoyed the President.' Again, no one believed Grant was that sort of fellow.

After the end of his disastrous administration, Grant suffered a new business failure in 1884 and hardship returned. Before he died, he wrote his memoirs in which he claims never to have uttered a 'profane expletive', not even when in charge of a train of pack mules during the Mexican war, 'but I would have the charity to excuse those who may have done so'. The book became an instant bestseller.

Grant was helped by professional writer Adam Badeau. A homosexual, Badeau had joined Grant's staff during the Civil War in 1864 and the two men remained close for the rest of Grant's life. Badeau wrote several books about Grant but they lack a certain intimacy.

One night in 1852, when he was thirty, Grant's successor Rutherford Hayes found himself overwhelmed by physical desire. He was attending a lecture by Professor Agassiz at the Young Men's Mercantile Library Association in Cincinnati, when saw a young woman in the audience and was deeply attracted to her.

After the lecture was over, he found himself compelled to follow her out into the street. In the pouring rain, he followed her down towards the river where she disappeared into a shabby house. It was only then that Hayes realized that the girl was a prostitute, and he knew that it was a matter of the greatest urgency that he get married.

Up until then, the closest relationship he had had was with his sister Fanny. He doted on her and she reciprocated. 'I love you like my own life,' she told him once.

As a young lawyer, he became emotionally involved with one of his clients, a serving girl name Nancy Farrer. She was accused of poisoning four people. He managed to save her from the gallows, but only by getting her committed to an insane asylum instead.

Hayes was undoubtedly popular with women from a young age. At fifteen, he wrote to a friend: 'Tell me how A. Pickett flourishes with girls. Tell him I flourish like a green bay tree.'

At twenty-two, he confided to Fanny: 'Between you and me, a little squad of girls have spent a great deal of time and pains in trying to get acquainted with me.' But he put them off by letting it be known that he was engaged to a girl in Columbus, Ohio. She did not exist.

He started 'numerous courtships, smitten, but not in love' in Lower Sandusky, now Fremont, Ohio, where he then lived. One evening, he climbed the fence of the Catholic convent for a tryst. The liaison ended as Fanny heartily disapproved of this interest in village girls.

'Do not fall in love with any of the Sandusky beauties,' Fanny wrote. 'Perhaps I am prejudiced, but I wish you to take into consideration that you will not always live in Sandusky. So do not marry a wife you will blush for anywhere. Do forgive me, brother, if I am meddling; if you do not like such interference, say so, and I shall forbear in the future.'

Hayes decided that the woman he should marry must be the image of his sister Fanny. He rejected Julia Buttles of Columbus, Ohio, who, according to Fanny, 'turned sick at your name' when he would not court her.

He was slow off the mark in wooing the twenty-one-year-old blue-eyed niece of Judge Lane and found her surrounded by other suitors. Then he fell for the Lanes's house guest Fanny Perkins. In a long and heartfelt letter to his sister, he explained that this Fanny had all the attributes that his sister Fanny would have required in his wife. But Fanny Perkins rejected him, so he went a-wooing a 'Miss W-', a Yankee girl in Columbus.

Hayes longed to get married. At twenty-one he had bet $25 that he would get married by the time he was twenty-five. With a year still to go, he lamented to Fanny: 'I have had no loves yet.'

He claimed to be 'one of the sunniest fellows in the world', but he confided that he really wanted a wife 'to take charge of my correspondence with friends and relatives. Women of education and sense can always write good letters, but men are generally unable to fish up enough entertaining matter to fill half a sheet.' He was deadly serious. In 1850, he ended one flirtation with a Miss H. because she was too flirtatious.

In the end, it came to a straight choice between two girls – a friend of Fanny's called Helen Kelley and a straitlaced graduate of Cincinnati's Wesleyan Female College called Lucy Webb. Helen was 'a gay figure in the world of fashion'. She was sophisticated, coquettish and surrounded by a number of suitors with 'fast' reputations.

Plainly a passionate woman, she excited Hayes sexually, but she frightened him as much as she attracted him. Besides Helen's assertive personality sometimes clashed with Fanny's. The dour Lucy on the other hand soothed him. She was a strict Methodist and a safer bet. Hayes's indecision lasted eighteen months.

Helen was certainly Fanny's choice. Fanny thought that if they married, Helen would keep Hayes near by in Columbus, but if he married Lucy she might take him away.

Meanwhile, Helen toyed with Hayes, first encouraging him, then distancing herself, professing her love for him, then seeing other suitors. Judging by his diaries, Hayes derived a certain masochistic pleasure from this.

Then in 1852, Hayes threw caution to the wind and married Lucy. Nevertheless, he remained almost unhealthily attached to his sister Fanny, despite the fact that she was now married with children. When Fanny died in childbirth, Hayes told Lucy: 'You are sister Fanny to me now.'

Lucy was a passionate opponent of slavery and convinced her husband to take an abolitionist position. She was also an early advocate of women's rights. When her husband was a Congressman, she accompanied him on official visits to schools, hospitals and prisons.

To the men of the 23rd Ohio Volunteer Infantry, her husband's Civil War regiment, Lucy was known as 'Mother Lucy' for her tireless efforts in ministering to the wounded and comforting the dying. In the White House, she became 'Lemonade Lucy' because she banned alcohol from the premises.

In office, Hayes had to confront problems with America's changing attitudes to sex. His own cousin John Humphrey Noyes founded a group of Bible Communists, called the Perfectionists, who practised 'complex marriage'. They were hounded out of Vermont as promiscuous adulterers and established the Oneida Community, dedicated to free love, in New York.

The major political problem, however, was the Mormons who were still practising polygamy. He took a tough line with them, arresting those who married more than once and excluding those who advocated polygamy from office.

Anti-pornography campaigner Anthony Comstock pushed through a Federal Law banning obscene material from the mail in 1873. In June 1878, Ezra Hervy Heywood, founder of the New England Free Love League, was arrested for sending a pamphlet advocating the abolition of marriage through the posts.

'A man guilty of circulating, writing or publishing obscene books – books intended or calculated to corrupt the young – would find no favour with me,' Hayes said. But when Heywood was sent to jail, Hayes pardoned him on the grounds that his 'writings were objectionable but were not obscene, lascivious, lewd, or corrupting in the criminal sense'.

Despite her ban on alcohol, Lucy Hayes was a popular First Lady. Praise from prominent people filled six Morocco-bound volumes. Poems were penned by Henry Wadsworth Longfellow, Oliver Wendell Holmes, John Greenleaf Whittier. Mark Twain also made a wry contribution. 'Total abstinence is so excellent a thing,' he wrote, 'that it cannot be carried to too great an extreme. In my passion for it I even carry it so far as to totally abstain from Total Abstinence itself.'

11

GARFIELD THE GAY?

James Garfield was the last of the 'log cabin' presidents. His father died when Garfield was two years old. He helped his mother work their small farm in Orange, Ohio, taking what schooling he could during the winter months. When he was seventeen, he worked driving the horses and mules that pulled flatboats along the Ohio canal.

Life on the canal was different from the stifling existence he had known in Orange. The young men were largely interested in one thing, and their trips took them down to Cleveland, a major port known for its abundance of brothels. Across the river in what was called Ohio City in 1849, it had been necessary to pass a law banning 'lewd and lascivious behaviour in any of the streets, lanes, alleys or public places'.

With the money he earned on the canals, Garfield enrolled in a local school run by the Disciples of Christ, a strict sect. He had a genuine conversion and became a preacher, working as a carpenter during the summer to put himself through Geauga Seminary in Chester, Ohio. Five years later, he repented of his life on the canal.

'Oh, at that time I was ripe for ruin and an active and willing servant of sin,' he wrote. 'How fearfully I was rushing with both soul and body to destruction.'

By that time, he had become excessively worried about masturbation. At the Seminary, he pored over Henry Ward Beecher's *Seven Lectures to Young Men*, the Reverend John Todd's *The Young Man* and Orson S. Fowler's *Amativeness: Embracing the Evils and Remedies of Excessive and Perverted Sexuality, Including Warning and Advice to the Married and Single*, a tract utterly condemning masturbation. Garfield fervently wished that there were 'ten thousand copies ... in every town in the United States'.

In his book, the Reverend Todd warned that nine out of ten boys indulged. It was okay for farmers and canal hands to waste their energies that way, but those, like Garfield, who were trying to rise in the world had to be self-sufficient and in control of their sexual desires. Masturbation was not just criminal and sinful. It doomed those who practised it to poverty and insanity.

Fowler warned of the 'pallid, bloodless countenance ... hollow, sunken and half-ghastly eyes [and] half-wild, half vacant stare' of the masturbator. The signs were obvious for all to see: 'carrying of the hands frequently to the sexual organs by way of changing their position'; 'lascivious expression on observing females'; and 'unwillingness to look other people in the face'.

Garfield felt he suffered from all of these symptoms and struggled with the 'total abstinence' that Fowler recommended. Then a phrenologist examining his head noticed an over-developed 'bump of amativeness' at the base of the skull. This, it was believed, governed sexual desire, something Garfield plainly had too much of.

To cure himself, Garfield would take frequent cold showers – first publicly at one of the little dam mills on the Chagrin river when there were no women about. Later he built his own shower bath at Hiram College.

During this period, Garfield took an inordinate interest in homosexuality. He studied what the Bible had to say on the subject and, as a classical scholar, read Cicero, Virgil, Plutarch and Seneca. This may have been because many nineteenth-century writers associated the excessive masturbation that so plagued the young Garfield with homosexuality.

However, more than one writer has concluded that Garfield had a juvenile homosexual infatuation with a young man named Oliver B. Stone. Throughout his life, his diaries reveal a deep uncertainty about his masculinity.

Garfield paid his way through the Western Reserve Eclectic Institute (now Hiram College) by teaching English and ancient languages. He was a passable poet and an accomplished classics scholar. He would astound friends by writing Greek with one hand and Latin with the other, simultaneously.

As a youth, Garfield had been deeply inhibited around young women and was frequently shocked by their forwardness. However, at the Eclectic College, he fell under the spell of Almeda A. Booth, one of the teachers whose early love affair had been ended prematurely by the death of her fiancé. The relationship was purely platonic, but she helped knock the rough edges off the crude canal boy.

At the same time, Garfield fell in love with Mary Hubbell, one of his students. He poured out his heart to her in poetry and love letters, and took her for walks in the moonlight. Garfield called the affair an 'adventure' and lapsed into coded Latin in his diary to describe the 'tender game' he played with Mary. She let her guard slip and they became close, perhaps even intimate, at Garfield's boarding house.

During this passionate affair, Mary and her family thought that the couple were engaged. When Garfield came down with a cold, they invited him into their house and put him through the standard treatment of the day. He was stripped, wrapped in a cold, wet sheet and laid in an unheated room for two hours. Then he was put to bed. Mary's parents went off to visit one of their other daughters and left Garfield alone in the house with Mary for a day. Mary nursed him, apparently attending to his every need – another coded note appeared in Garfield's diary.

Suddenly Garfield's ardour cooled. It is often thought that Garfield's attitude changed as marriage grew closer. His mother's second marriage had been a disaster. After a year, she had simply packed her bags and moved back home. In the Cuyahoga Court of Common Pleas, she was found 'guilty of gross neglect of duty as a wife' and divorced, her reputation forever tainted.

Garfield began seeing other women. He had become more relaxed in their company. After he met another student at the college, Lucretia Rudolph, he announced that he and Mary were not going to marry and that they had never been engaged. Mary's family were outraged and threatened to make his love letters public. The ladies of Hiram blackballed him out of sympathy for their dishonoured sister and his name was dirt on campus.

Garfield himself was bitter. After all, he had never asked Mary to marry him. 'To the first view, life – the world and society – seem pleasant and alluring,' he wrote, 'but when their depths are penetrated, their secret paths trod, they are found hollow, soulless and insipid.'

From his humble beginnings, Garfield craved to become respectable. To this end he asked Lucretia 'Crete' Rudolph, the daughter of one of the founders of the Eclectic College, to marry him. She consented and he was allowed to visit her, unchaperoned, in the privacy of her bedroom.

Nevertheless, as the nuptials approached the thought of marriage sent him into a black depression. They had planned to marry in 1854 when Garfield graduated, but he managed to postpone the wedding for two years while he took a BA at Williams College in Williamstown, Massachusetts. Again he supported himself there by teaching.

Only once during his time at Williams did he return to Hiram to visit Lucretia, but he frequently found time to visit the Disciples of Christ at Poestenkill, New York. There he met Mrs Maria Learned, who was bored with her unfeeling husband and formed a deep attachment to Garfield.

When she learnt that he was to be married to Lucretia Rudolph in Ohio, she encouraged him to strike up a relationship with Rebecca Selleck, a frequent visitor to the Learned household. Sister Rebecca was much more passionate than the sedate Lucretia, and she and Garfield spent much time alone in a room they called the Prophet's Chamber. His letters make it clear that they made love there, with the collusion, if not the participation, of Maria Learned. The three of them began to refer to themselves as the 'holy trinity' and the 'triangle'.

After he graduated from Williams in 1856, Garfield returned to his teaching post at Hiram at a salary of $600 a year, but he wrote regularly to Rebecca who kept his desirous love letters in the cleavage between her breasts.

Rebecca came to visit Garfield in Hiram, but Lucretia suspected nothing. She even dismissed campus gossip about Garfield's divided affections as baseless lies.

Garfield then attempted to establish a new 'triangle' by encouraging Rebecca and Lucretia to become friends. They got together at Garfield's nightly Bible readings, but he found it difficult to explain the exact nature of what he was proposing to the prudish Lucretia.

After being back in Hiram for over a year, the question of marriage was pressing once again. Garfield knew that he could not dodge it this time. He took one last trip to Poestenkill, to the 'holy trinity' there. On his return, he confessed all to Lucretia. She forgave him, but could not find it in her heart to forgive the duplicity of Rebecca who she thought was her friend.

Lucretia offered to release Garfield from his engagement, so that he could marry Rebecca, but it was respectability he craved, not passion. He would go through with the wedding 'with all its necessities and hateful finalities'. What Garfield feared most was the 'narrow exclusiveness of marriage'. Lucretia was well aware of his indifference, but after their four-year engagement the marriage simply had to go ahead.

'I don't want much parade about our marriage,' wrote Garfield, coldly. 'Arrange that as you see fit.'

There was no honeymoon and both of them were soon deeply unhappy. Garfield confessed that the marriage had been 'a great mistake' and took frequent business trips alone. Then the Civil War came and he joined the Union Army.

After the Battle of Shiloh in 1862, his health began to deteriorate. He was sent home to convalesce. Lucretia nursed him and her tenderness during that period rekindled their romance. She worked out that, during the first four and three-quarter years of their marriage, they had been together less than twenty weeks. She vowed from then on that they would never be parted.

However, Garfield was not to be corralled. He found excuses to travel to New York on business and he dropped by on Rebecca Selleck. In the autumn of 1862, he had an affair with Mrs Lucia Calhoun, an eighteen-year-old reporter for the *New York Times*. The affair was brief and Garfield confessed to Lucretia. She forgave him, but in 1867, he went to visit Mrs Calhoun again, explaining that he had to collect indiscreet letters that he had written to her which might damage his political career. Lucretia feared that the affair might start all over again and prayed that 'the fire of such a lawless passion would burn itself out unfed and unnoticed'.

On that occasion, Garfield probably resisted, but it seems likely that at other times he could not contain his sexual passion. During the 1880 election, there were allegations that he had visited a prostitute in a New Orleans brothel.

Four months after being elected, he was shot by a disgruntled office-seeker in the Baltimore and Potomac railroad depot in Washington, DC. He died on 19 September, 1881. Long after death, talk of his womanizing continued. For the remaining thirty-six years of her life, Lucretia Garfield lived in seclusion in Ohio, vehemently denying all rumours of her husband's infidelity.

12

THE PRIVATE PRESIDENTS

The twenty-first President of the United States, Chester Arthur, burnt all his private papers the day before he died which has made it difficult for biographers to discover anything much about the private side of Arthur's life. However, it is safe to assume, particularly in this case, that if someone is hiding something then there is something to be hidden.

There were certainly plenty of things that Arthur did not want disclosed. For example, he may not have been eligible to be the U.S. President. He was not a 'natural born citizen' as the Constitution demanded, but was probably born in Canada, and therefore a British subject.

Arthur was close to New York's Republican Boss, Senator Roscoe Conkling. Under Conkling's patronage, Grant appointed Arthur collector of the Customs House in New York harbour, well known as a home of graft, theft and bribery. In 1877, the Jay Commission exposed the corruption in the authority and the newly elected President Rutherford Hayes demanded Arthur's resignation.

Arthur's wife, Ellen Herndon, was seven years his junior. Her father was in command of a mail packet sailing from New York, when she met 'Chet' Arthur, a young lawyer. Arthur fell for young 'Nell' and, when her father was lost in a storm off Cape Hatteras in 1859, they married. As part of Senator Roscoe Conkling's political machine, they became rich. But Ellen became distressed by the fact that he spent so much time away from home, ostensibly drinking and smoking with his political cronies. She felt lonely and neglected, and there was talk of separation.

In January 1880, he was away in Albany when she attended a benefit concert in New York and caught a cold waiting for her carriage. When he heard the news of her illness, he jumped the milk train but by the time he arrived at her bedside she was unconscious. Two days later, she died.

Later that year, he was nominated for the vice-presidency and when Garfield was shot he became president. 'Honors to me now are not what they once were,' he wrote. In the White House, he kept a picture of his wife and put fresh flowers in front of it every day. He also presented a commemorative stained glass window to St John's Church. It was on the south side, so he could see it from the White House at night.

No woman could replace his 'Nell' as First Lady, but Arthur persuaded his youngest sister, Mary McElroy, to spend several months each year as 'Mistress of the White House'.

While publicly, Arthur played the grieving widower, privately he was having a high old time. He left his daughter in New York with a governess and sent his son to Princeton, where he majored in girls, wild parties and expensive clothes.

President Arthur then threw himself into a round of state dinners and private suppers. Commentators said that he was 'almost seeming to act in a conscious effort to forget the death of his wife'. Guests were confronted with fourteen-course meals with eight different wines. The White House was full of women.

Ex-President Hayes railed against 'liquor, snobbery and worse', but to most Washington socialites this was a refreshing change from the White House of 'Lemonade Lucy'. 'No President since the war has been so universally popular here,' wrote one Washington newspaper.

Arthur had always been a dandy. In the White House, it was rumoured that he would try on twenty pairs of trousers before settling on the ones he would wear. He wore tweeds during business hours, frock coats in the afternoon, and a dinner suit in the evening.

As President, Chester Arthur was the most eligible widower in the land. Mothers with marriageable daughters, widows eager to be consoled and hosts of romantic girls who saw President Arthur as a reincarnation of the legendary King Arthur flocked to his court. He paid a compliment to one, presented a posy to another and strolled in the White House gardens with a third. Gossips were constantly linking his name with eligible women.

He occasionally travelled with female companions, but he knew how to cover his tracks. When one nosey lady enquired a little too persistently into his love life, Arthur snapped: 'Madam, I may be President of the United States, but my private life is nobody's damned business.'

In fact, his very private, private life took up most of his time. His staff found it almost impossible to get him to give any of his attention to the affairs of state. It once took him a month to copy out a letter of condolence, which had already been drafted by the State Department and was destined for a European court. A White House clerk said later: 'President Arthur never did today what he could put off until tomorrow.'

After his first year of office, Arthur discovered he was dying of Bright's disease, a fatal kidney condition, and he seemed determined to enjoy what remained of his life.

How precisely he did that we shall never know. Whatever evidence there was went up in smoke on 15 November, 1886.

Grover Cleveland was the twenty-second President of the United States and the twenty-fourth, the only man to have returned to the White House after being voted out of office. In between came Benjamin Harrison, a stiff and formal man, nicknamed 'the human iceberg'. During his time at the White House, electric lights were installed, but he did not dare switch the light on in his bedroom, and he left the lights in the halls and living rooms on all night, fearing a shock if he touched the switch. The White House electrician had to turn them off when he reported for work in the morning.

Harrison did genuinely care for women. One of the few campaign promises his administration did fulfil was providing pensions for Civil War widows. However, this drained the treasury and put his administration into terminal decline.

Harrison's first wife, who was the first President-General of the Daughters of the American Revolution, became ill in 1892 and her widowed niece, Mrs Mary Scott Dimmick, took over as official hostess. Harrison was reluctant to leave his ailing wife to campaign for re-election. Ever the gentleman, his opponent Grover Cleveland refused to take advantage of the situation. This made for a lack-lustre campaign, the only excitement coming from the rise of a third party, the Populists. The result was a landslide to Cleveland.

In October 1892, before Harrison left office, his wife died of tuberculosis. After a service in the East Room of the White House, her body was returned to Indianapolis for burial.

Harrison returned to his law practice in Indianapolis and, in 1896, married Mary Scott Dimmick. This caused something of a scandal in the family and neither his son nor daughter from his first marriage attended the ceremony. The following year Harrison became a father again at the age of sixty-three. He died of pneumonia in Indianapolis on 13 March, 1901 and is buried in Crown Hill Cemetery, Indianapolis, alongside his two wives.

13

ROVER CLEVELAND

Grover Cleveland survived a sex scandal to get into office and is the only president to get married in the White House. He wed his twenty-one-year-old ward – twenty-eight years his junior – provoking another scandal.

Cleveland was also a draft dodger. He was called up in 1863 to fight in the Civil War, but he exercised his legal right under the Conscription Act and paid a young Polish immigrant named George Benninsky $150 to fight in his place. While the war was on, Cleveland built up his law practice in Buffalo and spent a great deal of time eating, drinking and gambling. He was particularly fond of the beer, sausages and sauerkraut at Schenkelerger's restaurant. His weight soared to 250 lbs. The only exercise he got was on fishing and hunting trips, and his occasional visits to local brothels.

From 1871 to 1874, he was sheriff of Erie County and personally hanged murderers, rather than inflict the onerous task on his deputies. He then returned to private practice. 'The law,' he said, 'is a jealous mistress.'

Not that jealous. Around that time, he became involved with a widow, Mrs Maria Halpin. She was thirty-six; he thirty-seven. She gave birth to a son. There was no proof that the child was his. Indeed, she named him Oscar Folsom Cleveland after Cleveland's law partner, but the other men Mrs Halpin had been seeing were all married, so Cleveland gallantly admitted paternity. Mrs Halpin demanded marriage. Cleveland provided only child support.

In the 1884 presidential election, the Republican candidate was James G. Blaine and the battle between Cleveland and Blaine was one of the dirtiest campaigns in American history. While in Congress, Blaine had accepted $100,000 in bribes from the railroads. Even the corrupt New York Republican Boss Conkling, when asked why he had not backed Blaine's nomination, said: 'I do not engage in criminal practice.'

Democratic newspapers ran huge features showing how Blaine had got rich in political office. The Republicans countered with stories about Cleveland's illegitimate child. Cleveland took the bold step of admitting all. He announced that he had once formed an 'illicit connection with a woman and a child had been born and given his name'. He denied that he had ever entertained a woman 'in any bad way' while he occupied the governor's mansion in New York and wired his campaign managers the simple message: 'Whatever you say, tell the truth.'

This audacious plan paid off handsomely. The more that came out about the Halpin affair, the better the light Cleveland appeared in. He had dutifully maintained an interest in the child's welfare. When Mrs Halpin began drinking heavily, he arranged for the boy to go to an orphanage while she was confined to a mental institution. When she escaped and kidnapped the child, Cleveland found a prominent New York family to adopt the boy and he grew up to be a respected doctor.

Meanwhile, the Democrats discovered that Blaine's first child had been born just three months after his marriage. When Cleveland was given the evidence, he tore it up, saying: 'The other side can have the monopoly on all the dirt in this campaign.'

The story leaked out anyway, but instead of coming clean, Blaine claimed that due to a mix-up involving the death of his father, there had been two marriage services. The first, he said, had occurred six months earlier. He produced no evidence to this effect and no one believed him. The contrast between the two candidates could scarcely have been more vividly drawn.

It was also discovered that Blaine had lied to a House committee investigating railroad contracts; and in a letter to a railroad executive, Blaine had solicited false testimony. The letter concluded with the incriminating line: 'Burn this letter.'

The campaign dissolved into a slanging match. Democratic mobs would chant: 'James G. Blaine, the continental liar from the state of Maine' and 'Burn this letter'. Republicans would yell: 'Ma, Ma, where's my pa?' The Democrats would counter with: 'Gone to the White House, ha, ha, ha.'

At an election meeting in Chicago, one of the electorate eloquently summed up the position. 'We are told,' he said, ' that Mr Blaine has been delinquent in office but blameless in private life, while Mr Cleveland has been a model of official integrity, but culpable in his personal relations. We should therefore elect Mr Cleveland to the public office which he is so well qualified to fill, and remand Mr Blaine to the private station which he is admirably fitted to adorn.'

As the election drew closer, the race was neck and neck. Everything depended on the vote in New York, where Cleveland was unpopular. A week before the election, Blaine went to New York to woo the Irish Catholic vote. His mother was a Catholic and his sister was a mother superior. At a meeting of five hundred clergymen called

131

to condemn Cleveland over his illegitimate child once again, the pastor of Murray Hill Presbyterian Church stood up and dubbed the Democrats the party of 'Rum, Romanism and Rebellion'.

New York Democrats seized on this anti-Catholic remark and swung the state. Cleveland won the election by 219 electoral votes to Blaine's 182, although he was ahead in the popular vote by just 1,100.

In 1876, Cleveland's partner Oscar Folsom – probably the father of Mrs Halpin's baby – had been killed when he was thrown from a buggy. Cleveland was executor of Folsom's estate and looked after his widow and her eleven-year-old daughter Frances. For years, Cleveland saw a great deal of the two of them. No one suspected that his interest in his young charge was anything more than avuncular.

Frances and her mother missed the inauguration, but they visited the White House that spring. It was rumoured that Cleveland was going to marry Mrs Folsom. In fact, Cleveland had often told friends who enquired why he was not married that he was waiting for his wife to grow up.

Soon after the visit, Cleveland wrote to Frances proposing marriage, and once she had graduated from Wells College, they became engaged.

On 2 June, 1886, in the Blue Room in the White House, in front of fewer than forty guests, President Cleveland and Frances Folsom were married in a revised and shortened service. The word 'obey' was omitted. When the ceremony was over, a twenty-one-gun salute sounded from the navy yard and all the church bells in Washington peeled out.

At the reception and supper in the state dining room, Cleveland and his bride received a telegram of congratulations from Queen Victoria and one of the table decorations was, appropriately enough, a model of the full-rigged ship *Hymen* made out of pansies and pink roses.

There was, of course, intense public interest in the President's youthful bride. The story circulated that he had bought her first baby carriage. The press followed them on their honeymoon to Deer Park in Maryland, camping outside their honeymoon cottage and observing the newly-weds through telescopes. Cleveland commented that the reporters were 'doing their utmost to make American journalism contemptible'.

The President and his wife were, after all, rather an odd couple. She was twenty-one, tall, graceful, dark-eyed, attractive. He was 260 lbs, bull-necked, physically unprepossessing. In fact, newspapers wrote scandalous editorials warning the young bride of the dangers of intimate relations with a man of such weight and girth. But the marriage was successful and they had five children.

In the 1888 election, Cleveland was sunk by his own side. Enemies in New York's Tammany Hall circulated a scurrilous pamphlet charging Cleveland with bestial perversions during his Buffalo days and brutal treatment of his young wife. Although he won the popular vote, he lost the electoral vote by 168 to Benjamin Harrison's 233. On leaving the White House on 4 March, 1889, Mrs Cleveland said to the staff: 'Take good care of the furniture and ornaments in the house . . . for I want to find everything just as it is now when we come back again. We are coming back just four years from today.'

Frances Cleveland was not just the youngest First Lady, she was one of the most popular. Even while her husband was out of office, she never lost her place in the public's affection and she returned to the White House four years later as if she had been gone just a day.

In 1895, during his second term in office, Cleveland heard from Mrs Halpin again. She was now remarried and living in New Rochelle, New York. In a letter to the

President, she demanded money and threatened to publish her side of the story. Nothing came of it.

Frances wept when she left the White House a second time, after William McKinley's inauguration. So did many of the staff. They moved to Princeton. Cleveland was happy there and she was at his side when he died in 1908. Four-and-a-half years later, she married the Professor of Archaeology at Princeton. She survived until October 1947.

Cleveland's successor William McKinley had a dizzying view of women. During his youth he repeatedly read *Noble Deeds of American Women,* which was one of the few books his father owned.

He was a staunch Unionist and vehemently anti-slavery. When war came he joined up and fought fiercely. Returning as a war hero, McKinley was popular with girls. He had a muscular body and dressed foppishly, with a black frock coat and purple ties. Eager to get married, he often escorted local belles and his name was linked romantically with several of them. But then he fell for Ida Saxton.

McKinley first set eyes on her working as a cashier in her father's bank. She was beautiful and attracted a number of young male depositors who often brought bouquets in with their money. Soon McKinley had vanquished his rivals and Ida's father said: 'You are the only man I have ever known to whom I would entrust my daughter.'

They married in 1871 and honeymooned in New York. Their first daughter was born later that year. At his wife's prompting, McKinley became a leader in the temperance movement, though as President he enjoyed whiskey, wine and a good cigar. Ida was very possessive and called her husband 'the Major', after the rank he attained during the Civil War.

Soon after their second daughter's birth in 1873, phlebitis and epileptic seizures rendered her an invalid. The child finally died, closely followed by her older sister. They had no more children.

Ida believed that her illness was a punishment from God. If it was, it punished her husband too. Her possessiveness became an obsession. She forbade him to leave her side and took bromides to sleep. Although she regularly seemed to hover on the brink of death, she always rallied and somehow managed to survive another thirty-four years.

McKinley was devoted to her. He organized his burgeoning political career around her. She was never far from his side when he served as a Congressman and Governor of Ohio, spending most of her waking moments in a small rocking chair. If he could not be with her he would send a note saying: 'Receive my evening benediction of love.'

In the White House, she was lavishly dressed and received guests sitting in a blue velvet chair. She held a small bouquet so that she would not be expected to shake hands. Contrary to protocol, she would be seated next to her husband at formal dinners. If he saw a seizure coming he would throw a napkin over her face until it passed. Although it was known that Ida's health was 'delicate' the press did not report the facts of her illness and they only came to light long after she died.

During his presidency, McKinley would often leave important business to attend to his wife. His political patron Mark Hanna once remarked: 'President McKinley has made it pretty hard for the rest of us husbands here in Washington.'

However, he also had his vices. He was a vain man and never wore his spectacles in public. He had a huge wardrobe and changed his clothes three or four times a day when they became wrinkled.

He also liked to dance and was extremely gallant with his partners. One can only speculate on how a virile man with an invalid wife would feel dancing with a personable young female partner.

When President McKinley was shot by a Polish anarchist, his dying thoughts were of his wife. After his death, she was nursed by her younger sister in Canton. She died five years later, at the age of fifty-nine, and was laid to rest beside her husband in a memorial tomb.

14

ROUGH RIDER

As a 'Rough Rider', Theodore Roosevelt was the only U.S. President to have a condom named after him. As teddy bears were also named after him, it could be said that he is the only president to have gone to bed with children all over the world.

Born on 27 October, 1858 at 28 East 20th Street, New York City, Roosevelt was a weakling, an asthmatic child. Too ill to attend school, he was given private tuition at home, which he supplemented with voracious reading.

At thirteen, the young Roosevelt was too weak to defend himself against two bullies and he persuaded his father to let him take boxing lessons. The incident, he said, 'did me real good' and he continued to use boxing to build up his strength.

At the age of sixteen, he became interested in girls. His favourite was Edith Carow. They had attended dancing classes together as children and Roosevelt mentioned in his diary that she was 'a very pretty girl'. He picnicked with Annie Murray, went rowing with Nellie Smith and riding with Fanny Smith. Fanny later recalled being overwhelmed by the 'unquenchable gaiety' of his personality. 'As a young girl I remember dreading to sit next to him at any formal dinner lest I become so convulsed with laughter at his whispered sallies as to disgrace myself and be forced to leave the room,' she said.

While at Harvard, Roosevelt went to parties in all the best houses of Boston. 'I have been having a very gay time,' he wrote. 'Some of the girls are very sweet and bright.'

His name was linked with Miss Fiske, Miss Wheelright, Miss Andrews and Miss Richardson – 'the prettiest girl I have seen for a long time'. And there was always Edith Carow.

Roosevelt compared all other girls to Edith. During a sleigh ride he mentioned that 'one of the girls looked quite like Edith – only not so pretty as her Ladyship'. Later Edith came to visit him at Cambridge, Massachusetts. 'I don't think I ever saw Edith look prettier,' he wrote to his sister. 'Everyone admired her little Ladyship immensely and she behaved as sweetly as she looked.'

By this time, Roosevelt had become quite a dandy, with his English-cut suits, silk cravats, cameo pins, beaver hat, fob watch and cane. He agonized over whether he should wear a frock coat or a cut-away in the afternoon.

In the summer of 1878, Roosevelt asked Edith Carow to marry him. She refused and he discovered that she had a romance. They quarrelled and Roosevelt 'was not very nice'. It was then that he met Alice Hathaway Lee, the daughter of a Boston banker.

'See that girl? I am going to marry her,' he told a friend. 'She won't have me, but I am going to have her.'

It was true. Alice was not at all impressed by Roosevelt. She claimed that a faint smell of formaldehyde clung to him. She certainly had no intention of marrying him. But he said: 'I loved her as soon as I saw her sweet, fair, young face.' He called her 'enchanting', 'flowerlike', 'radiant' and even rhapsodized over her to Edith, once they had made it up after their spat.

Roosevelt pursued Alice with the relentless energy he brought to bear on everything else in his life. Despite turning him down several times, she eventually consented to marry him after watching him box. Although he was totally outclassed, he showed such courage in the bout that everyone was impressed. Even when he had won her, he was so afraid of losing her that he bought a pair of French duelling pistols.

'How I love her!' he wrote. 'She seems like a star of heaven, she is so far above other girls; my pearl, my pure flower. When I hold her in my arms there is nothing on earth left to wish for.'

Roosevelt let his feelings run away with him and at least one teacher suggested that he was not entirely masculine. But Roosevelt did not apologize for his sensitivity. Nothing, he said, disgusted him more than the 'male sexual viciousness', which made a wife the servant of her husband's lusts.

While Roosevelt's fellow students had been carousing in the seamier parts of Boston, he had held himself inviolate. In October 1880, when he married Alice, he was still a virgin. He wrote in his diary: 'Thank Heaven, I am at least perfectly pure.'

In other passages, he had asked God's help to stave off temptation 'and to do nothing I would have been ashamed to confess'. When his wayward cousin Cornelius 'distinguished himself by marrying a French actress!' Roosevelt was outraged. 'He has disgraced the family, the vulgar brute,' Roosevelt wrote. 'P.S. She turns out to be a mere courtezan! A harlot!'

Alice, too, was a virgin. He called her his 'baby wife'. The picture of her he loved most showed her at fourteen. But of their wedding night, all Roosevelt would confide to his diary was: 'Our intense happiness is too sacred to be written about.'

Together, on their honeymoon in New York, they would devour the newspapers – 'our only intercourse with the outside world'. His attraction to her was passionate and physical. Their honeymoon was 'a perfect dream of delight'.

'When we are alone, I can hardly stay a moment without holding her in my arms or kissing her,' he wrote. 'She is such a laughing, teasing, pretty little witch ... I cannot help petting and caressing her all the time.'

They travelled on to Europe by boat and Alice became so seasick that she thought she was going to die. In the National Gallery in London, Roosevelt admired the Rembrandts, but disapproved of the Rubens nudes. 'I do not believe that you can get a "grand Greek Aphrodite",' he wrote, 'by merely exhibiting a scantily attired Dutch housewife.'

Roosevelt had robust views on such things. He condemned the writing of Emile Zola, saying: 'Of course, the net result of Zola's writing has been evil. Where one man has gained from them a shuddering horror at existing wrong which has impelled him to try to right that wrong, a hundred have simply had the lascivious, the beast side of their natures strengthened and intensified.'

Even Tolstoy was 'a sexual degenerate ... for erotic perversion frequently goes hand in hand with a wild and fanatical mysticism'. This was largely because he saw Tolstoy as being against marriage, which Roosevelt thought was proper except for shiftless and worthless people. While divorce, he thought, should not be easy for anyone.

Roosevelt called Alice 'Sunshine'; she called him 'Teddykins'. However, their love life was not without problems. Alice had to undergo gynaecological surgery in 1882 before they could have children.

Then tragedy struck. On Valentine's day 1884, both Roosevelt's mother and his wife – who had given birth to a baby daughter just two days before – died of typhoid fever. He wrote in his diary: 'The light has just gone out of my life.'

His obituary of Alice was terse: 'Alice Hathaway Lee. Born at Chestnut Hill, July 29th, 1861. I saw her first in Oct. 1878; I wooed her for over a year before I won her; we were betrothed on Jan. 25th, 1880, and it was announced on Feb. 16th; on Oct. 27th of the same year we were married; we spent three years of happiness greater and more unalloyed than I have ever known to fall to the lot of others; on Feb. 12th 1884 her baby was born, and on Feb. 14th she died in my arms, and my mother had died in the same house, on the same day, but a few hours previously. On Feb. 16th they were buried together in Greenwood. On Feb. 17th I christened the baby Alice Lee Roosevelt. For joy or for sorrow my life has now been lived out.'

He was just twenty-five.

Later, he published a book called *In Memory of My Darling Wife*. In it, he pays her a more glowing tribute: 'She was beautiful in face and form, and lovelier still in spirit; as a flower she grew, and as a fair young flower she died. Her life had been always in the sunshine; there had never come to her a single great sorrow; and none ever knew her who did not love and revere her for her bright, sunny temper and her saintly unselfishness. Fair, pure, and joyous as a maiden; loving, tender, and happy as a young wife; when she had just become a mother, when her life seemed to be just begun, and when the years seemed so bright before her – then, by a strange and terrible fate, death came to her.

'And when my heart's dearest died, the light went from my life for ever.'

Roosevelt lost three successive elections and left for Dakota, where he took up the life of a cowboy. He returned to New York two years later to marry again, this time to his childhood sweetheart Edith Carow. They had remained friends throughout Roosevelt's marriage to Alice. However, Edith secretly admitted that she was 'passionately in love with him' but had moved to England with her mother.

When Alice died in 1884, Roosevelt wanted to be true to her for ever and avoided seeing Edith. But Edith was determined and returned to New York. The two of them met by accident and the old flame re-ignited.

'I have never loved anyone else,' Edith wrote to him. 'I love you with all the passion of a girl who has never loved before.'

Roosevelt went through torments of self-recrimination for not being constant in his heart to Alice.

'I utterly disbelieve in and disapprove of second marriages,' he wrote to his sister Bamie. 'I have always considered that they argued weakness in a man's character. You could not reproach me one half as bitterly for my inconstancy and unfaithfulness as I reproach myself.'

But he was still young and he wanted a family. Secretly they got engaged. To shuttle so eagerly from the arms of Alice to those of Edith, after having done the reverse seven years before, was hardly the act of a gentleman, let alone a politician famous for his public moralizing.

They married in London in 1886. By the time, they returned to the U.S., Edith was pregnant. They settled at Sagamore Hill, in Oyster Bay, New York, in the house Roosevelt had built for Alice, and had five children over the next ten years.

In the 1890s, eager for high political office, the Roosevelts were drawn into the political circle of Henry Adams, the grandson of John Quincy Adams and great-grandson of John Adams. They met in Adams's book-lined living room in Lafayette Square near the White House in Washington, DC. Although they talked politics, the group was riven with sexual intrigue.

Adams was in love with the wife of another Senator J. Donald Cameron of Pennsylvania. She was said to be the most beautiful woman in Washington. John Hay, former secretary to Abraham Lincoln, who went on to become Secretary of State, though married, was having a clandestine affair with Nannie Lodge, the wife of Roosevelt's best friend Henry Cabot Lodge. Clarence King, the brilliant geologist, had a black common-law wife who bore him five children. Adams was also captivated by Edith, Roosevelt's 'sympathetic little wife'. She obviously had power over Roosevelt. 'He stands in such abject terror of Edith,' Adams said.

From Adams's house in Lafayette Square, Roosevelt began to turn his eyes towards the White House, but in 1892, he was almost ruined by scandal.

Katy Mann, the former maid of Roosevelt's alcoholic brother Elliott, claimed that Elliott was the father of her illegitimate child and demanded $10,000 for the child's upkeep. She had a locket and letters to back her story, plus the testimony of the other servants. Elliott, who had been addicted to morphine and laudanum since an accident, vehemently denied the charges. The family hired an 'expert in likenesses' who examined the child and promptly concluded that Katy's story was true.

Roosevelt thought that marital infidelity was a hideous crime which reduced its perpetrator to the level of a 'flagrant man-swine'. He believed that any sex between Elliott and his wife Anna should cease until Elliott's 'hideous depravity' had been expunged by 'two or three years of straight life'. The family paid Katy off, but Elliott collapsed under the pressure. He took another mistress, a Mrs Evans, and resumed his heavy drinking. Terrified of ruin, his wife wanted to seize control of Elliott's $170,000-estate before he blew it, and moved to have him declared legally insane. Roosevelt, himself, applied for the writ. The press found out and had a field day.

Later, Roosevelt got his own back. He made his famous assault on 'muck-rakers'. In 1913, he sued the editor of the obscure Michigan paper, *Iron Age*, who said that he frequently got drunk. Roosevelt won the case and just six cents in damages.

When the assassination of McKinley brought Roosevelt to the presidency, Edith filled the White House with children and pets. She tried to keep the family in the background while reporters focused on her flamboyant husband, though the debut of one daughter and the wedding of another took place in the White House. She was also an accomplished political hostess, aristocratic enough to play the game.

One of Roosevelt's closest friends in Washington was Jules Jusserand, the French ambassador to the U.S. from 1902 to 1924. The two men would going swimming together naked, in the Potomac, though Jusserand would keep his gloves on 'in case we meet a lady'.

Roosevelt, though prudish, showed no such shame.

15

A PRESIDENT FRUSTRATED

Weighing over three hundred pounds and standing six foot tall, William Howard Taft was the largest president but he spent his life under the heel of two small, slim women. He was plainly a man who liked to be dominated and he found the perfect dominatrix in his wife Helen.

His masochism began with his domineering mother, Louisa. She and her sister, Delia, had travelled together as young women and had vowed not to marry. When Louisa took up with Alphonso Taft, seventeen years her senior and a man who could bring her the social status she craved, Delia wrote despairingly: 'Oh Louise, Louise, how can I live the rest of my life without you? I am but one half of a pair of scissors.'

Alphonso had been married before. His first wife described the marriage as an 'unbroken sea of unhappiness'. He was stiff and Victorian. His second marriage was equally cold. Louisa always referred to her husband as Mr Taft. When he died, she resumed her travels with her sister.

Louisa constantly complained that Taft was large for his age, grew fatter every day and 'he has such a large waist that he cannot wear any of the dresses that are made

145

with belts.' But it was her constant chiding that made him overeat.

When Taft left home, he found himself unhappy. He was used to Louisa dominating his life. Soon he found the perfect substitute, Helen 'Nellie' Herron. She had a personality much like his mother's. He pursued her with ardour for two long years. She did not respond with passion, but slowly began to realize that Taft could help her to fulfil her lifelong ambition to be First Lady.

At the age of seventeen, Helen had stayed in the White House as a guest of President Hayes. She had not 'come out' yet, 'so I couldn't spend my time in the White House as I would have liked in going to brilliant parties and meeting all manner of charming people,' she lamented. However, she got a taste for Washington and in 1912 she told a *New York Times* reporter that she had vowed to marry only a man 'destined to be President of the United States'.

In fulfilling that ambition, Nellie has been compared to 'chilled steel', but otherwise, she was neurotic. As a girl, she shied away from the social whirl because she feared sexual relationships. Young men made her tremble. She hated them. She got on better with married men ten or more years her senior.

'This matter of fancying people is inexplicable,' she wrote in her diary. At twenty-two, she still claimed to be 'utterly indifferent' to men. However, she and her girl-friend Sally visited a 'Bohemian' barroom opposite the Music Hall in Cincinnati, where they drank beer and smoked cigarettes. This, she boasted, was 'rather fast'.

The year after her visit to the White House, Nellie had invited childhood friend William Taft to one of her 'salons', where they talked about Washington. From the beginning he adored her, but she tried to calm his passion.

146

'Friendship is infinitely higher than what is usually called love,' she wrote, 'that fatal idealization which is so blind and, to me, so contemptible.'

Taft, though, was hopelessly smitten.

'Oh Nellie, you must love me,' he pleaded. 'Any act, any expression, any look of yours, Nellie, that shows me you hold me dear . . . sets me wild with delight. Every such act, or expression or look I regard as evidence, with however little ground, that there is dawning in your heart the love I am so hungry for.'

Taft assured her that his love 'grew out of friendship' and was 'founded on a respect and admiration for your high character . . . and your intellectual superiority'. If they married, he promised, she would be 'senior partner' for life.

Even when they became secretly engaged, she remained frigid. He forgave her for this. Taft said she was 'afraid I shall think you too cold and you want to be forgiven for it. Why, Nellie, dear, do you think I think you are any less tender in your feeling because you do not talk about it? Ah, my dear, I know you better than you think I do. You are reserved. That is your nature.'

Helen only married Taft in 1886 because, as she wrote to her mother, 'a lot of people think a great deal of Will. Some people even say that he may obtain some very important position in Washington.'

Taft's own ambition was to be Chief Justice of the Supreme Court, but Helen steered him relentlessly towards the presidency. When pleased, she called him 'the dearest sweetest boy that ever lived' or 'my dear darling, lovely, beautiful, sweet, precious boy'. He called her his 'guardian angel'.

But still she kept her distance. She frequently left him to go on trips and extended holidays alone. He felt lost if he was away from her for even a day or two and would bombard her with letters. She rarely replied.

SEX LIVES OF THE U.S. PRESIDENTS

'I shall understand silence, my darling, to mean that you are having a good time,' he bravely conceded.

When she did write, it was not any better.

'I was very much puzzled by your letter,' he replied on one occasion. 'I read it over and over again. There was no word of endearment or affection from one end to the other and the tone of it sounded to me so hard and complaining.'

But even masochists are grateful for small mercies. When he discovered the merest hint of affection, he exalted that it was 'all the sweeter that it is so unusual in you'.

She chided him on his excessive eating, saying that she found his obesity physically repulsive. But she did not try to curb it as it gave her the excuse not to have sex with him. It was this sexual frustration that led him to seek comfort in food in the first place.

'Oh Nellie, do say that you will try to love me,' he begged. 'Oh, how I will work and strive to be better and do better. Oh Nellie, you must love me.'

In *William Howard Taft – An Intimate History*, the author Judith Icke Anderson concludes that the more pathetic of Taft's letters tell us that he got very little gratification as an adult.

But he did get one piece of satisfaction. After he left the White House – which he described as the 'lonesomest place in the world' – President Harding appointed him Chief Justice. So both Helen and Taft got what they were after.

16

THE BERMUDA TRIANGLE

In 1884, when Woodrow Wilson was about to be married, he had a mental breakdown. The physical symptoms included an eye tic and a paralysed right hand, something Sigmund Freud could have made much of in his famous psycho-analytical study of Wilson.

Wilson complained at the time that he was 'ignorant of women' and 'shut up in his own heart'. He wrote to his fiancée, Ellen Axson, confessing in barely concealed sexual terms: 'It isn't pleasant or convenient to have strong passions. I have the uncomfortable feeling that I am carrying a volcano about with me. My salvation is in being loved.'

He was twenty-eight and still a virgin. Freud concluded that the cause of Wilson's breakdown was that he was tortured by the power and intensity of his own libido, as his periodic fits of depression continued during both his first and second marriages.

Wilson had been in love before he met Ellen Axson. When he was twenty-three he had fallen for his cousin Hattie and he wrote ardent letters to her.

'His increased masculinity for the moment led him no closer to the body of a woman,' Freud wrote of this correspondence.

Headaches and indigestion plagued him that time too, so much so that he had to drop out of the University of Virginia without a degree. Acutely unhappy, he proposed to Hattie. She refused him.

There seems to have been some sexual activity even earlier. On vacation in Columbia in 1878, when he was twenty-two, he wrote to friends that he was at 'the scene of some old love adventures' and joked about 'a walk and a kiss'. He also said that religious camp meetings he had attended made flirtation easy.

'Certainly one can hardly find courage enough to blame the young men and women for yielding to temptation which everything conspires to make almost irresistible,' he said. 'I know well enough that I could pretty safely predict my own course under such circumstances.'

On that holiday, he certainly made a monumental effort to keep away from the many pretty girls who attended the amateur concerts and went for moonlight excursions on the river. In Wilson's young mind, sexual stirrings were the work of the devil.

However, Wilson seems to have had a relatively happy 'romp' with Katie Mayrant, the attractive niece of Mrs J. Reid Boylston who owned the boarding house he stayed at in Atlanta, shortly before he met his first wife to be.

The feelings of depression and loneliness that tormented Wilson throughout his life – attributed, by Freud and others, to his fear of his own powerful sex drive – didn't make his wooing of Ellen all gloom and doom. He wrote to her saying: 'I long to be made your master – only however, on the very fair and equal terms that, in exchange for the authority over yourself which you relinquish, you shall be constituted supreme mistress of me.'

He also joked that during a brief separation they formed 'an interstate love league (of two members only, in order that it may be of manageable size)'.

In 1885, they married. He took various professorships at Bryn Mawr College, Pennsylvania, and the Wesleyan College, Connecticut. During separations they exchanged letters daily. Even ten years after his marriage, his correspondence indicates an intense passion. In 1895, he wrote: 'Then I come myself, to claim you, to take possession of you – of all the time and love you can give me: to take you in my arms and hold you till I have made sure, by feeling your heart beat against mine and by seeing once more the very depths of your eyes, that I am really at home once more, with the woman who has made me and kept me what I am. I tremble with a deep excitement when I think of it. I verily believe I never quivered so before with eager impatience and anticipation. I know that I was not half so much excited on the eve of our marriage.'

Elsewhere he called himself her 'intemperate lover' and, shortly before returning home one time, he asked: 'Are you prepared for the storm of love making with which you will be assailed?'

In 1902, Woodrow Wilson became president of Princeton. During this time particularly, he made inordinate efforts not to be away from home at night. On the other hand he spent time translating from the French a highly erotic bedroom scene from Théophile Gautier's *Mademoiselle de Maupin*. At the same time, he seemed to have developed over-active sexual fears. When he heard that his wife's young sister, Margaret Axson, then eleven, was going to live with relatives in Athens, Georgia, he became alarmed that she would be in a college town where 'the restraints upon the intercourse of the two sexes are at a minimum' – though he conceded: 'It must be the riotous elements in my own blood that make me fear so keenly what even the most honourable young fellows might be tempted by mere beauty to do.'

151

He was concerned that, as an academic himself, his own daughters were also exposed to the attentions of students. At Princeton, he fenced them in. When a student lent one of them a volume of poems by Edward de Vere, Earl of Oxford, which celebrated love a little too lustily for a staunch Presbyterian like Wilson, he confiscated the volume and burnt it.

He was extremely jealous of his wife, envying men who sat next to her at dinner. He also told her that he was not worthy of her and that she should pray that he be less subject to temptation.

Even in 1908, after more than twenty years of marriage, Wilson was writing that his love continued to grow 'deeper and more passionate'. Around this time, his mother died and his father took up with a Mrs Gannis, which Wilson found disturbing. He was glad when they broke up.

A mass of sexual contradictions, Wilson was embarrassed when he heard jokes about sex, but he was not above telling a risqué story himself. What's more, the dry-as-dust scholar had a mistress.

Wilson met Mrs Peck in 1907. She was a vivacious, witty, sophisticated woman of forty-five, a gourmet cook, an accomplished pianist and an excellent dancer. Born in 1862, in Grand Rapids, Michigan, as Mary Allen, she married Thomas Harbach Hulbert in 1883. Their marriage was a happy one. She had one child, a son, before her husband died suddenly six years later.

The young widow went to live in Rome with her recently widowed father-in-law and his young woman companion who he later adopted. After two years, she quit this bizarre *ménage à trois* and returned to America to have an operation to correct injuries sustained during childbirth.

In 1840, she married Thomas Dowse Peck, a widower with two daughters, and moved to Pittsfield, Massachusetts. She found her husband to be cruel and mean, and fell into a deep depression. However, a sympathetic doctor recommended that she holiday alone on Bermuda, which she did each winter after 1892. It was there, in 1907, that she met Wilson. He was on his first vacation alone without Ellen. He found an 'instinctive sympathy' between them and one topic of conversation, not unnaturally, was marital unhappiness.

When Wilson returned to Princeton after his vacation, he continued to write to Mrs Peck. They met again in 1908, when Wilson was holidaying alone in Bermuda once more. They walked along the beach together, reading verse. Soon they were deeply in love. One letter, which Wilson never sent, began: 'My precious one, my beloved Mary.'

At the same time, Wilson was writing home to Ellen, describing Mrs Peck and the platonic friendship they had struck up. Ellen was not convinced. When he returned to Princeton that autumn, there was a blazing row and Ellen refused to accompany her husband on his trip to Great Britain that year as she had in 1906.

However, when he returned from England, they made up as husband and wife and became lovers again. She even accompanied him on a visit to the Pecks in Pittsfield, and invited Mrs Peck to come and stay with them in Princeton. When Mrs Peck accepted the invitation and actually turned up in Princeton, it caused quite a stir.

In 1909, Wilson and Mrs Peck discussed separation and divorce from their respective partners. Wilson urged caution and circumstances conspired to keep them apart. Wilson, though, wrote to Mrs Peck that he thought of her 'a thousand times' and he grew jealous when he heard that Mrs Peck was considering an invitation from the Governor of Bermuda, a bachelor whose name had also been linked to hers romantically.

That winter, there was no correspondence between Wilson and Mrs Peck. It is clear that he visited her in New

York. He was in or near the city at least six times in November, December and January. His other correspondence indicates that sex was very much on his mind that winter. Ironically, Mrs Peck's apartment was at 39 East 27th Street, only five blocks from the house where Wilson's father had received 'love ministries' from Mrs Gannis.

Mrs Peck began divorce proceedings in 1912. Wilson secured the Democratic nomination at the party's convention that same year and there were rumours that he might be named in the suit. It was even said that the judge had been given one of Wilson's love letters in evidence. Wilson's presidential opponent Theodore Roosevelt, who was running for a third time, dismissed the gossip.

'You can't cast a man as a Romeo when he looks and acts so much like an apothecary's clerk,' Roosevelt said.

Mrs Peck's divorce was granted and she reverted to calling herself Mrs Hulbert. Wilson, however, was already well on his way to the White House and any whiff of scandal could have cost him the presidency. When he won the election though, he took his entire family to Bermuda for a holiday. Mrs Peck joined them there. She also visited Wilson in Washington, but the couple were always chaperoned by Ellen or Wilson's cousin, Helen Bones.

In the last year of her life, Ellen Wilson told Cary Grayson, the White House doctor, that the Peck affair was the only unhappiness that her husband had caused her during their long marriage. In 1915, he confessed to what he called the contemptible error and madness of a few months – November, December and January of 1909–10, perhaps? – that had left a stain on his whole life.

Mrs Peck and Wilson kept up a lively correspondence and she visited him at the White House in 1915, after Ellen had died from kidney disease. There was speculation that they might marry. Wilson certainly supported her financially, but by then he had already met Mrs Edith Bolling Galt. Less than a year after his first wife died, Wilson turned his attention to the forty-three-year-old widow. They met when Helen Bones, who had taken on the duties of First Lady when Ellen died, invited her to tea. Wilson was out playing golf, but came home early. He invited her to dinner; two months later, he proposed. Mrs Galt could give him no answer. Wits said she was so shocked that she fell out of bed.

Wilson was determined to ensnare her. He sent her flowers daily and had a private wire installed between her home and the White House so that they could communicate secretly. They may not have slept together in the White House before they were married, but their letters indicate that they were physically intimate during a secret vacation in New Hampshire.

Back in Washington, Wilson's colleagues found him hopelessly in love. He put aside all but the most pressing business of state to be with his sweetheart. With the European powers already embroiled in World War I, it was not the time to have a lovesick president.

His ministers were terrified of the political repercussions if Wilson married again so soon after the death of his first wife, but they dare not tell him that. Instead, to remind him of the political dangers he faced, they told him that Mrs Peck was circulating his letters around town. The plan backfired. Wilson rushed over to Mrs Galt's house, spilt the beans about Mrs Peck and begged her to stand by him. She did and agreed to marry him. Wilson wrote a sickeningly schmaltzy press release and sent it out to the papers.

Fortunately for the standing of the President, the *New York Times* chose to paraphrase his statement rather than print it in full. But his luck could not hold. On 9 October 1915, the *Washington Post* made one of the most embarrassing typos in history.

In a story about Wilson and his fiancée's first appearance in public, the *Post* intended to say: 'The President spent much of the evening entertaining Mrs Galt.' Instead, it reported: 'The President spent much of the evening entering Mrs Galt.'

The editors spotted the error once the first edition had hit the streets and recalled the paper from the newsstands, but some of the issue had already been sold. The story got around and it confirmed the public's worst suspicions.

Soon Wilson was facing a hostile press. Rumours circulated that he was neglecting Ellen's grave. It was even alleged that Mrs Galt had been behind a bizarre plot to murder the first Mrs Wilson. The outraged women of America began to protest.

To limit the political damage, Wilson decided to marry as soon as possible and he and Mrs Galt were wed in December 1915. The new Mrs Wilson was not as tolerant as the old one when it came to Mrs Peck. She was banned from the White House. There is evidence that Wilson paid Mrs Peck off. It was said that she was paid $15,000 never to reveal the details of their extra-marital affair. However, within four years she was reduced to selling books door-to-door. Nevertheless, when she was offered $300,000 for his letters, she refused. Finally, in 1933, long after he was dead, she published her side of the story in her autobiography, *The Story of Mrs Peck*.

After World War I, Wilson proposed the setting up of the League of Nations, but Congress opposed him. Against the advice of this doctor, Admiral Grayson, he started a nationwide tour to drum up popular support. He had got as far as Pueblo, Colorado, when he collapsed with a stroke affecting the left side of his body. The train turned around at Wichita, Kansas, and took him back to Washington. For months, the President was bedridden, unable to carry out his duties.

During the illness, his wife Edith was rumoured to be the 'secret president'. In her memoirs, published in 1939, she calls this period her 'stewardship'. Others talked of 'Mrs Wilson's regency', 'Petticoat government' and referred to Woodrow Wilson as the 'First Man'.

She effectively ran the White House but claimed: 'I, myself, never made a single decision regarding the disposition of public affairs. The only decision that was mine was what was important and what was not, and the very important decision of when to present matters to my husband.'

Wilson died three years after leaving office, but Edith lived long enough to ride in President Kennedy's inaugural motorcade.

17

IN THE CLOSET

Warren Gamaliel Harding was a small-town politician who was forced into the presidency by an ambitious wife and a scheming party boss.

'I knew this job would be too much for me,' he said. However, though he was a total failure as a president, overseeing the most corrupt government in the history of the Republic, he did manage to maintain two steady mistresses, see other women and attend drunken orgies – an accomplishment unequalled until John F. Kennedy entered the Oval Office.

Born on 2 November, 1865 in Blooming Grove, Ohio, Harding was educated at a local school and learned the printing trade in the offices of the *Caledonia Argus*, a newspaper which his father bought in 1875. In 1880, he went to Ohio Central College, where he was a horn player in the band and editor of the year-book. He graduated with a BSc and returned to his family who then lived in Marion, Ohio. After a short period as a teacher, he began work as a journalist on the *Marion Mirror*. He was the first journalist to become president.

In 1884, Harding and two partners bought the *Marion Star* for $300. By 1886, he had bought them out. To improve the paper's profitability, he abandoned the *Star*'s non-partisan stance and began taking Republican advertising. In 1886, he was appointed a member of the Republican County Committee. After that, he left the running of the paper in the hands of his wife Florence.

'I went down there intending to help out for a few days and remained for fourteen years,' she said.

Florence Harding used her immense acumen to make her hard-drinking, poker-playing husband President of the United States. But she had a shaky start.

When she was just nineteen, Florence eloped with twenty-one-year-old Henry De Wolfe. He was a wastrel and spendthrift, and soon abandoned her. She returned shamefaced to Marion, Ohio, with a baby son. Despite her plight, she refused to live at home, renting rooms and earning money by teaching the piano.

She married Warren Harding in 1891, defying her father's objections. Harding was twenty-six; she was thirty-one. His motivation seems to have been sexual. Divorcees were considered racy in the 1890s, but he got less than he bargained for. After her early ardour had caused her so much grief, Florence had grown cold and passionless.

She was a plain woman. Harding called her 'Duchess' and often followed her advice, which was sometimes based on her consultations with an astrologer. There was little romance in their relationship and Harding took up with Mrs Carrie Phillips, the wife of a friend.

The affair began in 1905, when Florence was in hospital for the removal of a kidney, and continued for around fifteen years. Mrs Phillips was tall, high-breasted and had a reddish tinge to her golden hair. She was sophisticated, charming, mercurial and the love of Harding's life. At the time, she had an eight-year-old daughter, but she had just lost a son and needed consolation. Harding provided that and he quickly fell deeply in love.

With Carrie Phillips, he experienced physical desire and emotional release together. He loved both her mind and her body. He had only known this type of love once before, during a brief and passionate affair with one Pearle McWilliams.

They met and made love in her house on Main Street, but discretion forced them apart. When they were separated, Harding bombarded her with letters, sometimes thirty or forty pages long, full of romantic verse, doggerel and rhymed jokes. He rhapsodized about the feel of her thighs, the sound of her voice, the warmth of her personality, her hair, her cheekbones, her earlobes, how he craved her kisses, how he yearned for her breasts, how he longed for her caresses.

Harding pushed his political career on to a state-wide footing, largely so that he could get away from home. With the paper to run, Florence could hardly follow him. Carrie would find some excuse to get away from her doting husband and consummated her passion with Harding in countless anonymous hotel rooms.

At home in Marion, the Hardings and the Phillipses would be seen socially together and when Harding bought his first car the foursome would go out for early evening drives together. They even went on holiday together to Europe in 1909. On the boat, Harding and Carrie would slip out of their staterooms and meet in the shadows on deck. Part of the excitement, it seems, was finding ways to have sex practically under the noses of their respective spouses.

Even at home in Marion, it was amazing what they got away with. The small town was sometimes abuzz with gossip about them but somehow the managing editor of the local newspaper, Florence, did not seem to hear it.

At one point, Carrie asked Harding if he would leave his wife for her, but he was already too embroiled in his political career for that. She said she planned to take her daughter and go to live in Germany. At Christmas, Harding gave her a photograph of himself and begged her not to go. Carrie did go to Germany, briefly, but the outbreak of World War I forced her back into his arms and they quickly became lovers again.

John Phillips eventually found out about his wife's infidelity in 1920, but harboured no lasting resentment towards Harding. If Mrs Harding knew about it, she did not make a fuss.

However, Florence took against his other long-term mistress, Nan Britton, from the start. At thirteen, Nan had become obsessed with Harding, who was running for the Senate at the time. She was passing by the Hardings's house one day with her mother when they stopped to chat with the candidate. Nan admitted that she had decorated her room with Harding's campaign posters. Harding said that he was sure that she would like to have a real photograph of him to go with her collection. Florence neither smiled nor spoke and the atmosphere turned to ice.

Clement Wood, in his book *Warren Gamaliel Harding – An American Comedy*, maintains that Harding immediately fell for the child, who was already well developed, and took her to the newspaper office where she sat on his lap. But it is generally accepted that their wooing took considerably longer.

When Nan's father died, her mother turned to Harding for help. He found her a job as a substitute teacher and promised young Nan if he could ever 'do something for her' all she had to do was ask.

Three years later, she did just that. On graduating from secretarial school in New York, she wrote to him asking whether he remembered her and if he could help her get a job in Washington. He wrote back saying that he did indeed remember her – 'you may be sure of that, and I remember you most agreeably too' – and he would be delighted to help her. He would 'go personally to the War and Navy Department to urge your appointment'. He also mentioned that there was 'every probability' that he would be in New York the following week and that he would like to phone or to look her up and would 'take pleasure in doing it'.

She replied quickly saying that she thought that 'an hour's talk would be much more satisfactory', so that 'I could give you a better idea of my ability . . . and you could judge for yourself as to the sort of position I could competently fill'. This, she said, 'would please me immensely'.

The reply was a long handwritten letter on Senate notepaper saying 'I like your spirit and determination' and assuring her of 'my very genuine personal interest in your good fortune'.

Early the following morning, before she had time to reply, Harding phoned from Manhattan, saying that he had arrived in New York and she should meet him at his hotel. She hurried over. They walked through the reception area arm-in-arm and sat down on a settee. She blurted out all her schoolgirl feelings for him. He suggested that they go up to his room so that they would not be interrupted. Because of a convention in town, he explained, there was only one spare room in the hotel – the bridal suite.

'We had scarcely closed the door behind us when we shared our first kiss,' she wrote later. Between each succeeding kiss he would sigh 'God! God! Nan' or plead with her to 'tell me it isn't hateful for you to have me kiss you'.

Harding admitted that he had come from Washington solely to see her. He needed a woman. Nan pointed out that she was a virgin and was not ready to explore the 'lovely mystery' of sex despite the urgings of the fifty-

162

seven-year-old Harding. Nevertheless, Harding tucked $30 into the top of her new silk stockings.

Somehow between kisses, they managed to discuss her job prospects. He suddenly decided that it would not be a good idea for her to work in Washington. It was a goldfish bowl, full of gossip. Instead he would find her a job in New York.

After lunch he took her to the headquarters of U.S. Steel. In the taxi on the way he decided to test her shorthand. 'I'll dictate a letter to you and you tell me whether you get all of it,' he said.

He began: 'My darling Nan: I love you more than the world, and I want you to belong to me. Could you belong to me, dearie? I want you ... and I need you so ... ' He could not finish it because Nan smothered him with the kisses that he was pleading for.

At U.S. Steel, he introduced her to the president of the corporation who fixed her up with a job. When they got back to the hotel, Harding fell over when he got out of the cab. 'You see, dearie,' he said, red-faced, 'I'm so crazy about you I don't know where I'm stepping.'

Back in the bridal suite, she snuggled into his lap in a big armchair. 'We were made for each other,' he sighed. 'I'd like to make you my bride.'

Before she began her new job, Nan went off to visit her sister in Chicago. Harding sent her a picture of himself on the steps of the Capitol and a rambling forty-page letter. In her reply, she made her first casual request for money. He sent $42 – an odd amount that could appear as payment for possible work, he explained.

Harding had a speaking tour of the Mid-West booked at the time and, within a week, Nan received a letter asking her to meet him in Indianapolis. He was at the station when she arrived. They checked into separate rooms at the Claypool Hotel. She pretended to be his niece. They spent most of the night together, but she still withheld what she referred to as 'love's sweetest intimacy'.

The next day they travelled to Connersville, where Harding had a speaking engagement. This time Nan checked in in Harding's secretary's name, Elizabeth N. Christian. Then they went by train together back to Chicago.

'Dearie, are you going to sleep with me?' he asked on the way to the station. He booked a berth, which they shared, but still she coyly resisted.

'I had earlier reached this conclusion,' she wrote later. 'People got married and undressed and slept together; therefore, one must be undressed in order for any harm to come to them. I remember that this belief was so strong in my mind that when, during our ride together from Connersville to Chicago, I experienced sweet thrills from just having Mr Harding's hands upon the outside of my nightdress, I became panic-stricken. I inquired tearfully whether he really thought I would have a child right away. Of course this absurdity amused him greatly, but the fact that I was so ignorant seemed to add to his cherishment of me for some reason. And I loved him so dearly.'

In Chicago, they tried to check into a hotel as a married couple, but the disbelieving desk clerk said that if they could prove they were man and wife he would let them have the room for free.

Back in New York after their 'kissing tour', Nan could resist no longer. She gave way to what she called 'climatic intimacy'. It was a hot July day in 1917 and Harding had taken her to the Imperial, a second-rate hotel on lower Broadway which friends had recommended for such 'unconventional' activities.

'I remember so well, I wore a pink linen dress which was rather short and enhanced the little-girl look which was often my despair,' she wrote. 'There were no words going up in the elevator. The day was exceedingly warm and we were glad to see that the room which had been assigned to us had two large windows. The boy threw them open for us and left. The room faced Broadway, but we were high enough not to be bothered by street noises.'

It was a torrid afternoon and they stripped off and got into bed. 'I became Mr Harding's bride – as he called me – on that day,' she said.

As they lay in bed together afterwards, the telephone rang. Harding answered it. 'You have the wrong party,' he said.

At that moment, there was a knock on the door. A key turned in the lock and two detectives burst in. They demanded to know Nan's name and address. She turned to Harding. 'Tell them the truth,' he said, disconsolately. 'They have got us.'

As the detectives took down their details, Harding begged them to let Nan go, explaining that they had hurt no one.

'You'll have to tell that to the judge,' they said. A paddy wagon was on its way.

Then one of the detectives picked up Harding's hat. He noticed the name W.G. Harding stamped on the sweat-band and realized that they had just arrested a U.S. Senator. They became respectful – obsequious – and left the room. The two lovers dressed and the detectives led them to a side exit. On the way, Harding slipped them $20. In the taxi afterwards, he said: 'Gee, Nan, I thought I wouldn't get out of that for under a thousand dollars.'

This brush with danger did nothing to calm Harding's passion. He would travel up to New York once a week to sleep with her. She would meet him at Penn Station. They would go and see Al Jolson at the Wintergarden or a musical comedy on Broadway. Then they would have a discreet dinner in a dark restaurant.

'We were so sweetly intimate and it was a joy just to sit and look at him,' she wrote. 'The way he used his hands, the adorable way he used to put choice bits of meat from his own plate on to mine, the way he would say with a sort of tense nervousness, "That's a very becoming hat, Nan," or "God, Nan, you're pretty!" used to go to my head like wine and make food seem for the moment the least needful thing in the world.'

They talked freely about what they would do if Mrs Harding died. He would buy a place for them and they would live together in the country.

'Wouldn't it be grand, Nan?' he said. 'You'd make such a darling wife.'

They would talk about the day when he would be done with politics. He would get a farm with dogs and chickens and horses and, of course, a bride. But, for Nan, there was little appeal in life in the country. She liked the way, when people saw him, they'd say: 'There goes Harding.' She was already convinced that he was going to be president.

After dinner, they would check into one of the nondescript hotels that littered lower Manhattan as man and wife.

Sometimes, if Harding had a speaking engagement elsewhere in the country, he would write to Nan, giving her instructions on how to get there, when to arrive and which hotel he was staying at.

'I shall never forget how the sun was streaming in at the windows of the hotel when Mr Harding opened the door in his pajamas in answer to my rather timid knock,' she wrote of one tryst. 'His face was all smiles as he closed the door and took me in his arms. "Gee, Nan, I'm s'glad t'see you!" he exclaimed. I just loved the way he lapsed into the vernacular when we were alone together.'

Their lovemaking, apparently, was not confined to hotel bedrooms. 'We strolled out into the country,' Nan recalled. 'He could have chosen no lovelier a spot than the sunny meadow where we spent the morning. It sloped gently down to a winding stream, and on one side there was a thick wood. The ground was soft and the grass was high ... '

She moved into a room on West 136th Street in New York City, so they could have more privacy. There, she said, 'his pangs seemed almost virginal in their intensity and surpassed any longings he had ever experienced in his life'. But far from being virginal, Harding was having sex with Carrie Phillips – and perhaps even his wife – at the same time.

During boring debates in the Senate, he would crank out thirty-, forty-, sixty-page love letters to Nan. Nowhere except in French had he ever read anything comparable to the love letters they used to write to one another, Harding used to say. These letters were in addition to the huge missives he was still writing to Carrie Phillips. It was surprising that he got any work done at all.

He also sent Nan money regularly and five-pound boxes of her favourite Martha Washington candy. On her twenty-first birthday, he gave her a gold watch.

Sometimes Nan would travel down to Washington. This was more risky, but once they spent the whole afternoon and evening together in his rooms at the Senate Office building.

Other times he would turn up unexpectedly in New York and she would take the afternoon off to be with him. Her boss at U.S. Steel was very understanding. Indeed, the whole office knew that she had a lover who was a high roller in Washington who she referred to simply as 'my man'.

One midwinter, she borrowed a friend's apartment for one of their afternoon assignations. Harding got out of the lift on the floor below to allay the suspicions of the elevator man. Then they spent 'the most intimate afternoon' together.

'How indelible is my memory of Mr Harding sitting on the day bed, his back against the wall, holding me in his arms and looking down at me with a smile that was so sweet that it made me want to cry from sheer contentment!' she wrote.

'Happy, dearie?' he would ask. Nan loved it when he called her 'dearie'.

In 1918, Florence started suffering from her kidney complaint again and left Washington for treatment at Camp Meade. With her away, Harding grew bold, almost reckless. He brought Nan to Washington to show her off, parading her in public with extraordinary indiscretion. He even took her on a stroll down Pennsylvania Avenue, chewing gum and pointing out the sights.

Nan registered in various hotels under the name of Harding's secretary, though sometimes he took her over to the Senate Office building and made love to her there. He became increasingly careless about the use of contraceptives. 'And, of course, the Senate offices do not provide prevention facilities for use in such emergencies,' Nan complained.

Harding had long been convinced that he was sterile. As a boy he had had mumps and his testicles had swollen. The doctors told him that he was probably infertile. Neither his wife nor Mrs Phillips had been impregnated by him, though they had both had children by other men. He told Nan that he had wanted to adopt a child, but Mrs Harding would not hear of it.

In January 1919, Nan proved Harding wrong. She conceived. She was thrilled. Once she was sure she was pregnant, she wrote to him. He wrote back in a panic, but assured her that, however serious the trouble, he could handle it. They met in a room at the New Willard Hotel.

He was nervous and upset. There were beads of perspiration on his forehead.

'We must go at this thing in a sane way,' he said. 'We must not allow ourselves to be nervous over this.'

The way he suggested going at this thing was by handing over a bottle of Dr Humphrey's No. 11 tablets. She said they would not work. 'No faith, no works, Nan,' he said. But if she did not want to take the tablets, she did not have to. He himself would prefer 'the knife', he said. Nan explained that she had no intention of having an abortion. The thing she wanted most in the world was to have his child. Harding knew he was courting disaster. If word of this got out he would be finished politically, and there was be the redoubtable Florence to face.

None of this would cut any ice with Nan though. So he humoured her. It would be 'grand' to have a 'young lieutenant', he said. She was his 'shrine of worship', 'the perfect sweetheart and the perfect mother'.

'As he talked his voice grew tense,' Nan recalled. 'His hands trembled visibly. I took one of them in mine and held it tightly. His gaze was directed out of the window and he spoke to himself. I had to blink very hard to keep back my tears. I had never seen him so moved, so shaken ... '

He gave a reprise of their fantasy life together down on the farm.

'I would take you out there, Nan darling, as my wife,' he said.

Suddenly he freed his hands and grasped both her arms tightly.

'Look at me, dearie,' he cried. 'You would be my wife, wouldn't you? You would marry me, Nan? Oh, dearie, if I only could ... if we could only have our child – together.'

His voice tailed off. To Nan, it seemed like he was praying. It was 'the yearning of a heart laid bare!'

'I nodded wordlessly,' she said. 'The very air seemed sacred.'

However, Harding kept urging in his letters that she have an abortion. Her sister in Chicago agreed and bought Nan some 'bitter apple' medicine. Nan refused to take it. Back in New York, Harding continued to visit as usual. They even made love in a secluded corner of Central Park. And he bought her a sapphire ring.

'We performed a sweet little ceremony with that ring,' Nan wrote, 'and he declared that I could not belong to him more utterly had we been joined together by fifty ministers.'

In July 1919, the signs of her pregnancy were becoming obvious – 'Milk of a lovely richness was already coming from both of my breasts'. She moved out to Asbury Park in New Jersey, where she went under the name of Mrs Elizabeth Norton Christian again. She was to tell acquaintances there that she had been married to a Lieutenant Christian who had been posted to Europe almost at the close of World War I. Her mother, she was to say, disapproved of the match.

On the afternoon of 22 October, 1919, Nan gave birth to a daughter. She named her Elizabeth Ann. Six weeks later, she went to New York to do some Christmas shopping and call Harding – she did not feel safe calling from Asbury Park. When she got him on the phone, he said 'hello' then nothing more. She began to cry. She said she wanted him to come to New York for a brief visit. He said that he was coming to New York, but he would not visit her there. He did not think it wise for them to be seen together. At the time, his political patrons had asked him to run for president.

'It is a good thing that I am not a woman, I would always be pregnant,' Harding told friends in the Press Club. 'I just can't say no.'

Harry Daugherty, the skilful political manipulator who ran the Ohio Republican Party, foresaw with astonishing accuracy that the Republican National Convention in Chicago in 1920 would be deadlocked. He told a reporter: 'After the other candidates have failed ... the leaders, worn out and wishing to do the very best thing, will get together in some smoke-filled room about 2:11 in the morning. Some fifteen men, bleary-eyed from lack of sleep, and perspiring profusely with excessive heat, will sit down around a big table. I will be with them and present the name of Senator Harding. When that times comes, Harding will be selected.'

It happened almost exactly as he predicted, right down to the time. Harding was called into this original 'smoke-filled room' – suite 404–6 on the 13th floor of Blackstone's Hotel – and asked whether there was any reason why he should not be given the nomination. He excused himself for ten minutes, to phone Nan Britton. She was staying at her sister's apartment in Chicago where Harding visited her several times. Their daughter was there too, but Harding had always managed to miss seeing her. In fact, he never once saw the child.

When Harding returned from the phone, he told the political grandees in the smoke-filled room: 'No gentlemen, there is no such reason.'

It was a lie, of course, as the party bosses soon discovered. After a few days snatched with Harding in Marion, Carrie Phillips and her husband – who now had to be told of his wife's adultery – were paid by the Republican Party to take a world cruise during the election. Harding's men also gave her an outright bribe of $20,000 plus a monthly stipend to be paid while he was in office, as long as she kept quiet about their affair. It is, perhaps, a measure of her love for him that she accepted without a moment's hesitation.

Nan watched from the gallery as the cheering convention nominated Harding Republican candidate for the 1920 election. In a showdown in Marion, Harding admitted to Nan's sister that he was the father of her child. In return for their silence, he agreed to support Nan and offered her sister $500 a month if she and her husband would adopt the child.

However, once Harding was in the White House, things became more problematic. Nan began writing letters marked 'personal' and 'private and confidential' to Harding, but they were opened in the White House mailroom. They contained pictures of Nan's child, who bore a remarkable resemblance to the President, and asked for money. White House staffers dutifully destroyed them.

The enforced celibacy of the White House was too much for Harding. He sent for Nan. A White House aide was despatched to pick her up at the station. She was wearing a black crêpe dress with cerise braiding and a floppy picture hat. Driven direct to the White House, she was led in through the portico, down the main hall and into the Cabinet Room, where Harding was waiting.

He led her through into his private office where, stiffly, he embraced her. There was a sentry marching up and down outside the huge windows looking out over the White House lawn and Harding was terrified of being seen.

'He introduced me to the one place where, he said, he thought we might share kisses in safety,' she recalled. 'This was a small closet in the anteroom, evidently a place for hats and coats, but entirely empty most of the times we used it, for we repaired there many times in the course of my visits to the White House, and in the darkness of a space not more than five feet square the President of the United States and his adoring sweetheart made love.'

They worked out a method of her getting letters to him privately, by addressing them to the trusted White House valet. He would pass them on. After Harding had committed their message to memory he would burn them. She was to burn his letters too.

Until January 1923, Harding and Nan would regularly make love in that closet. Afterwards they would sit on a dilapidated leather sofa in the anteroom. Each time he would give her several hundred dollars. She was to be careful how she spent it. Expensive jewellery or fur coats would attract attention. Harding was terrified of being found out.

When Nan's daughter Elizabeth Ann was two-and-a-half, she had got locked in the bathroom and Nan had had to call the fire department to rescue her. The local newspapers carried a picture of Elizabeth Ann being carried down a ladder by the fireman. Harding was beside himself when he saw it.

Once Nan and Harding were almost caught *in flagrante*. They were in the closet when Mrs Harding turned up at the door to his office. The Secret Service man barred her way. She demanded that he stand aside, but he said that it was a Secret Service rule that no one was allowed in when the President had asked not to be disturbed.

Mrs Harding quickly made off to get into Harding's office via his secretary's. The Secret Service man banged on the closet door. Nan and Harding stopped their lovemaking and Harding bundled Nan out of a side door just in time.

Harding often complained of this sort of inconsiderate behaviour by his wife.

'She makes my life hell for me,' he told Nan.

Meanwhile, Harding's own father was making news back in Marion with his blooming romance with a buxom local woman five years younger than Harding himself. They eventually eloped and had a quickie wedding in Ohio. Harding was terrified that his father's behaviour would draw attention to his own peccadillo.

Nan was also giving Harding trouble over their daughter. She would bring pencil-written letters from Elizabeth Ann and would often cry while he read them. Nan was slowly sinking into a deep depression. Elizabeth Ann had now been officially adopted by her sister and her husband, and Nan wanted to come and work in Washington so that she could be near her lover. He did not think that was a prudent idea.

He tried to get her a new job with the New York Customs House, but she was neither a good stenographer nor typist. Harding was also becoming afraid that she would go and marry someone else and would tell her over and over about the farm in Ohio they would have when he left office. The two of them were still deeply in love.

The situation could not last. A shady private detective named Gaston Means claimed that he was summoned to the White House by Mrs Harding around this time. She told him her husband faced a career-wrecking scandal.

'Warren Harding has had a very ugly affair with a girl named Nan Britton from Marion,' Mrs Harding said. 'It goes back to the actual childhood of this girl. When she was but a child, she was a greatly over-developed child and wore extremely short dresses above the knees. It was not considered quite decent. And she was always doing everything on earth that she could do to attract Warren's attention. This over-development tended to attract men on the streets and, together with her unusually short dresses, she attracted attention of course and in not a very nice way. Why, I have watched men watch her even before she was in her early teens.'

Mrs Harding explained that Nan Britton had a child and claimed that Harding was the father of it.

'I don't believe it,' she added.

She hired Means to investigate Nan Britton. He took the job in full knowledge that what she really wanted him to do was to prove that Nan and Harding were not lovers and that someone else was father of the child.

Means sent his men to Marion and quickly discovered that Nan Britton was not the sort of woman that Mrs Harding had so vividly described. At school, she had been good and virtuous, some said a prude. She did not care for boys. Former landladies said that she was prudent and thrifty and that, although many young men pursued her, she turned them all down. There was only one picture on her dresser – Harding's. Means quickly concluded that Nan was indeed Harding's lover and that she was faithful to him.

Means claimed to have broken into Nan's sister's apartment in Chicago and purloined letters and diaries. He told Mrs Harding about them.

'She gazed at me in amazement,' he said. 'Her frozen countenance for the moment forgot its mask of immobility. The muscles and nerves of her face worked. She swallowed hard once or twice.'

She asked to see them. Means refused. He said that she had asked only for information, not for stolen goods.

'Are you a machine or a human being?' she asked. 'Have you no heart in you? Don't you know I've got to have and see those letters?'

Means continued to resist, but eventually she badgered him into handing them over. The letters were tied up with pink silk corset ribbon. She tore the bundles open and began frantically scanning the contents. Her face went white as chalk and her hands 'transparent like wax'. As Means slipped quietly out of the room, he could hear her moaning: 'Could you believe it?'

This was not the end of the matter. The Duchess was now convinced that Nan was Harding's lover, but that was only the half of it.

'Warren Harding is not capable of having a child,' she told Means. 'Therefore he is not the father of Nan Britton's child.'

When Means expressed doubt, she repeated the argument that, as she had proved her ability to have a child and had never been impregnated by Harding, he must be sterile. Means then went on a round of doctors' offices and eventually dug up medical records that indicated that Harding could have children.

The Duchess still refused to believe it and said that the only way to prove it one way or the other was to look into the face of the child. Means was to bring the child to her.

'Mrs Harding,' he asked, 'you want to turn me into a kidnapper?'

Mrs Harding did not. Instead, she summoned the President to her rooms in the White House and confronted him with the evidence. Harding turned on Means.

'By what authority have you put the President of the United States under surveillance?' Harding demanded.

Means replied that he had not put the President under surveillance, only the President's mistress and his illegitimate child. That did not matter, said Harding. Means would be indicted within twenty-four hours.

Then Harding turned on his wife.

'You have ruined me,' he said, shaking his fist at her. 'You have ruined me – you and your contemptible detectives.'

'Warren, Warren,' she pleaded. 'Think of our young love ... '

'Young love?' he screamed. 'Our young love! Love? I never loved you. You want the truth. Now you've got the truth. Young love? You ran me down.'

Harding did not stop seeing Nan Britton. He continued to have her smuggled into the White House and, according to Means, was even caught red-handed by his wife. Means was eventually indicted and spent a term in Atlanta Penitentiary.

However, the Duchess took on the duties of First Lady with renewed fervour. She opened the White House and grounds to the public again – it had been closed during President Wilson's illness – and established garden parties for veterans as a regular event.

Although Prohibition was in force, liquor was served at private parties in the White House. Harding's small town habits had certainly not changed. He still played poker with his cronies every night, played golf, went to baseball games and chased women. Harding, it was said, 'could no more resist a pretty girl or woman than he could resist food when hungry'.

Harry Daugherty's house on H street was used for drunken orgies with chorus girls. Women who took the President's fancy – and there were many of them – were rewarded with highly paid government jobs.

One woman, a former campaign worker who was banned from the White House by Mrs Harding, tried to blackmail the President with some love letters he had written. This cost Daughtery $15,000.

Harding's cabinet was, naturally, made up of poker and drinking buddies and people to whom he owed political debts. The Attorney General was Harry Daugherty and justice was bought and sold. The Secretary of the Interior Albert B. Fall accepted a $100,000 bribe to lease U.S. oil reserves at Teapot Dome to private interests. Daugherty was brought to trial but, after sixty-six hours' deliberation, the jury could not agree. Fall was convicted, though, and went to jail.

There was also corruption in the Veterans' Bureau, the Prohibition Bureau and the Bureau of Investigation – the forerunner of the FBI.

'I have no trouble with my enemies,' Harding said. 'But my damned friends, they're the ones that keep me walking the floor nights.'

In 1922, the mid-term elections brought the Democrats back to power in Congress. In an attempt to restore his flagging popularity, Harding set out on a nationwide whistlestop tour. On the way back from Alaska, he stopped for a dinner in Vancouver, where he contracted food poisoning. In San Francisco, he took to his bed in the Palace Hotel. On 2 August, 1923, his wife was reading the newspaper to him when he suffered a fatal cerebral thrombosis.

In the face of the corruption engulfing his government, his sudden death seemed a little too convenient and it was rumoured that it had been precipitated by Mrs Harding to save him from impeachment.

For weeks after Harding's death, while the President's corpse lay in state in the White House and then in the Capitol Rotund, smoke could be seen curling from the White House chimney even though it was mid-summer. Mrs Harding was burning her husband's papers. She died fifteen months later, having done all she could to salvage his reputation.

Nan Britton was away in France, at Harding's expense, at the time of his death. When she returned to New York, she married a Norwegian sea captain who soon abandoned her with considerable debts. Three years later, Nan wrote a sensational 440-page book about her relationship with the President and the child she bore him. It was called *The President's Daughter*. Her co-author was Richard Wright, whose wife sued for divorce naming Nan as co-respondent.

The book was nearly suppressed when the Society for the Suppression of Vice entered the printing plant and seized the plates, but a magistrate's court ordered them to give them back. Book shops refused to handle it and reviewers ignored it. Nevertheless, Nan managed to sell 90,000 copies at $5 a time under the counter. The great campaigning journalist H.L. Mencken took up the story in the *Baltimore Sun*, and used it to attack the Republican administration.

The government quickly closed ranks. White House staff were paraded in front of the public saying that they had never heard of Nan Britton and that she was a liar. The former editor of the *Buffalo Times*, Joseph DeBathe, wrote a book called *The Answer*, claiming that Nan's book was a tissue of sexual fantasies, deliberate falsehoods and criminal libel. Nan sued and lost. Then Gaston Means, the private detective Mrs Harding had used to spy on her husband, came forward with a book called *The Strange Death of President Harding*, claiming that Mrs Harding had poisoned her husband and murdered other of his associates when she had discovered his affair. The book was a runaway bestseller.

Carrie and John Phillips had lost all their money in the Great Depression and separated. John died in 1939, while Carrie supported herself by breeding Alsatian dogs. She moved to a house on Gospel Hill in Marion, nearer to Harding's old home. By 1956, she was so frail and decrepit that a court order was taken out to put her in Willetts Home for the Elderly in Marion, where she died in 1960. When her possessions were auctioned off, a box was found containing ninety-eight letters written by Harding. They reveal that Harding was lonely and sexually starved at home, and sought love and sexual fulfilment elsewhere. One letter, dated 1911, read: 'I love you garbed, but naked more ... ' The word 'naked' was underlined twice. In another, there is a poem which begins: 'Carrie, take me panting to your heaving breast.'

The letters were exactly like those Nan Britton described in her book and substantiated many of her claims.

Warren Harding was succeeded by his Vice-President Calvin Coolidge. He was aptly named. Coolidge was cool.

He was Calvinistic. The title of William Allen White's biography of Coolidge describes him fittingly as *A Puritan in Babylon*.

Coolidge was the personification of the New England conservative virtues of honesty, modesty and frugality. His economy with words was legendary. Apocryphal stories circulated about it. One was that a young lady who sat next to him at dinner took a bet that she could get more than two words out of him. In an effort to strike up conversation with him, she told him about the wager. Coolidge simply replied: 'You lose.'

Born on 4 July, 1872 in Plymouth Notch, Vermont, John Calvin Coolidge was a shy, industrious, red-headed boy. 'Calvin could get more sap out a maple tree than any of the other boys around here,' his father said.

As a young teenager, he attended parties where he played kissing games with girls, but his grandma, who thought dancing was sinful, gave him a dollar if he promised not to.

He studied classics at Amhurst College where he led a rather solitary life. Most of his contemporaries were guilded youths, keen on parties and girls, but as Coolidge did not dance, he became a wallflower. He did not join in the social and sports events and, in his own words, 'did not seem to get acquainted very fast'.

Girls began to scare him and he was certainly not attractive to women. Theodore Roosevelt's daughter, Alice Roosevelt Longworth, said that Coolidge looked 'as if he had been weaned on a pickle'.

A college acquaintance wrote of Coolidge: 'In appearance he was splendidly null, apparently deficient in red corpuscles, with a peaked, wire-drawn expression ... As he walked there was no motion of the body about the waist. The arms hung immobile.'

Apparently there was little motion below the waist either. Shy with the college girls, sometimes he managed to overcome his reserve and go out with girls from the town. He even proposed marriage to one redhead. She turned him down.

Grace Coolidge was everything her husband was not – warm, friendly, outgoing and gregarious. She was brought up in Burlington, Vermont, and was teaching at a school for the deaf in Northampton, Massachusetts, when she met Coolidge. The first time she saw him was through the window of a friend's house, where he was staying. He was shaving, wearing just his long underwear and a hat.

In the relationship, she made the running, taking him out picnicking, buggy-riding and sailing. For her sake, he tried dancing and skating but was singularly unsuccessful at both of them. Nevertheless, she was the only woman who ever attracted his attention.

He was certainly not the wooing type, but Grace fell for him anyway. Later she explained: 'Mr Coolidge had deeper sentimental feeling than most people whom I have known, but he did not reveal it in outward manifestations.'

Coolidge's grandmother suggested that, as he had no other prospect, he marry Grace. He went straight to her father and asked for permission. He had not even informed Grace of his intentions; nor did he ask her for her hand. Once he had her father's consent, he told Grace simply: 'I am going to be married to you.'

He was so unromantic in his approach that Grace's mother tried to break up the match. But he fought for his bride and they were married in October 1905 in her parents' home. It was raining that day and someone remarked that it was a bad omen.

'I don't mind the weather if I get the girl,' he said.

They headed off to Montreal for a two-week honeymoon. It was plainly unsatisfactory. After a week, he told her he wanted to go home. He was running for a seat on the School Committee and he wanted to make a campaign speech.

Although restricted to the modest income of a small-town lawyer, Grace kept up appearances and worked tirelessly to promote her husband's political career. When he became Governor of Massachusetts, she stayed at home bringing up their two boys, while he lived in rented rooms in Boston.

In Harding's Washington, Coolidge was totally out of place. Not for him, the wild parties with chorus girls that Harding's cronies organized. He stayed at home with his wife, mooning over her like a lovesick schoolboy.

A contemporary noted: 'The man would not have been what he was without the woman, and most of all precisely because of her infinite, exquisite tact in effacing herself.'

Entering Washington society as the wife of the Vice-President, Grace quickly became the most popular woman in town. Once established in the White House, she introduced a more restrained and dignified air to entertaining, following the excesses of the Harding years. Even the sudden death of her younger son did not distract her from her public duties. She was voted one of America's twelve greatest living women.

The White House under Coolidge was as different from Harding's administration as 'a New England front parlour is from a back room speakeasy'. Coolidge soon had a sure hand on the levers of state. He kept the good men from Harding's cabinet and got rid of the rest. The Republican Party rallied behind him and he mollified a fractious Congress, promising to continue the policy of returning to 'normalcy'. Above suspicion in the midst of a sea of corruption, he soon earned the confidence of the electorate. He went on to win the 1924 election with the slogan 'Keep cool with Coolidge'.

He certainly took little interest in the fair sex. When an associate drew his attention to a pretty young woman whose stockings had been splashed up to the knee, Coolidge commented on the state of the pavement.

However, he was very jealous of his wife and was deeply suspicious of the Secret Service agents detailed to protect her. One day in the Black Hills of South Dakota his wife went for a walk with her guard, James Haley. They got lost and turned up over two hours late. Coolidge was beside himself. Haley was sacked and Coolidge's tantrum made the headlines.

Soon after, there was a rumour that Coolidge and his wife planned to divorce after he left the White House. He decided not to contest the 1928 election, but stayed with his wife until, on 5 January 1932, he died of a coronary thrombosis. Hearing Coolidge was dead, humorist Dorothy Parker remarked: 'How can they tell?'

After Coolidge's death in 1933, Grace embarked on an adventurous life, travelling to Europe and flying in an aeroplane. She died in 1957.

Sadly, for the purposes of this book, Herbert Hoover's sex life was nowhere near as interesting or bizarre as his namesake and contemporary J. Edgar Hoover's was. There is no evidence that Herbert Hoover pored over pornography, liked dressing-up in women's clothing, gave oral sex to his deputy or liked being masturbated by a young boy wearing rubber gloves while another leather-clad youth read passages from the Bible.

Herbert Hoover was born on 10 August, 1874 in West Branch, Iowa, and was the first president to be born west of the Mississippi. His father, a Quaker, was a blacksmith, who died of typhoid fever when Hoover was six. His mother died of pneumonia three years later and at the age of ten Hoover travelled with his bed-roll and a wire basket filled with chickens from West Branch to Newberg, Oregon, to live with his uncle. He earned his keep there chopping wood, milking cows and caring for his uncle's horses.

Hoover attended a Quaker school and developed a crush on his teacher Miss Gray. With her help, he entered Stanford University in 1891 where he won a student election by marshalling the votes of the 'queeners' – that is, the co-eds.

Graduating with a degree in engineering in 1895, he went to work in a mine in Nevada. Two years later, he left for Australia where he headed gold-mining operations for a British company and lived in rough mining communities.

There is evidence that Hoover had a torrid affair in Australia with a barmaid in Kalgoorlie. Years later, after his return to America, he is said to have written her a love poem which was quoted in the book *Those Were the Days* by Arthur Reid, published in Perth in 1933. The poem speaks eloquently of their passion:

Do you ever dream, my sweetheart, of twilight long ago,
Of a park in old Kalgoorlie, where the bougainvilleas grow,
Where the moonbeams on the pathway trace a shimmering brocade,
And the over hanging peppers form a lovers' promenade?

Years have flown since then, my sweetheart, fleet as orchard blooms in May,
But the hour that fills my dreaming, was it only yesterday?
Stood we two a space in silence, while the summer sun slipped down,
And the grey dove dusk with drooping pinions wrapt the mining town,
Then you raised your tender glances darkly, dreamily to mine,
And my pulses clashed like cymbals in rhapsody divine.

While the starlight-spangled heavens rolled around us where we
*   stood,*
And a tide of bliss kept surging through the currents of our blood,
And I spent my soul in kisses, crushed upon your scarlet mouth,
Oh! My red-lipped, sunbrowned sweetheart, dark-eyed daughter of the
*   south.*

I have fought my fight and triumphed, on the map I've writ my
*   name,*
But I prize one hour of loving, more than fifty years of fame.

Despite this great passion, Hoover returned to California
where he married his Stanford sweetheart Lou Henry.
They had two sons.

After a successful career in mining, Hoover 'on the
slippery slope of public life' organized relief during
World War I.

'We in America today are nearer to the final triumph
over poverty than ever before in the history of any land,'
said Hoover during the election in 1928. Within months
of his inauguration, the world was plunged into the Great
Depression.

Hoover also made his position on prohibition clear,
calling it 'a great social and economic experiment, noble
in motive, far-reaching in purpose'. He got that wrong
too. At a baseball match, he was booed and the crowd
chanted: 'We want beer! We want beer!'

18

THE SECRETARY OF STATE

Herbert Hoover was replaced by Franklin D. Roosevelt, a suave Martini-sipping patrician who did more than anyone to put America back to work. He also ran the most sexually disorderly White House in history.

Even at Harvard, FDR was a ladies' man. He loved to dance and flirted outrageously with pretty women. Among his special favourites were Muriel Delano Robbins, his niece Helen Roosevelt, Mary Newbold and Frances Pell. He was once forward enough to earn a sharp slap from Alice Sohier. He dated two girls from prominent Boston families, Dorothy Quincy and Frances Dana. He nearly married Frances, but she was a Catholic and his mother objected.

During his time at college, he fell under the influence of his distant relative, the President, Theodore Roosevelt, and met his niece Eleanor. She was an ugly duckling and was shocked and delighted that such a debonair man as Franklin Roosevelt should be attracted to her.

Many considered him in no way good enough for her. He already had a reputation as a womanizer, a drinker and a careless flirt. From the beginning, he continued to play the field. On a trip to England, he wrote to his mother: 'As I knew the uncivilized English custom of never introducing people ... I walked up to the best-looking dame in the bunch and said "howdy?" Things at once went like oil and I was soon having flirtations with three of the nobility at the same time.'

What he wrote to Eleanor about this incident, we will never know. She burned all the letters of their courtship, perhaps because they contained pledges of everlasting fidelity which he singularly failed to live up to.

However, her letters to him survived. In one, she quoted from Elizabeth Barrett Browning:

> *Unless you can swear, 'For life, for death!'*
> *Oh, fear to call it loving!*

He, apparently, swore and, in 1903, they became engaged.

Roosevelt's mother, Sara, was against the match and took him off on a five-week cruise of the Caribbean in the hope that he would forget Eleanor. During the trip, he had a shipboard romance with an attractive older French woman, which displeased his mother even more.

The lady in question must have made a great impression on him. As late as 1936, when he heard that she had moved to Trinidad, he tried to get in touch with her.

Despite this distraction, in 1905, the marriage went ahead with President Roosevelt giving away the bride. Their honeymoon was a European tour. They sailed on the *Oceanic*. In Brown's Hotel in London, they were ushered directly to the Royal Suite because of their kinship with the U.S. President. Roosevelt was delighted. Eleanor was not. It cost $1,000 a day. He also began calling her 'Babs', short for 'Baby', the nickname he used for the rest of their life together.

On their honeymoon, she was disturbed by two things – his sleepwalking, which was, she thought, a sign of an uneasy conscience, and his pattern of casual flirtation.

Never a good sailor, she had a particularly miserable voyage on the way home. When they landed in New York, she went straight to the doctor. He told her that she was pregnant. It was the first of six children, one of whom died in infancy.

During World War I, Roosevelt was in Washington where he spent a great deal of time partying with old friends from Harvard. Women flocked to him and there was the occasional flirtation.

Meanwhile, Eleanor spent more time at their holiday home in Campobello, leaving him to his own devices. Their intimate relations ended altogether in 1918 when Eleanor discovered that her husband was having an affair with her social secretary, Lucy Page Mercer.

Lucy was in her early twenties and extremely attractive. As she came from a prominent Maryland family that had fallen on hard times, it was not difficult for Roosevelt to include her in his circle of friends while Eleanor was away and he courted her quite openly. When Roosevelt was recovering from a bout of pneumonia, Eleanor decided to sort out his personal correspondence and came across a package of love letters from Lucy.

'The bottom dropped out of my own particular world,' she said.

She was devastated. His affair confirmed everything she thought about herself – that she was unattractive and unloved. After thirteen years of marriage, she offered Roosevelt a divorce.

'Don't be a goose,' Roosevelt replied.

At a family conclave, the couple agreed to stay together – a divorce in those days would have finished his political career. Sara said that she would cut off her son without a penny if he left Eleanor. The most decisive factor in

188

Roosevelt's mind was that Lucy was a Catholic. Even if he had divorced Eleanor, Lucy would not have married him.

Although, Eleanor said that she would remain married to Roosevelt, she would not share his bed. The truth was that she had never really enjoyed physical intimacy. Sex, she explained to her daughter, was a burden that a woman had to endure.

'Father and mother had an armed truce that endured until the day he died,' wrote their son James.

Eleanor also insisted that Roosevelt give up his mistress. He agreed but, behind Eleanor's back, continued to see Lucy until his death, twenty-seven years later.

In fact, the affair continued with hardly a pause for breath. Lucy had already left Eleanor's employment and joined the Navy as a yeomanette. She worked in the Navy Department in Washington and lived near by. Although Eleanor delayed her departure to their holiday home at Campobello that summer to keep an eye on her wayward husband, as soon as she had gone, the affair resumed.

Roosevelt's letters talk of boat trips down the Potomac and long drives in the country with a circle of friends that usually included Lucy. To allay Eleanor's suspicions, he employed British diplomat Nigel Law as a 'beard'. He was a good friend and would pretend to escort Lucy on any occasion the three of them might be seen in public.

However, Eleanor may not have been totally fooled. Her cousin Alice Longworth once spotted Roosevelt and Lucy out alone together for a drive. She told him: 'I saw you twenty miles out in the country. You didn't see me. Your hands were on the wheel but your eyes were on that perfectly lovely lady.'

Lucy and Roosevelt were, after all, physically well suited. She was beautiful. He was handsome. Young women in Washington would stop in the street to watch him stride by. Alice even had Roosevelt and Lucy to dinner at her home. Roosevelt 'deserved a good time,' Alice said, 'he was married to Eleanor.'

But that did not stop Alice trying to spill the beans to her cousin. She told Eleanor that Roosevelt had a 'secret'.

'She inquired if you had told me,' Eleanor told Roosevelt later, 'and I said that I did not believe in knowing things which your husband did not wish you to know so I think that I will be spared any further secrets.'

This may have been disingenuous. Roosevelt's son James said that his mother had evidence that Roosevelt and Lucy had checked in together in a hotel at Virginia Beach as man and wife and had spent the night together. This was at a time when Roosevelt was Secretary of the Navy and America was mobilizing for war.

In 1919, Roosevelt took on a new secretary, Marguerite 'Missy' Alice LeHand, who soon became his mistress. Eleanor became aware of the liaison, but tolerated it, perhaps because she considered Missy of a different social class; or it may have been because, after 1920, Eleanor's interests had changed. Many of her closest friends were lesbians.

Eleanor even learned to tolerate his reputation as a flirt, bottom-pincher and knee-holder – a reputation that increased with age and was thought to reflect the innocent charm of the man. During the 1920 campaign, Roosevelt flirted outrageously and, for the first time, Eleanor could joke about the 'lovely ladies who served luncheon for my husband and who worshipped at his shrine'. By this time, she seemed to have reconciled herself to her womanizing, playboy husband, and even to the fact that Missy LeHand was constantly on hand.

Meanwhile, Lucy had become a governess, employed by Winthrop Rutherfurd, a wealthy sportsman and dog breeder. His wife had died leaving him with five children. Lucy and Rutherfurd married in 1920. She was twenty-

nine; he fifty-eight. Roosevelt was stunned when he overheard news of the marriage at a party.

In 1921, while vacationing on Campobello Island in
New Brunswick, Roosevelt went swimming in the Bay of
Fundy and was struck down with polio. His mother wanted him to retire to Hyde Park but his advisers thought it
best that he keep his interest in politics alive. While
Roosevelt underwent a systematic programme of hydro-
therapy in the hands of Missy LeHand, Eleanor attended
political meetings and acted as his eyes and ears.

Since the Lucy Mercer affair, the Roosevelt's marriage
had become more of a working partnership than a romantic relationship. Throughout her life Eleanor remained a staunch supporter and political helpmate to
her husband. Gradually she used her position to begin a
political career of her own.

Roosevelt and Missy LeHand lived together more or
less openly on a houseboat on winter holidays in Florida,
where Roosevelt tried strengthening his legs by swimming. This was not Eleanor's scene at all and she seldom
visited.

Although Missy ostensibly had her own room on the
boat, she had to go through Roosevelt's bedroom to get
to the bathroom. The houseboat's inhabitants were often
to be seen lolling around in pyjamas, nighties and bathing suits. It was what one guest called a 'negligée existence'. When Eleanor visited, she usually came with one of
her lesbian friends.

Roosevelt also established a foundation for the care of
polio victims at Warm Springs, Georgia. Eleanor seldom
went there either, and the Roosevelt cottage at Warm
Springs was presided over by Missy LeHand. When Eleanor did stay, she was a guest and Missy the hostess.

Despite years of therapy in Georgia, Roosevelt never
recovered the use of his legs and his suffering gave him a
new determination.

'If you have spent two years in bed trying to wiggle your big toe,' he once remarked, 'everything else seems easy.'

After 1923, Roosevelt and Eleanor were rarely together. She had set up homes for herself in Greenwich Village and Val-Kill, near Springwood, but in her letters to him, Eleanor still addressed him as 'Dearest Honey', told him 'We all miss you dreadfully', and signed off 'Ever lovingly'. In his letters to her, Roosevelt expressed his growing admiration for her energy, determination and political activities.

In 1929, she took up with a young man named Earl Miller. She was forty-five. He was thirty-two, a body builder and a well-known womanizer. Roosevelt was Governor of New York at the time and had assigned Miller to Eleanor as a bodyguard. They spent a great deal of time together, reading aloud, singing and playing the piano. He coached her at tennis and taught her how to shoot and to dive. He was totally devoted to her, checking her bills and squiring her around her public duties. Some of her lesbian friends were distressed to see him 'manhandle' her, especially when they were in bathing suits. They would walk hand-in-hand and he would touch her knee. He claimed that she would have made a better president than Roosevelt and called her not 'Mrs Roosevelt', but 'Lady' or 'Dearest Lady'. Nevertheless, he hardly gets a mention in her autobiography.

When it seemed likely that Eleanor would become First Lady, there was talk of her running away with Miller – she hated the thought of being imprisoned in the White House so much. It was then, curiously, that Miller had an affair with Missy LeHand. Miller claimed that Missy had put him on night duty at Warm Springs so that he could come to her room. But after two years of clandestine romance, he says she found out that he was also 'playing around with one of the girls in the Executive Office', and took to her bed and cried for three days.

There has been speculation that Roosevelt actually engineered the affair to prevent Eleanor running away with Miller, which would have destroyed his presidency.

Not only did Eleanor take Miller's affair in her stride, she actually encouraged his romances. She managed to keep a hold over him even during his three marriages, which all ended in divorce. After Roosevelt's death, the affair almost hit the headlines. On 13 January, 1947, the New York *Daily News* columnist Ed Sullivan wrote: 'Navy Commander's wife will rock the country if she names the co-respondent in her divorce action!!!'

In the White House, Missy LeHand had her own suite, though she was often seen visiting the President's room in her night attire. She shared meals with the family and, alone, called him 'F.D.'

Meanwhile, on the north side of the house, Eleanor lived with cigar-smoking Associated Press-reporter Lorena Hickok, a well-known lesbian who had openly lived with other women before. She had first met Eleanor in 1928. As a reporter, she had gone to interview the First Lady of the Empire State. In her report, she eulogized Eleanor's 'long, slender hands' and her 'lace-trimmed hostess gown'. Later she joined Eleanor on the 1932 campaign trail. The two of them became inseparable and her flattering columns – cooked up with Eleanor herself – were syndicated throughout the United States and helped build Eleanor's image.

The other press syndicates soon realized that AP were getting all the exclusives and assigned women reporters of their own to cover Eleanor's activities.

Hickok was singularly unattractive. She was five foot eight but weighed almost two hundred pounds, smoked cigars, cigarettes and pipes, drank Bourbon on the rocks and was very much 'one of the boys'.

She and Eleanor went to great lengths to hide their affair. Hickok even edited and retyped Eleanor's letters, burning the originals. Still explicit expressions of love slipped through. Eleanor wrote to Hickok, saying: 'I wish I could lie down beside you tonight and take you in my arms'; 'I ache to hold you close' and 'Most clearly I remember your eyes, with a kind of teasing smile in them, and the feeling of that soft spot just northeast of the corner of your mouth against my lips ... '

They even exchanged rings and had jealous lovers' tiffs. When Roosevelt was first elected they had walked across Lafayette Park to the White House together.

The White House staff soon spotted what was going on. White House maid Lillian Parks recalled that Eleanor and Hickok would disappear together for long periods in Eleanor's bathroom, claiming that it was 'the only place they could find privacy for a press interview'. The staff considered this 'hardly the kind of thing one would do with an ordinary reporter, or even with an adult friend'.

In fact, coping with the Roosevelts' bizarre domestic arrangements was a nightmare for the White House staff, especially as FDR despised Hickok and was once heard yelling: 'I want that woman kept out of this House.'

The only four-term president, Roosevelt certainly revelled in the role. Every year on his birthday, Roosevelt would hold a drinks party at the Cufflinks Club. He would dress as a Roman emperor and his female guests would be expected to appear as Vestal virgins.

In 1940, when Roosevelt won an unprecedented third term in the White House, everyone was jubilant except Missy LeHand. She was concerned for his health and wanted him to retire, perhaps so that he could divorce Eleanor and marry her.

The atmosphere in the White House was not improved when Hickok, still in residence, fell in love with a female tax-court judge. Eleanor had a relationship with the youthful Joseph Lash which further enraged the President. Lash had a security file and Eleanor was outraged when she discovered that the room where she had spent time with him in the Blackstone Hotel in Chicago had been bugged by Army Intelligence. The tapes 'indicated quite clearly that Mrs Roosevelt and Lash engaged in sexual intercourse', an FBI report said. Later, Lash was refused an Army commission. A number of indiscreet letters from Eleanor to Lash surfaced. Lash was engaged to be married at the time.

Meanwhile, a sex scandal hit the White House from a most unexpected quarter. Roosevelt's special envoy, first to Hitler and Mussolini, then to Churchill, was Under Secretary of State Sumner Welles. In January 1941, FBI director J. Edgar Hoover informed Roosevelt that Welles was a homosexual and provided him with affidavits signed by a number of porters on a Pullman train who said Welles had propositioned them. Roosevelt stuck by him, but the matter was leaked and the gossip forced Welles from office.

Missy LeHand had an affair with William Bullitt, Roosevelt's pre-war ambassador to the Soviet Union. Then, in 1941, she suffered a cerebral haemorrhage. She was moved out of the White House and died three years later.

The loss of Missy left Roosevelt short of female companionship. Laura Delano and Margaret Suckley, two unmarried cousins, became such frequent visitors that Eleanor called them his 'hand-maidens'; and he had a wild flirtation with Crown Princess Martha of Norway.

Then Lucy Mercer returned. In fact, Roosevelt had kept in touch with her over the years without Eleanor's knowledge. She had been at the Democratic National Convention in 1936 when he made his acceptance speech and secretly attended all four of his inaugurations.

In 1941, while Winthrop Rutherfurd lay dying after a severe stroke, Roosevelt and Lucy began meeting again regularly in Washington. Secret service agents would drive him out to Canal Road, beyond Georgetown, where she would be waiting for him in her car. They would usually drive about for a few hours before he would return to the White House. On at least one occasion, they had an assignation at Hobcaw Barony, Bernard Baruch's estate in South Carolina, where Roosevelt had gone for a rest. There is a famous story of Roosevelt's railroad car being shunted off into a siding near the Rutherfurd estate at Allamuchy, New Jersey, for a secret rendezvous.

After her husband died, Lucy visited Roosevelt in the White House, while Eleanor was away with Lash. She was at Roosevelt's side in the cottage in Warm Springs when he died. Laura Delano and Margaret Suckley were there too, but while they stayed on, Lucy Mercer Rutherfurd had to pack quickly and leave.

Roosevelt had just been re-elected yet again in 1944 by a popular majority of two-and-a-half million over Thomas E. Dewey of New York. He died of a massive cerebral haemorrhage, less than a month before the end of the war in Europe and four months before the fall of Japan.

When Eleanor left the White House, she told reporters: 'My story is over.'

She was wrong. Longtime friend Bernard Baruch proposed marriage. She refused, but continued her active sex life and went on to become a delegate to the United Nations and one of the authors of the Declaration of Human Rights. She died in November 1962 and was buried at Hyde Park alongside her husband.

By contrast, Harry S. Truman was a true man. He married his childhood sweetheart and said that she was so beautiful he never looked at another woman. He was even embarrassed if they looked at him, which mostly they did not.

The courtship was one of the slowest ever. It began when he was six. They got engaged when he was thirty and married when he was thirty-three. In the eighty-two years they knew each other, they were only separated briefly by World War I. While in France as an artillery officer, he visited the *Folies-Bergère*, which he dismissed as a 'disgusting performance'. In Marseilles, though, the dancer Gaby threw him a bunch of violets, which he caught. He returned from the war fond of swearing and full of off-colour jokes.

His wife Elizabeth 'Bessie' Virginia Wallace Truman was a private person, though she stood by his side on election platforms and served as his secretary when he was elected Senator.

'She is worth every penny I pay her,' he quipped.

She said that she was not much interested in the 'formalities and pomp or artificiality which ... surround the family of the President'. After nine months in the White House, *Newsweek* reported that she had done her Christmas shopping alone. No one recognized the First Lady in Washington stores.

19

I LIKE IKE

While Roosevelt was womanizing his way through the war and Truman was keeping himself to himself, General Dwight D. Eisenhower, commander of the largest amphibious assault force ever marshalled and soon to be the thirty-fourth President of the United States, was in London having a fling with his English driver; or rather, not having a fling. Though they tried several times, the great general proved to be impotent. There were, plainly, other things on his mind. One can only wonder what damage the German propaganda machine could have done if they had found out about it.

Eisenhower's family life was strict and religious, but he was interested in girls from an early age. He was in luck – in his high school in Abilene, girls outnumbered boys by two to one. The boys tended to drop out before graduation too, so in Eisenhower's graduation class there were twenty-five girls and just nine boys.

However, Ike was shy around girls and he wanted to impress his classmates that he was a regular guy. Paying the girls too much mind was considered sissy. So Ike deliberately dressed badly, mussed up his hair and, on the few occasions he was forced on to the dancefloor, proved to be a terrible dancer.

After graduating, Ike took a summer job in a creamery and began to lose his shyness. He had a half-serious romance with a redhead called Ruby Norman.

Then, on his way to West Point, he stopped off to visit his brother Edgar at Ann Arbor. One evening, the two boys rented a canoe and paddled down the Huron river with a couple of college girls. It was 'the most romantic evening I had ever known,' Eisenhower later recalled.

That evening caused him to regret abandoning his plan to study law with Edgar at the University of Michigan in favour of a career in the army. 'It looked to me as if he were leading the right life,' he said.

Eisenhower was a keen sportsman who enjoyed fishing, baseball, football and, later, golf. A knee injury sustained during a game at West Point put an end to his hopes of fame as a running back. Otherwise, Eisenhower was an average student, graduating 61st academically and 125th in discipline in a class of 164 in 1915.

He was posted to Fort Houston at San Antonio, Texas. There, one Sunday afternoon, as officer of the day, he was inspecting the guard. On the lawn outside the Officers' Club, there was a gaggle of women. One of them, Mrs Lulu Harris, wife of Major Hunter Harris, saw Eisenhower and called out: 'Ike, won't you come over here? I have some people I'd like you to meet.'

He refused.

'Sorry,' he said. 'I am on guard and I have to make an inspection trip.'

'Humph!' said Mrs Harris, turning to her companions. 'The woman-hater of the post.'

Then she called out at Ike: 'We didn't ask you to come over to stay. Just come over here and meet these friends of mine.'

Ike walked over. Later he recalled: 'The one who attracted my eye instantly was a vivacious and attractive girl, smaller than average, saucy in the look about her face and in her whole attitude.'

She was nineteen-year-old Mamie Geneva Doud, the daughter of a Denver meat packer. He was twenty-five. There followed a whirlwind romance and, on St Valentine's day 1916, he proposed. In June, he organized a ten-day leave. They married in the Douds' spacious home on 1 July. Eisenhower did not sit down until the ceremony was over, afraid of destroying the knife-edge creases in his pants. Afterwards, they had a two-day honeymoon in Eldorado Springs, Colorado.

Back at the post, Ike did not settle easily into married life. He often showed a marked reluctance to return to the married quarters, preferring to play poker in the evening with his friends instead.

Less than a month after her marriage, Mamie Eisenhower discovered that she would always be number two in her husband's life. As he was packing to move to a new posting, he told his nineteen-year-old bride: 'My country comes first and always will. You come second.'

Despite frequent rows about this, they began a family.

Good to his word, he stuck with the army. Over the following thirty-seven years' service to his country, Mamie estimated that they moved house twenty-seven times.

During World War II, Ike was appointed Supreme Commander in Europe and was posted to London. Because of the bombing, Mamie stayed behind in Washington, DC.

When Ike landed in Prestwick, Scotland, he was met by young driver Kay Summersby. She was a former model and movie actress, who had enlisted in the transport section of the Women's Royal Army Corps. She was assigned to Eisenhower because of her encyclopedic knowledge of London. Though born in County Cork, Eire, Kay was actually a British subject.

'She is also very pretty,' Eisenhower wrote tactlessly in a letter home to Mamie. 'Irish and slender and I think in the process of getting a divorce, which is all that worries me.'

Fortunately, his aide Harry Butcher forgot to mail this letter. Butcher also recorded in his own diary that Eisenhower's feelings towards Kay were rather more carnal.

'Ike defines this member of the WAC as "a double-breasted GI with a built-in foxhole",' he wrote.

Kay played an important part in Eisenhower's life. As well as driving him around, making his coffee and providing him with some well-earned relaxation, he turned to her for emotional support when the going got rough.

After the letter that was never sent, Eisenhower discreetly omitted any reference to Kay Summersby in correspondence with Mamie. As Supreme Commander, however, his every move was reported on and Kay appeared in almost every press shot of the General, close beside him.

Even though Kay was engaged to a young American officer, Colonel Richard A. Arnold at the time, gossip flourished. Some of it inevitably got back to Mamie. Ike constantly reassured her and told her that he wished she was there with him, if it was not for the bombing.

Eisenhower was ill at ease with women generally, but Kay Summersby made him feel comfortable. He enjoyed her charm, her good looks and her flirtatious manner, even if she was twenty years his junior. As well as being his driver, she was appointed his secretary at AFHQ and he drove her like a slave from dawn to dusk. They were seldom out of each other's sight. Her light touch with high-powered military men and senior politicians was invaluable. She even accompanied him to meetings with

Churchill and King George VI. They went together on a trip to Algiers, Egypt and Palestine. They would dine together and she would be his partner at bridge. They went horseback riding. Her youth and humour were a convenient escape from the pressures of war and death. She found it easy to fall in love with her middle-aged boss, while he found excuses to touch her, or brush her knee. Gradually their relationship grew beyond mere flirtation.

Brigadier General Everett Hughes recorded in his diary: 'Kay will help Ike win the war.' Nevertheless he foresaw a terrible scandal.

Mamie's letters continually harped on her worries about him being surrounded by attractive young women in London. He would tell her 'not to worry your pretty head about WAACS' but she was still concerned about 'tales I heard about the night clubs, gaiety and loose morals'.

The gossip, he said, was without foundation. How could anyone be 'banal and foolish enough to lift an eyebrow at an old duffer such as I am in connection with WAACS – Red Cross workers – nurses and drivers?' he wrote. Her suspicions and his prevarication continued.

'If you want me to get you a lot of vital statistics I'll have [his aide Tex] Lee form them up, march them in here, and I'll give each a questionnaire,' he wrote shirtily.

Then Mamie mentioned that she had read in *Life* magazine that his 'London driver' had joined him on a trip to Algiers.

'She is terribly in love with a young American Colonel and is to be married to him come June, assuming both are alive,' Ike wrote back. 'I doubt that *Life* told that.'

Besides, he said ruefully: 'I'm old – my days of romance may be all behind me but I swear I think I miss you more and love you more than I ever did.'

Nevertheless, Mamie's suspicions drove her slowly to drink.

General Hughes mentioned in his diaries that after one party, he sat around with Eisenhower and 'discussed Kay'.

'I don't know whether he is alibi-ing or not,' Hughes wrote. 'Says he wants to hold her hand, accompanies her to her house, doesn't sleep with her'.

Even the most casual observer could see that something was going on between this middle-aged general and a woman young enough to be his daughter. 'The other day Kay and I were out riding and a soldier yahooed at us,' Eisenhower told General Patton.

Asked whether the affair was just a matter of rumour, war correspondent John Thompson of the *Chicago Tribune* replied: 'Well, I have never before seen a chauffeur get out of a car and kiss the General good morning when he comes from his office.'

The gossip had gone almost as far as it could when, on the eve of their wedding, Kay's fiancé was killed by a land mine. Eisenhower consoled her in her grief and told Mamie that she 'cannot long continue to drive – she is too sunk!' But she wasn't and they began a passionate affair.

'It was like an explosion,' Kay wrote in her memoirs. 'We were suddenly in each other's arms. His kisses absolutely unravelled me. Hungry, strong, demanding. And I responded every bit as passionately. He stopped, took my face between his hands. "Goddamn it," he said, "I love you."

'We were breathing as if we had run up a dozen flights of stairs. God must have been watching over us, because no one came bursting into the office. It was lovers' luck, but we both came to our senses, remembering how Tex had walked in earlier that day. Ike had lipstick smudges on his face. I started scrubbing at them frantically with my handkerchief.'

Unfortunately, they were seldom alone, but one evening, he and Kay found themselves alone for a nightcap.

'Ike refilled our glasses several times,' she recalled, 'and then, I suppose inevitably, we found ourselves in each other's arms in an unrestrained embrace. Our ties came off. Our jackets came off. Buttons were unbuttoned. It was as if we were frantic. And we were.

'But it was not what I expected. Wearily, we slowly calmed down. He snuggled his face into the hollow between my neck and shoulder and said, "Oh, God, Kay. I'm sorry. I'm not going to be any good for you." '

Eisenhower could not get an erection. Kay put this down to the fact that he had a lot on his mind; or it may have been his innate sense of morality.

So that he and Kay could spend more time together, Ike fixed them up with a rural retreat, Telegraph Cottage. He bought her a dog which they called Telek, combining *Tele*graph and *K*ay. They tried to make love several times at Telegraph Cottage, too, but again without success.

Kay was by Eisenhower's side as he saw off the D-Day assault force and saw the tears in his eyes. She toured the battlefields of Normandy with him and stayed with him at his new headquarters at Versailles. As late as March 1945, members of Eisenhower's staff discussed the General's affair, but slowly his relationship with Kay Summersby had begun to cool.

He travelled more, leaving her behind at his headquarters. Mamie was giving him hell, he told General Hughes. With the war drawing to a close there would be no further place for Kay in his life.

However, in June 1945, he wrote to his superior, General Marshall, chief of the general staff, asking permission to divorce Mamie and marry Kay. Marshall was furious.

He threatened to break Eisenhower through the ranks and 'see to it that the rest of his life was a living hell' if he married Kay Summersby.

Mamie had known of Eisenhower's intentions and thought it for the best but Eisenhower accepted Marshall's decision, realizing that 'from every stand-point of logic and public relations the thing is impossible'. He wrote to Mamie with the bad news and comforted her with the thought that 'you cannot be any more tired than I of this long separation'.

Eisenhower was ordered home for a whirlwind tour of the United States. Mamie met him at the airport. After their years apart, she gave him only the briefest kiss and a hug before he was hustled off to the Pentagon. They had a week together at White Sulphur Springs before he went back to Germany, alone even though the European war and the threat of bombing were over.

Their time together had done little to ease the situation. When Eisenhower had to pay a brief visit to Belfast, Mamie remarked in a letter that he seemed 'highly interested in Ireland'. Eisenhower explained wearily that he had travelled with two male aides and 'carried out a schedule that would kill a horse'.

Mamie was right to be suspicious. Eisenhower and Kay had one last attempt at lovemaking on his birthday, 14 October, 1945.

'I remember thinking, the way one thinks odd thoughts at significant moments, wouldn't it be wonderful if this were the day we conceived a baby – our very first time,' she wrote. 'Ike was tender, careful, loving. But it didn't work.

' "Wait," I said, "you're too excited. It will be all right."

' "No," he said flatly. "It won't. It's too late. I can't."

'He was bitter. We dressed slowly. Kissing occasionally. Smiling a bit sadly.'

The pressure of war was over. Now Ike was suffering a new pressure from the Pentagon and from his wife.

Kay was still a problem. She was British and could not go on working under Eisenhower's occupation command, but he managed to find her a job with General Lucius Clay in Berlin, explaining to his friend Walter Bedell Smith that Kay 'feels very deserted and alone'.

Soon she left the WRAC, took out U.S. citizenship and moved to New York. In 1947, she got engaged and sent Eisenhower an invitation to the wedding. When he refused to attend, she broke off her engagement.

The following year she ran into Eisenhower 'accidentally' in New York. He was curt, saying simply: 'Kay, it's impossible. There's nothing I can do.'

Mamie returned to Europe with her husband when he was appointed to head NATO and played hostess at their chateau there. Kay eventually reconciled herself to her loss and, in 1952, married.

That same year, just a few days before Eisenhower's presidential campaign began, a new woman took on the Kay Summersby role. She was Ann Whitman who had been at supreme allied headquarters with him during World War II. This time she stayed with him as his aide for eight years.

Mamie's last temporary quarters were the White House. Some say that the marriage was never mended after his affair with Kay Summersby. Mamie began to have trouble with her balance, due to a problem in the inner ear. Rumour attributed it to the abuse of alcohol and her visits to Western health spas were portrayed as efforts to dry out.

However, in the White House, Ike and Mamie still slept together. Mamie said she liked to reach over in the middle of the night 'and pat Ike on his old bald head any time I want to'.

The couple retired to the farmhouse they had bought in Gettysburg, Pennsylvania, in 1948. It was the only home they ever owned together. Mamie died ten years after her husband in 1979 and was buried beside him in a small chapel beside the Eisenhower Library in Abilene, Kansas.

In 1948, Kay Summersby wrote a bowdlerized book called *Eisenhower Was My Boss*. Then she threatened to tell the whole sordid story in a series of articles in *Look* magazine. The affair caused a lot of sniggering when Eisenhower ran for president, but it was not until five years after his death in 1972 that she published *Past Forgetting: My Love Affair with Dwight D. Eisenhower*, revealing the full extent of their wartime romance. If what she says is true, one of the Allies' greatest wartime generals was impotent throughout his victorious campaign. But perhaps, as General Hughes said in 1943, Kay Summersby did help Eisenhower win the war.

20

SOME LIKE IT HOT

John Fitzgerald Kennedy never really stood a chance. Womanizing ran in the family. His father Joe Kennedy, pre-war U.S. Ambassador to London, was known as an ardent skirt-chaser. He facilitated his sexual adventures by investing heavily in Hollywood. There he could indulge himself in an endless stream of beauties willing to take a chance on stardom.

In 1927, he met Gloria Swanson. An aggressive businessman, he quickly took over the interests of the biggest star of the time, creating a new company for her, Gloria Productions Inc.

'In two months, Joe Kennedy had taken over my entire life,' Swanson said. His interest did not stop at business. One evening he turned up at the door of her room in a Palm Beach hotel. 'He just stood there, in his white flannels and his argyle sweater and his two-toned shoes, staring at me for a full minute or more, before he entered the room and closed the door behind him. He moved so quickly that his mouth was on mine before either of us could speak. With one hand he held the back of my head, with the other he stroked my body and pulled at my kimono. He kept insisting in a drawn-out moan, "No longer, no longer. Now.'' He was like a roped horse, rough, arduous, racing to be free. After a hasty climax he lay beside me, stroking my hair. Apart from his guilty, passionate mutterings, he had still said nothing cogent.'

In 1928, at a party in New York, Joe Kennedy confessed to stunned guests that he wanted to have a baby with Swanson. There had been no Kennedy baby that year. He begged her to visit his wife Rose and the children with him. She refused. Later he managed to get the three of them together on a ship returning from Europe. Rose seemed oblivious to what was going on.

'Was she a fool, or a saint?' Swanson wondered. 'Or just a better actress than me?'

In 1929, Cardinal O'Connell paid her a visit and warned her not to go on seeing Joe Kennedy. As divorce was out of the question for the Catholic Kennedy, he had sought the Church's permission to separate from Rose and set up a second household with Swanson.

The affair ended after two box office bombs and when Swanson discovered that the gifts Joe was plying her with were actually charged to her own company.

Joe Kennedy did not limit his philandering to Hollywood starlets and showgirls. No good-looking woman was safe, not even the wives of business associates or the girlfriends of his own sons were off limits.

'Be sure to lock your bedroom door at night,' Jack told female visitors. 'The Ambassador has a tendency to prowl.'

Joe Kennedy even brought his mistresses home to visit. One stayed for several months and joined in family activities.

Nor did his interest drop off with the years. In the 1950s, he made a play for the actress Grace Kelly. In his early seventies, he was seen fondling a young hooker brought to a Kennedy party by international playboy Porfirio Rubirosa.

Jack was encouraged to follow in his distinguished father's footsteps. Once when he got home from school, he found his bed covered with sex magazines the old man had bought. They were all opened to display naked women in the most explicit of poses. This, Kennedy explained, was 'Dad's idea of a joke'.

Jack Kennedy had lost his virginity at the age of seventeen with a prostitute in a brothel in Harlem which he had visited with his school-friend Lem Billings. The girl, who was white, charged $3 each.

Back at school, the youngsters panicked. Convinced that they had contracted venereal disease, they plastered themselves with creams and salves. Even this was not good enough for Kennedy, who woke a doctor in the middle of the night, demanding an examination.

Kennedy quickly overcame his fear of VD and visited a number of other brothels. He especially favoured those south of the border. In May 1936, he wrote to Billings about his adventures with school-friend Smokey Wilde.

'Got a fuck and suck in a Mexican hoar-housse [sic] for 65c, so am feeling very fit and clean,' he boasted. 'Smoke and I set out yesterday, went over the border and arrived at a fucking Mexican town. Met a girl there who is really the best thing I have ever seen but does not speak English. Am writing to her tonight to get a date with her because she wouldn't go out with me last time and it is really love at first sight. They have the best-looking girls in those towns. Anyways Smoke and I ended up in this two-bit hoar-house and they say that one guy in five years has gotten away without just the biggest juiciest load of clap – so Smoke is looking plenty pallid and even I occasionally think of it, so boys your roomie is carrying on in true 9 South style and is upholding the motto of "always get your piece of arse in the most unhealthy place that can be found".'

He did indeed get a dose of clap from this escapade and signed a later letter to Billings 'your gonnereick roomie'.

Back at college, the action continued.

'Went down to the Cape with five guys from school – EM [Eddie Moore] got us some girls thru another guy – four of us had dates and one guy got fucked three times, another guy three times (the girl a virgin!) and myself twice – they were all on the football team and I think the coaches heard as they gave us a hell of a bawling out. The guy who got the virgin just got a very sickening letter, letting [him know] how much she loved him etc and as he didn't use a safer he is very worried. One guy is up at the doctor's seeing if he has a dose and I feel none too secure myself. We are going down next week for a return performance, I think.

'Regards to Ripper and the boys – the name of the drug store where I buy my rubbers is Billings & Stower – Regards, Kennedorus.'

Sadly, a new coach was brought in who 'found out about our little party and I am now known as "Play-boy" '. Kennedy complained of the crack down and lamented that 'I will have to wank plenty to "tame" it down'.

'He was very successful with girls,' said Billings. 'Very.'

At Harvard, he devoted much of his time to chasing women.

'I can now get tail as often and as free as I want which is a step in the right direction,' Kennedy boasted to his friend. When he was intending to visit Billings at Princeton he asked: 'Get me a room way away from all the others and especially from your girl as I don't want you coming in for a chat in the middle as usual and discussing how sore my cock is.'

Moving on to Stanford, in California, one of the first co-eds to be 'branded' by Kennedy's 'red-hot poker' was Susan Imhoff.

'Because of his bad back he preferred making love with the girl on top,' she recalled. 'He found it more stimulating to have the girl do all the work. I remember he didn't enjoy cuddling after making love, but he did like to talk and had a wonderful sense of humour.' Like his father before him, Jack Kennedy went for the quick fling and eschewed any emotional attachment.

'He was like a kid,' recalled Tip O'Neill. 'He really liked girls. But Kennedy never got emotionally involved. He'd sleep with a girl and he'd have Billy take her to the airport the next day.'

'The young girls,' a friend of his sister's said, 'the secretaries and the air hostesses – they were safe grounds. They were not going to make any intellectual or strong demands on him which he wasn't ready to fulfil.'

He used to call his penis 'Lay More', but after he was circumcized in 1938 he began calling his newly renovated member 'J.J.' Soon, he told Billings it 'has never been in better shape or doing better service'.

He also began courting high society. He pursued Frances Ann Cannon, a rich beauty from North Carolina studying at Sarah Lawrence. Next came Charlotte McDonnell, daughter of a New York stockbroker. There was rumour of an engagement, but Charlotte's father disapproved. Kennedy was labelled a 'moral roustabout' and Mr McDonnell forbade him from seeing his daughter again.

There were other serious dates. Olive Crawley dropped him when he disappeared during a date to seduce the hatcheck girl at the Stork Club. He dropped Harriet 'Flip' Price when she would not oblige. They had talked of marriage but Kennedy was not that serious. His favourite expression, he confessed, was still: 'Slam, Bam, Thank You, Ma'am.'

In 1938, Kennedy and his older brother Joe Junior accompanied their father to the U.S. embassy in London.

Joe Senior had to impose a curfew on the two young men to limit their pursuit of women. Kennedy remained obsessed.

With war imminent, Kennedy joined the U.S. Navy and was posted to the Office of Naval Intelligence in Washington, where he quickly gained a reputation as a playboy. One of his lovers was Ingrid Arvad, a former Danish beauty queen. In the 1930s, Hitler had cited her as the perfect example of Nordic beauty. According to an FBI report, she had actually been to bed with the Führer. She had also been the mistress of a Swedish journalist who had been pro-Nazi.

Suspected of being a German spy, Ingrid's phone was tapped and her apartment bugged by the FBI. FBI boss J. Edgar Hoover got tapes of Kennedy making love to 'Inga Binga'. She called him 'Honeysuckle' or 'Honey Child Wilder'. Early in his political career, Kennedy boasted that when he got to Washington he would get the tapes back. He never did.

'He'd always be walking around with a towel around his waist,' Ingrid's son Ronald said his mother told him. 'That's all he ever wore in the apartment – a towel. The minute he arrived, he'd take off all his clothes and take a shower . . . If he wanted to make love, you'd make love – now. They'd have fifteen minutes to get to a party and she'd say she didn't want to. He'd look at his watch and say we've got ten minutes, let's go.'

Ingrid also told her son that she was pregnant when she married and she did not know whether his father was her husband or Kennedy.

After just ninety days with Naval Intelligence in Washington, Kennedy was on the verge of being cashiered as a security risk. Political influence kept him in uniform. He was quickly posted to Charleston, South Carolina. That did not stop the young Kennedy from seeing Ingrid though. On numerous occasions, they made love in

Room 132 of the Fort Sumter Hotel, South Carolina. Once he even went AWOL to visit her in Washington. The FBI soon had the hotel rooms where they met for their trysts bugged. J. Edgar Hoover got still more tapes of the future president's activities. On one memorable recording, Ingrid tells Kennedy that she is pregnant and accuses him of enjoying the pleasures of youth without the responsibility.

Kennedy wanted to marry Ingrid and took her to Hyannis Port, but his father opposed the match. Ingrid was not a Catholic, but that did not stop the old man from trying to seduce her himself.

When he was finally posted to active duty, commanding a PT boat, fellow officers nicknamed him 'Shafty' and complained that he spent more time chasing models than chasing enemy submarines.

'Girls were an obsession with him,' one recalled. 'We liked them too, but we didn't make a career out of it.'

At a Hollywood party after the war with Ingrid, he tried to woo actress Olivia de Havilland. She resisted his charms and said she was leaving. He leapt to the door to open it, only to find that it was the closet door. Rackets and tennis balls rained down on him.

After Ingrid, Kennedy filled the void with a series of chorus girls and models, notably Angela Greene who went on to become an actress.

Kennedy briefly became a journalist, but he spent most of his time at parties, trying to seduce rich, often married women. There were iceskaters, Hollywood starlets and strippers such as the well-endowed Tempest Storm. Divorcees were his particular favourite as, being a Catholic, there was no danger of marriage. The names were legion – one that stood out was English actress Peggy Cummins. With her, he made gossip columns though he never got her into bed.

Anita Marcus outlined the Kennedy technique: 'I think that the main thing was that when he talked to you, he looked you straight in the eye and his attention never wandered. He was interested in finding out what I was doing there – why I was there. It was a drawing-me-out thing. It was undivided attention. I was the most envied girl in the room. He had a way with women. There is no question about it.'

When he began his political career, he ran on his good looks and charm. Women responded viscerally.

'The older ladies seemed to mother him,' a volunteer said, 'all of the young ones fell in love with him.'

During his 1946 congressional campaign, an election aide caught him making love to one of the campaign workers on the desk in his office. Later, the girl missed her period. Kennedy said: 'Oh shit.' And moved on.

When he arrived in Washington, three hundred correspondents voted him 'the handsomest member of the House'. Fellow congressman Frank 'Toppy' Thomson of New Jersey said: 'I could walk with Jack into a room of a hundred women and at least eighty-five of them would be willing to sacrifice their honour and everything else if they could get into a pad with him.'

State Department official Lucius Battle recalled having to drag his wife away from him.

Campaigning for Kennedy's second congressional term, Massachusetts Governor Paul Denver told a crowd: 'I hear it being said that my young friend Jack Kennedy isn't working down there in Washington, that he's too fond of girls. Well, let me tell you ladies and gentlemen, I've never heard it said of Jack Kennedy that he's too fond of boys.'

There is some evidence that Kennedy married Florida socialite Durie Macolm in 1947. Her printed family history states that among her numerous husbands was one 'John F. Kennedy, son of Joseph P. Kennedy, one time

Ambassador to England'. If true, this would mean that America's first Catholic president was, in fact, a divorcee.

In 1951, Kennedy had another brush with marriage, this time with Alicia Purdom, wife of British actor Edmund Purdom. The anti-British Joe put a stop to that. An Italian magazine said that he paid her half-a-million dollars to back off. It further alleged that she was pregnant. Danger did not end there. In the summer of 1960, during the presidential race, Alicia sued for divorce. Her husband countersued, naming Kennedy as co-respondent. A friend of the Kennedy's contacted Alicia. A discreet divorce was arranged in Mexico and the whole thing was hushed up.

In 1952, after defeating the long-term incumbent Henry Cabot Lodge in the Massachusetts Senatorial race, Kennedy locked himself and his date in a closet at a white-tie benefit in Newport, Rhode Island. Guests had to wait to get their coats back until Senator Kennedy had finished his lovemaking.

There came a time – politically – when Kennedy had to get married. Who better for a bride than Jacqueline Bouvier, the daughter of John Vernon 'Black Jack' Bouvier III, an alcoholic and notorious New England womanizer. Jackie, at least, would know what to expect.

Ostensibly Jacqueline Bouvier was 'the classic virgin princess'. In every way, her education surpassed Kennedy's own. She was beautiful and classy. When he used the old-fashioned words 'prick', 'fuck', 'nuts' and 'son of a bitch', she was shocked. However, one of their first sexual encounters took place over the river from Washington, DC, in Arlington, Virginia, in the back seat of Kennedy's convertible. They were disturbed by a policeman. Embarrassed when he recognized 'the playboy senator' as the press were already calling him, the cop left the couple alone to get on with their amorous business.

Jackie quickly broke off her engagement to John Husted, but there were no flowers or candies from Kennedy. He proposed by telegram. The wedding in 1953 was the society event of the year.

The marriage was strained to start with. Jackie was a patrician. Kennedy was a bog-trotting, street-fighting politician. To expect her to fit into his world was, a friend said: 'Like asking Rocky Graziano to play the piano.'

The most difficult problem she faced was Kennedy's flagrant philandering. She did not expect fidelity. She had witnessed her father's many affairs, but she had not prepared herself for the all-encompassing sweep of her husband's dalliances. These were not just casual entanglements. Kennedy and his congressional friend George Smathers established an apartment at the Carroll Arms Hotel in Washington, where they could entertain young women.

'Jack liked to go over there and meet a couple of young secretaries,' Smathers recalled. 'He liked groups.'

Worse, he would often bring lovers along to receptions where Jackie would be present. Sometimes he would employ a 'beard' such as his brother-in-law, actor Peter Lawford. He also employed other tactics. While Jackie was away in Europe, he arranged to go to various 'house parties' in Maine. Uneven numbers of men and women at these parties were supposed to throw the press off the scent; or a respectable elderly lady would be employed to take a jaded Kennedy to Mass on a Sunday morning to allay suspicion.

In 1954, when Kennedy was required to declare against the witch-hunting techniques of Senator Joe McCathy – a friend of his father's – he got, diplomatically, ill. He spent a lot of his young life in hospital with various complaints, but found some comfort in the fact that this meant he was constantly surrounded by young nurses.

In his New York hospital room, there was, a series of young, so called 'cousins' who visited. Playing along, Jackie hired Grace Kelly to pretend to be his night nurse. When Jack opened his eyes, he thought he was dreaming, especially as his father had his eyes on the same prize.

In 1956, Kennedy met divorcee Joan Lundberg, a mother of two, in a bar in Santa Monica. They began by discussing the record she was about to put on the juke box, then moved on to a party at Peter Lawford's home.

Lundberg said that Kennedy loved threesomes with himself and two girls. She also said that he was a voyeur. The affair lasted three years. He paid her bills and for an abortion when she got pregnant. They even made love in Jackie's marital bed in Georgetown. The affair ended amicably when he won the Democratic nomination in 1960.

One night in 1958, a couple called Leonard and Florence Kater were disturbed by a man throwing pebbles at the window of their twenty-year-old lodger, Pamela Turnure, who was a secretary at Kennedy's Senate office. The man, who became a regular nocturnal visitor, was Kennedy himself.

Devout Catholics, the Katers took pictures of Kennedy sneaking out in the middle of the night and rigged a tape recorder to pick up sounds of the couple's lovemaking. In 1959, when Kennedy was running against Lyndon Johnson for the Democratic nomination, they mailed details of the affair to the newspapers. The press shied away from the story but J. Edgar Hoover heard about it, got the pictures and tapes from the Katers and gave them to Johnson, a long-time friend, to use in his campaign. In fact, Hoover had a bulging file on Kennedy which included 'affidavits from two mulatto prostitutes in New York'. At that time, Kennedy also maintained a private suite in Washington's Mayflower Hotel, which an FBI informant referred to as 'Kennedy's personal play-pen'.

When Kennedy won the nomination and then the election, the Katers, in frustration, demonstrated outside the White House, with placards complaining that there was an adulterer in the Executive Mansion. Nobody took any notice.

Pamela Turnure was rewarded for her selfless, nocturnal service, which continued for over three years. When Kennedy entered the White House, she was made press secretary to Jackie. Jackie knew what was going on, but did not object, figuring that if she made it that easy for her husband, he would get bored. When Kennedy was asked what it was like having his mistress work for his wife, he replied: 'Like living life on a high wire.'

Jackie was always one step ahead of her husband. At White House dinners, she would not hesitate to seat one of his lovers either side of him. That way, at least, he would have no access to fresh talent.

In 1957 and 1958, Kennedy slipped over to Cuba for assignations with Florence Prichett Smith, wife of the U.S. Ambassador to Havana under the Eisenhower administration. He had met her in the Stork Club in 1944 and some said that she was the love of his life. She was a model at the time, but later married, converted to Catholicism, then three years later divorced.

In 1947, she was back with Kennedy. In his appointment book for 28 June, she wrote: 'Flo Prichett's birthday: SEND DIAMONDS.' A year later, she married a millionaire, a much older man, Earl Edward Smith who Eisenhower despatched to Cuba.

While Kennedy was president, he also saw her in Florida. One time, when he had given his Secret Service agents the slip, a local policeman found Florence and Kennedy together in a swimming pool – and 'they weren't doing the Australian crawl,' he reported.

Kennedy was not ashamed of his activities. One FBI informant said that he saw Kennedy and Senator Estes

Kefauver have sex with two women in their apartment in front of other guests, then switch partners and do it again. On his desk, Kennedy had a photograph of himself and other men with several nude girls, taken on the deck of a yacht. He liked to make love on the floor of his office in the Senate Office building. Stories of his reckless woman-izing circulated in the Senate. He would hold orgies in his apartment at the Carroll Arms Hotel across the road from the Senate Office building while his colleagues were voting on various pieces of legislation. 'That sort of thing was his favourite pastime,' said Smathers, by then a fellow U.S. Senator.

'I am not through with a girl till I have had her three ways,' Kennedy told another colleague. What he meant by this, we can only surmise.

'Jack felt he could walk on water so far as women were concerned,' Senator Smathers said. 'There is no question about the fact that Jack had the most active libido of any man I've ever known. He was really unbelievable – absolutely incredible in that regard, and he got more so the longer he was married.'

Smathers even remembered a time when he, Kennedy and two girls had gone back to their private apartment, when a call came that he was wanted back at the Senate. He was halfway there when he realized that the Senate was no longer in session. When he got back to the apartment, he found Kennedy trying to have sex with both women.

'No one was off limits to Jack,' Smathers said. 'Not your wife, your mother, your sister.'

Kennedy's long-serving secretary Evelyn Lincoln ad-mitted that Kennedy was 'a ladies' man'. But she added: 'Kennedy didn't chase women. The women chased Ken-nedy.'

One time, Kennedy tried to seduce historian Dr Mar-garet Coit.

'Do you do this to all the women you meet?' she asked.

'Good God, no,' he said. 'I don't have the strength.'

During the 1960 election, Hoover released some material on Kennedy's sex life – which included a picture of Kennedy naked with an attractive brunette on a beach – to Republican candidate Richard Nixon. But Kennedy did not even tone down his behaviour during the campaign. He hung out in Las Vegas with Frank Sinatra during the filming of the ratpack movie *Ocean's 11*. One FBI report stated that 'showgirls from all over the town were running in and out of the Senator's suite'. One of these showgirls, a tall brunette, was later observed visiting the White House for sexual matinees.

In early March that year, Sinatra introduced Kennedy to twenty-five-year-old Judith Campbell and they began a long-term affair. Later that month, Sinatra also introduced her to the Mafia boss Sam Giancana and she became his lover too.

At the beginning of April, Jackie was pregnant again and had gone to Florida. So Judith was free to visit Kennedy in his house in Georgetown. Despite Joe Kennedy's enormous wealth, the Kennedy campaign was short of funds. Kennedy asked Campbell whether she could arrange a meeting with Giancana, whose Chicago Crime Syndicate – former proprietor Al Capone – turned over $2 billion a year. She did and, according to FBI wiretaps, the Mafia made huge campaign contributions which were used to pay off key election officials. Giancana later boasted to Judith that her boyfriend would never have made it to the White House without his help.

As the 1960 primaries drew to a close, Judith Campbell met Kennedy at Peter Lawford's suite in the Beverly Hilton Hotel for a late-night party. He lured Judith into a bedroom, where another woman was waiting, and suggested that the three of them make love together – 'I know you'll enjoy it,' he said.

'He assured me that the girl was safe and would never talk about it to a single soul,' Judith recalled, but she tearfully rejected him.

Later Kennedy wooed her back with flowers, telephone calls and a ticket to the convention. If he failed to win the nomination, the two of them would take off to a remote island, he promised, where they would never have to wear clothes. Judith got the impression that Jackie intended to leave him if he was not elected. The most Kennedy ever said about their marriage was that it 'had not worked out as they had hoped'.

On the campaign trail, the opportunities were irresistible. Women mobbed him. One student in Louisville shouted at him: 'We love you. You're better than Elvis Presley.'

Young women swooned over his pearly teeth and a teenage girl said that if she had the vote, she would vote for him, then fled into the school locker room in embarrassment.

Journalists began writing of the female 'jumpers', 'leapers', 'clutchers', 'touchers', 'screamers' and 'runners'. One wrote of the 'groans and moans and a frowzy woman muttering hoarsely to herself, "Oh, Jack I love yuh, Jack, I love yuh, Jack, Jack, I love yuh"'; or the harsh-faced woman peering over one's shoulder glowering, "You a newspaperman? You better write nice things about him or you watch out" (and she meant it).'

Although Jackie continued to play the part of the adoring political wife, her husband's relentless infidelity sent her into black depressions. She could not escape. Her beauty and grace were seen as vital vote catchers and she had to be at the candidate's side constantly.

Even as the election drew closer, Kennedy found time to party, usually at Peter Lawford's beach house north of

Santa Monica. Dean Martin said that Lawford acted as Kennedy's pimp and that 'the things that went on in that house were just mind-boggling'.

Lawford himself refused to talk about Kennedy and his 'broads' but 'all I will say is that I was Frank's [Sinatra's] pimp and Frank was Jack's. It sounds terrible now, but then it was a lot of fun.'

Lawford's mother said: 'I find it difficult to place my complete trust in a president of the United States, who always has his mind on his cock.'

There were rumours about his involvement with the beautiful brunette Janet des Rosiers, who travelled on the Kennedys' plane with him. She was his 'girl Friday' – or 'our stewardess' as Evelyn Lincoln called her – and massaged the candidate and combed his hair in a private compartment on board. Previously she had been employed to perform the same functions for Kennedy's father.

Before the first televized debate with Republican presidential candidate Richard Nixon, Kennedy casually asked an aide if there were any girls lined up. Ninety minutes before airtime, Kennedy disappeared into a hotel room with a prostitute. She had already been paid for her services and he spent fifteen minutes with her. He was so pleased with his relaxed on-air performance that he had a girl lined up before each of the subsequent debates.

The press knew all about these activities, but chose to keep quiet. In those days unless a politician's thirst for strong drink, womanizing or homosexual activities became so blatant that they would affect his performance in office, the press corps simply refused to report them. Nevertheless, Kennedy ruefully noted: 'I suppose if I win, my poon days are over.' 'Poon' is a slang term Kennedy picked up in his Navy days.

He was wrong, of course. Once elected, the press gave him even more latitude. Some time before his inauguration, Kennedy slipped off for two or three days in Palm Springs with actress Angie Dickinson. They disappeared into a holiday cottage and never emerged. A *Newsweek* reporter who travelled with the Kennedys barged in and caught Dickinson relaxing on the bed, but he promptly forgot what he had seen.

Angie Dickinson has been credited with saying of her affair with Kennedy: 'It was the best twenty seconds of my life.' Indeed, it has been widely reported that Kennedy, like his father, was a quick and inconsiderate lover, more interested in the conquest than the consummation. However, Dickinson has, in fact, maintained a respectful silence on the subject of her affair with Kennedy.

Kennedy also had sex with Jayne Mansfield while she was eight-months pregnant – he was 'very considerate of my condition'; with the actress Gene Tierney and stripper Blaze Starr, who he made love to in a closet while her regular boyfriend, Democratic Governor Earl Long, was at an election party next door.

Judith Campbell was invited to Kennedy's inaugural ball, but declined. She said she would not feel right with his wife and children there. Angie Dickinson did attend and went to a private dinner party with Kennedy. Jackie herself avoided many of the inaugural functions, having no wish to stand by while her husband was squeezed, hugged and pawed by the numerous actresses who had been invited. Jackie did, however, attend one ball with her husband at the Statler-Hilton. Even then he could not resist slipping out of the presidential box to attend a private party with Frank Sinatra, Angie Dickinson, Janet Leigh and Kim Novak. He returned sheepishly with a copy of the *Washington Post* under his arm as if the newly inaugurated President of the United States had had to slip out to buy a newspaper.

Later that night, JFK celebrated his inauguration in proper Kennedy style. He attended a party at columnist Joe Alsop's Georgetown house, where the first thing he asked was: 'Where are the broads?'

The place was packed with young girls and Hollywood starlets. The niece of one European ambassador was also on offer. Peter Lawford had provided six candidates. He lined them up and Kennedy picked two of them for a proper celebration.

Once in the White House, Kennedy was bombarded with the FBI files of people in his administrations. At first, he enjoyed reading them, especially as it told him which of the White House secretaries were 'available', but when he realized the extent of Hoover's snooping, he swore he would never read another dossier – though he admitted ruefully: 'I'd like to see what they have got on me.'

Judith Campbell was a regular visitor to the White House. She tells of a visit there one Saturday afternoon, kissing and cuddling in his bedroom to the sound track of the musical *Camelot*. She went into the bathroom to undress and when she returned, he was already in bed, lying in his favourite position on his back. Sometimes it made her feel as if she was just there to satisfy him sexually. This was one of over twenty visits Judith Campbell made to the White House. Despite Hoover's regular warnings about Judith Campbell's connections with the Mafia to the Attorney General Bobby Kennedy, the affair continued. In fact, Judith later played a vital role as go-between in the failed CIA–Mafia plans to assassinate Fidel Castro.

Judith met with Kennedy in his house in Florida, but he would also go there alone and have aides recruit talent from Palm Beach.

The painter Mary Pinchot Meyer visited the White House too. Veteran journalist Ben Bradlee and his wife often accompanied her to soirées there, but there were clandestine visits too, when they smoked marijuana together. A woman known only as Susannah M. claimed on a TV documentary to have had a four-year relationship with Kennedy, which included visits to the White House.

In fact, there was quite a stream of attractive young women making their way to the Presidential Mansion. Kennedy would often take them nude swimming in the White House pool. Male friends would send over nubile volunteers. One was a *Playboy* centrefold sent over by a columnist. Kennedy sent a note saying: 'Got your message – both of them.'

At one nude swimming party, Kennedy and a tall beautiful blonde were joined by Bobby, a male friend and several more naked girls. Suddenly they got a message that Jackie, who had left for Virginia, was on her way back to the White House. Everybody scrambled. But when Jackie had collected the things she had forgotten and was on her way again, the nude party resumed.

There were other nude parties at the White House, though for Kennedy they seemed to pall. At one, he slumped down in a chair to read Walter Lippmann. Later, he phoned a friend saying that he was in the Oval Office with two naked young women and he was reading the *Wall Street Journal.*

'Am I getting too old?' he asked.

He was not. The sheer numbers of women going through the White House gave the Secret Service headaches. They were supposed to give every visitor a full security check. It proved impossible to keep up and the Secret Service codenamed Kennedy 'Lancer' – a name supposedly with *Camelot* overtones.

One former Newfrontiersman said: 'It was a revolving door over there. A woman had to fight to get on line.'

White House staff were asked to comb the presidential apartments for lipsticks, dropped hairpins or other incriminating evidence. They cursed Kennedy's penchant for blondes. If he had one steady brunette, they complained, their life would have been much easier. They were not always as thorough as they might have been. On one occasion, Jackie found a pair of panties stuffed in a pillow case. She held them between her forefinger and thumb and presented them to her husband.

'Would you please shop around and see who these belong to?' she said. 'They are not my size.'

Presidential staff also had to work around Kennedy's womanizing. One young woman was in bed with Kennedy when there was a knock on the door of the Lincoln bedroom. Kennedy got up and let two advisers in. He slumped in a chair while he read the classified cables they had brought, gave his orders, then went back to bed with her.

Another White House staffer reported taking the lift up to the family apartment while Jackie was away, to be confronted with a naked blonde office girl running down the corridor.

During a Summit meet on the Bahamas with British Prime Minister Harold Macmillan and Foreign Secretary R.A.B. Butler, Kennedy complained: 'If I don't have a woman for three days, I get terrible headaches.'

He told others that he could not sleep properly unless he had had a lay.

'We're a bunch of virgins, married virgins,' lamented secretary of the cabinet Fred Dutton, 'and he's like God, fucking anybody he wants to any time he feels like it.'

Even during the Cuban missile crisis, his mind was on women. During a tense meeting when the fate of the world hung in the balance, Kennedy spotted an attractive secretary. He told Secretary of Defense Robert McNamara: 'I want her name and number. We may avert war tonight.'

After Kennedy's famous 'Ich bin ein Berliner' speech at the Berlin Wall, he pursued a German secretary named Ursula who worked at the U.S. embassy.

In the White House, there were two blonde secretaries – one twenty-one, one twenty-three – nicknamed 'Fiddle' and 'Faddle' by the Secret Service and referred to as the 'office amusements'. Both were attractive college graduates who ostensibly worked for White House press secretary Pierre Salinger and Evelyn Lincoln. In fact, they often travelled with the President and got calls to report on duty at all hours. Jackie called them the 'White House dogs' and introduced them to a French journalist once as 'my husband's two lovers'.

One night Kennedy and Peter Lawford tried amyl nitrate 'poppers' with Fiddle and Faddle, to test the drug's effect on sex. Drugs were used quite widely in the Kennedy White House. Kennedy used cortisone and Novocaine to dull the pain in his back, but he also employed Dr Max Jacobson – known to the stars as 'Dr Feelgood' – who injected him with amphetamine and steroids. The President and the First Lady had developed a strong dependence on 'speed' by the summer of 1961. Kennedy was high on speed during the Cuban missile crisis. Jacobson, himself an addict, was later struck off.

Peter Lawford had introduced Kennedy to cocaine and he took LSD in the White House while making love with Mary Pinchot Meyer. They joked about what would happen if the Russians dropped the bomb while he was tripping.

The Kennedy marriage was damaged beyond hope of repair long before they entered the White House. It was effectively over when Jackie gave birth to a still-born child in 1956. At the time, Kennedy was cruising in the Mediterranean with George Smathers and several accommodating young women. One of them, a stunning but not particularly bright girl named 'Pooh', fascinated Kennedy. Rather than fly back to be beside his grief-stricken wife, he chose to stay on in the Mediterranean. He only returned home three days later, after Smathers convinced him that any further delay would ruin his political career.

His callousness ruined their marriage, especially after Jackie learnt what Kennedy had been doing. She would bring it up constantly. When she left hospital, she moved back to her stepfather's estate and divorce was on the cards. The situation worsened when she discovered that their fifteen-year-old baby-sitter was pregnant and was naming Kennedy as the father. Joe Kennedy stepped in and made a financial settlement on Jackie, provided she did not leave her husband. Having little money of her own, she agreed but from then on, it was guerrilla warfare. She would constantly be on his back about pretty girls, indulge in punishing shopping sprees and flaunt herself in public with male friends to incite his jealousy. Once, in the White House, she got drunk on champagne and danced with every man in sight.

This was very effective as Kennedy was jealous of men who were mere acquaintances of Jackie's. It did not stop his own activities, however, which Jackie slowly became resigned to.

'I don't think there are any men who are faithful to their wives,' she told a friend. 'Men are such a combination of good and bad.'

She may well have had affairs of her own. There was possibly an affair with her security guard. Evelyn Lincoln believes that she had one affair with 'a dashing Italian count'. Jackie seems to have paid unusual attention to Gianni Agnelli, the owner of Fiat. Rumour has it that she was getting her own back because Kennedy had flirted openly with Signora Agnelli.

Jackie was so popular with the American public that she felt that nothing could hurt her – 'unless I run off with Eddie Fisher,' she said.

Somehow, the marriage struggled on. When a friend of Kennedy's was contemplating divorce, Kennedy advised: 'Try it the way I am doing it.'

The friend replied: 'I go home five nights a week. You're in this Arabian Nights never-never land of the White House. Some nights you don't go home at all.'

Kennedy thought about this. A few nights later, he called and said: 'You're right. If I had to go home three nights a week, I'd go up the wall.'

Evelyn Lincoln also believes that Jackie had begun her affair with Aristotle Onassis in October 1963, one month before her husband was assassinated in Dallas, Texas.

The FBI continued to keep track of Kennedy's every move. They bugged Judith Campbell's phone and did security checks on the prostitutes hired for Kennedy's parties.

Kennedy had had his eye on Marilyn Monroe since she first appeared in movies in the early 1950s. In 1954, when he was incapacitated after back surgery, he stuck her picture on his wall. It showed her standing feet apart, wearing shorts. He stuck it on the wall upside down, so that her legs were in the air.

They began their affair in the late 1950s. They were certainly lovers during the 1960 election campaign and made love in Los Angeles when Kennedy was there for the Democratic National Convention that year. Around that time Peter Lawford remembered taking photographs of Kennedy and Monroe together, naked in the bathtub. Marilyn was performing oral sex on Kennedy at the time. Another time, Kennedy aide Peter Summers saw them emerge from the same shower.

They appeared together at a nude swimming party at Lawford's beach house the night of his acceptance speech. Still Kennedy was shocked when he found that Marilyn wore no underwear when he put his hand up her dress that night at a dinner party in a restaurant.

On other occasions, heavily disguised with a black wig and sunglasses, Monroe was smuggled into Kennedy's suite at the Carlyle Hotel in New York and on to Air Force One. They made love on the beach at Santa Monica, spent the night at the Beverley Hilton and spent time together at Bing Crosby's estate in Palm Springs. She even called her masseur when they had an argument about anatomy and she put Kennedy on the phone to settle the point.

As newspaper reporters covered the lobby of the Carlyle, the Secret Service found another way into the hotel via a series of tunnels that ran from a nearby apartment building. The President of the United States would have to clamber past huge steam pipes, accompanied by two Secret Service men with torches and a map, for half an hour with Marilyn or his latest playmate.

Sometimes Kennedy gave his guards the slip to make a private tryst, leaving behind the army officer who had the nuclear security codes handcuffed to his wrist. If the Soviet Union had launched an all-out attack during the time they were separated, America would have been powerless to retaliate.

The FBI had Peter Lawford's house bugged and in November 1961, agents taped Kennedy and Monroe talking, disrobing and having sex on the bed. Hoover was delighted. He had overheard Bobby Kennedy discussing the possibility of firing him. Now he knew he was safe.

In March 1962, Hoover learned that Kennedy had visited Monroe again in California and the two of them had spent the night together. They met again in May in New York when she sang her famous 'Happy Birthday, Mr President' at a Democratic Party fundraiser at Madison Square Garden.

Knowing of their affair, Jackie had started taking long trips abroad on her own. Marilyn had the private number of the family apartment at the White House and Jackie would sometimes answer the phone when she called. She would hand the phone over to her husband and they would chat in her presence.

On the night of the birthday party, Jackie was out of town – a 'surprise contestant' at a horse show in Virginia. She was right to stay away. Marilyn appeared, sewn into a dress that veteran diplomat Adlai Stevenson described as 'skin and beads – only I didn't see the beads'. The sexual electricity between Kennedy and Monroe was visible even to the TV cameras. Photographs showing the President ogling Marilyn mysteriously disappeared from the picture agencies.

After Marilyn had finished her seductive rendition, Kennedy took the stage and said: 'I can now retire from politics after having had, ah, "Happy Birthday" sung to me in such a sweet wholesome way.'

That was the last time Kennedy and Monroe were together. Hoover had used his knowledge of the affair to secure his job. He had let it slip to Kennedy that Lawford's beach house was bugged 'very likely ... by the Mafia'. Kennedy could risk seeing Marilyn no longer.

Marilyn could not accept that the affair was over and fell into a deep depression. She turned to alcohol and barbiturates, and threatened to go to the press. Kennedy despatched his brother Bobby – who had already been seen hovering around Marilyn at his brother's birthday party – to calm her down. In the process they became lovers and slept together in the guest bedroom at Lawford's bugged beach house. They kissed openly and went to a nudist beach together. Bobby even promised to marry her. Hoover was delighted to hear this. Bobby Kennedy, as Attorney General, was Hoover's boss and, consequently, his arch-enemy. He proceeded to make things hot for Bobby. He told the Attorney General that the Mafia were intending to use their knowledge of the sexual exploits of Marilyn Monroe and Judith Campbell to prevent Bobby's continuing investigations into organized crime.

Kennedy was then forced to give up Judith Campbell and Bobby had to abandon Monroe. For Marilyn, this was one blow too many. Somehow she imagined herself First Lady with one or other of the Kennedy brothers. Once, she had even called Jackie in the White House and asked her to divorce Kennedy, so she could marry him and have his children, though she admitted that he was a lousy lay and 'brutal and perfunctory in bed'. He went for quantity not quality. Jackie, she knew, was not passionate. Kennedy had complained about it. Marilyn knew, too, that Jackie would never let him put his hand up her dress.

Losing both the Kennedy brothers destroyed Marilyn. She attended some orgies at Lake Tahoe arranged by Lawford and Sinatra, but it did not help. When she died of a drugs overdose, her former husband baseball star Joe DiMaggio, knowing who was responsible, banned the Kennedys from the funeral.

In 1963, in another attack on the President, Hoover leaked to the press information linking Kennedy to the Profumo affair. Kennedy had had sex, both in London and New York, with actress and model Suzy Chang who moved in the wealthy London circles associated with Profumo and his friends. Kennedy had met Chang at the 21 Club in London. After that, she took regular flights to the U.S. It was as much as Bobby could do to keep this material out of the papers.

Kennedy had also been seeing Ellen Rometsch, an East German refugee. The FBI picked her up in July 1963 as a suspected Communist plant and deported her to West Germany. The Rometsch affair was reported in the papers. The *Des Moines Register* said that the potential spy was

SEX LIVES OF THE U.S PRESIDENTS

a beautiful brunette who had attended parties with congressional leaders. The paper hinted that her lovers in-cluded high-ranking members of the executive branch.

Before the rest of the press could follow up, Bobby sent La Verne Duffy to Germany. He and a number of other men flashing U.S. security badges got Mrs Rometsch to sign a statement denying sleeping with important people in America. Senator Williams planned to raise the affair. Bobby had to quash his distaste for Hoover and phone him at home. Hoover gave a briefing to Senate leaders and the matter was dropped, but the Kennedy's were now in Hoover's debt. After that, when Kennedy was asked why he did not fire Hoover, he would reply simply: 'You don't fire God.'

On the surface, the Profumo scandal was considered an exclusively British affair, but it created near panic in Washington. Kennedy himself pored over the reports. If it were to be discovered that the President was involved in a British security scandal, impeachment would surely follow. Kennedy had been warned on numerous occasions that his womanizing would bring him down, but he did not listen.

'They can't touch me while I'm alive,' Kennedy told a friend, 'and after I'm dead, who cares?'

Well, apparently, people do. Forty years after Kennedy was assassinated in Dallas, his sex life made the headlines, yet again, when documents were released showing that he had an affair with a teenager while he was in the White House. Nineteen-year-old Marion 'Mimi' Beardsley came to 1600 Pennsylvania Avenue to interview Mrs Kennedy for Jackie's old school paper, but the First Lady was too busy to see her. It seems that the President had more time for the young lady and hired her to work in the press office, even though she had no relevant skills. She was then invited to pool parties and flown around the country on Air Force One to provide 'sexual release' for the commander-in-chief. She was even spotted at the 1962 Bahamas summit, where JFK discussed the British nuclear deterrent with Prime Minister Harold Macmillan, kneeling on the floor of the presidential limousine Lewinsky-style. Bearded by the New York *Daily News* outside her Fifth Avenue Presbyterian church in Manhattan in 2003, Mimi now appears to have learnt to keep her mouth shut.

Both Kennedy and Bobby used 'playgirls', according to FBI reports. There are also indications that Bobby became Jackie's lover after Kennedy was killed in Dallas. David Heyman, Jackie's biographer, claims that shared grief led them to have a long affair.

Until his mid-1990s marriage, Senator Ted Kennedy kept up the proud family tradition. His drinking and womanizing in Washington were constant sources of gossip. Both elements remained just below the surface in the incident at Chappaquiddick in 1969 which cost him a shot at the presidency in 1980. Late at night, he drove his car off an unmarked bridge. His companion, a young woman named Mary Jo Kopechne, was drowned.

The Kennedy family was engulfed in sex scandal again in March 1991, when Senator Edward Kennedy took his nephew William Kennedy Smith to Au Bar, a trendy nightspot in Palm Beach, Florida. Smith picked up Patricia Bowman, the twenty-nine-year-old stepdaughter of the prominent industrialist. They went back to the Kennedy compound and down to the beach. Smith swam naked in the sea, then they returned to the garden and had sex on the lawn. Smith maintained that it was consensual. Patricia said it was rape.

In a sensational, televised trial which went into every detail – including the number of grains of sand in Patricia's panties and where she bought her lingerie – Smith was acquitted. Though the verdict was controversial, everybody agreed about one thing – Ted Kennedy's performance on the witness stand was masterful.

21

WHEY, HEY LBJ

Lyndon Baines Johnson was a rival of Kennedy's in every way and considered it unjust that Kennedy's reputation as a womanizer outstripped his own.

'I have had more women by accident than he has had on purpose,' he said.

Johnson openly boasted of his conquests, which were numerous, but what was more remarkable about him was his ability to keep two long-term relationships going, without alienating his wife.

Johnson's womanizing career began early when he was fortunate enough to go to a college at San Marcos, where the women on campus outnumbered the men by three to one. It was easy to get a date. His brother, Sam Houston Johnson, recalled visiting him there. Lyndon came back to his room naked after taking a shower. He took his penis in his hand and said: 'Well, I've gotta take ol' Jumbo here and give him some exercise. I wonder who I'll fuck tonight.'

He loved to boast about his sexual conquests and was graphic in his descriptions of what went on. But he had his eye on the main chance. A poor country boy, if he wanted to get on he had to marry for money.

He dated Carol Davis, daughter of a rich businessman. Johnson would brag that when they went out, she picked up the tab. The relationship ended when she got engaged to someone else. Later Johnson courted Kitty Clyde Ross, daughter of the richest man in Johnson city.

From a young age, Johnson had been passionate about politics. When he began his political career, he worked so hard at it that he had little time for enduring relationships. For relaxation, he would pick up waitresses and spend the night with them. His sexual encounters were episodic, one night stands.

Too busy for conventional wooing, Johnson asked a woman friend who had refused him a date to fix him up with someone else. She introduced him to Claudia 'Lady Bird' Taylor, the daughter of a prominent businessman. They married in 1934.

In 1937, Johnson was elected to congress. Around that time, he met Alice Glass, the live-in lover of newspaper magnate Charles E. Marsh. Marsh had left his wife and children for her. Alice did not believe in marriage, but they had two children together.

Their Virginia home, an eighteenth-century-style manor known as Longlea, was a meeting place for politicians and journalists. At the time, Alice was involved in organizing efforts to get Jews out of Germany. Johnson lent a hand. Sometime in 1938 or 1939 they became lovers, meeting often in the Mayflower Hotel in Washington or at the Allies Inn.

This was a dangerous move as Marsh had become Johnson's political patron. His paper ran pro-Johnson articles and, when Johnson found he was having trouble getting by on his $10,000-a-year congressman's salary, Marsh helped out. He sold Johnson a tract of land at a knock-down price. It was actually Lady Bird's money that paid for the acreage. That one deal secured their financial future.

Lady Bird probably knew of Johnson's affair with Alice. When he went to spend the weekend at Longlea, she would discreetly fly back to Texas or stay in Washington and busy herself with domestic chores.

Once, when Johnson spent the weekend away with Alice in New York, he left his number with one of his staff. Marsh needed to contact Johnson and insisted that the man give him the number. Johnson was furious and gave the staffer a dressing down on Monday.

Marsh eventually found out about the affair. One night, when he was very drunk, he confronted Johnson and ordered him out of the house, but when Johnson returned later, Marsh said no more about it.

The affair lasted until 1967, when Alice found that she could no longer support Johnson over the Vietnam war. Alice married Marsh, but after six years, they divorced.

Johnson's other enduring love was Madeleine Brown. He met her at a reception in Dallas in 1948. He was a congressman. She was twenty-four and an assistant in an advertising firm.

'He looked at me like I was an ice-cream cone on a hot day,' she recalled.

They began a twenty-one-year affair. Three years after they met, Madeleine bore Johnson a son, who they called Steven.

Madeleine said her love for Johnson was 'purely physical'. Their affair was kept well hidden from his wife Lady Bird and their two children. In return, Madeleine was furnished with a two-bedroomed house, a maid, an unlimited charge card and a new car every two years.

When Johnson was in Texas they would get together. At one of the assignations at Austin's Driskill Hotel when Johnson was Vice-President, he explained that they were in trouble. At that time Kennedy was still trying to remove Hoover as head of the FBI. Hoover wanted Johnson to exert his influence with Kennedy. He knew about Madeleine and Steven. Johnson's solution was for Madeleine to marry someone else – on paper at least.

'I want you to go through with the marriage,' he told Madeleine, 'to help me get my balls out of Hoover's vice grip.'

The affair continued until 1969.

Johnson had been friends with Hoover since he first came to Washington in the 1930s. They were neighbours. Hoover would invite the Johnsons over for dinner or Sunday brunch and sometimes babysit their daughters. Privately, Johnson called Hoover 'that queer bastard'. But with his own closet bulging with skeletons – women, bent business deals and allegations of ballot-rigging in the 1948 election – he had to keep on the right side of him. This also had other advantages. Hoover would lend Johnson FBI files for light, bedtime reading. Johnson revelled in the sexual peccadillos of his colleagues and the information he gleaned helped him in his spectacular rise to power. He would regularly simply walk up to a senator and say: 'How about this little deal you have with this woman?'

At the 1960 Democratic Convention in Los Angeles, Johnson used some of what Hoover had told him in the dirty fight for the nomination. LBJ, it was said, stood for 'Let's Block Jack'. When Kennedy's money and superb organization won him the nomination, Johnson was furious. Early editions of the newspapers gave the names of three men Kennedy was considering as his running mate. Johnson's was not one of them. Johnson changed all that. He went to Kennedy and he said he would use the FBI material to blow Kennedy's 'family man' image out of the water if he was not included on the ticket. In 1960, even the information on Kennedy's wartime affair with Ingrid Arvad was dangerous. The war had only been over fifteen years and revealing that Kennedy had slept with a woman

239

so closely involved with Hitler could have lost the Democrats the vital Jewish vote.

Kennedy and his brother Bobby agonized over the decision, but could see no way out. Johnson had boxed them into a corner. Finally, Kennedy conceded.

'I'm forty-three years old,' he said. 'I'm not going to die in office. So the Vice Presidency doesn't mean a thing.'

Johnson saw it differently.

'I looked it up. One of every four presidents has died in office,' he said. 'I'm a gamblin' man, and this is the only chance I got.'

The next day Johnson was named as vice-presidential nominee.

As Vice-President, Johnson developed a close relationship with Kennedy's younger sister Jean. They travelled together to India in 1962. Jackie Kennedy was also very fond of Johnson, finding him 'very gallant, courtly'. At White House parties, she made a point of dancing with him. After Kennedy's funeral, she wrote to Johnson, thanking him 'for the way you have always treated me ... before, when Jack was alive, and now as President'.

Johnson's partnership with Hoover continued when he was in office, with Hoover providing him with any sleaze he could, especially if it concerned the Kennedys. Kennedy had been having sex with one of the hostesses on the family plane and brought her into the White House as assistant press secretary. Hoover supplied a full field investigation report on her, including some nude pictures she had posed for when she was still a senior at high school. When she came into the Oval Office to clear the Teletypes, Johnson would take the pictures out of their folder and examine them. It became quite a joke in the White House.

When Johnson became president and was pressed by a young aide to fire Hoover, Johnson replied famously: 'If you've got a skunk around, it's better to have him inside the tent pissing out, than outside the tent pissing in.'

Johnson used the White House secretaries as his own personal harem.

'One way, you could visualize Lady Bird as the queen in *Anna and the King of Siam*,' said one journalist who knew him well. 'It worked that way; you know the scene where she sits at table and all the babes – Lady Bird was the head wife.'

One 'very pretty young woman', a White House secretary, had sex with him on the desk in the Oval Office. Another, who was on secondment to the Johnson ranch in Texas, reported a nocturnal brush with LBJ. She was woken one night to find a man climbing into her bed.

'Move over,' he said. 'This is your President.'

Even Esther Peterson, head of the Women's Bureau in the Johnson administration, found that she 'had to bend a lot'. Johnson's humour, she noted, was largely based on women's sexual features.

When one aide reported that Congresswoman Green was giving a member of the administration trouble over an education bill, Johnson said: 'Tell him to spend the afternoon in bed with her and she'll support any god-damn bill he wants.' He told another aide to adopt similar tactics with a woman journalist who was criticizing his government. He took his own advice. He had regular sex sessions in the Oval Office with a female reporter from the *Washington Star*.

One blonde secretary was caught sitting on Johnson's lap. She said that she had tripped over a rug. He hired six beautiful secretaries and slept with five of them.

'I put high marks on beauty,' he said. 'I can't stand an ugly woman around or a fat one who looks like a cow that's gonna sit on her own udder.'

Johnson signed into law all the 1960s Civil Rights legislation. He was equally unprejudiced in his private life. One of his conquests was a beautiful black girl called Geraldine Whittington. Secretaries were not only entertained in the Oval Office. He also had sex with them on Air Force One and on *Sequoia*, the presidential yacht. If Johnson spotted a pretty woman outside the White House gates, he would send an aide out to get her.

'He may have been just a country boy from Texas,' said press secretary George Reedy, 'but he had the instincts of a Turkish sultan.'

Lady Bird knew of her husband's philandering. One Secret Service agent even claims that she caught Johnson having sex with one of his secretaries on a couch in the Oval Office. She accepted it stoically. 'That's just one side of him,' she said. Years later she explained to a television producer: 'You have to understand, my husband loved people. All people. And half the people in the world are women. You don't think I could have kept my husband away from half the people?'

Johnson told one young aide that he saw nothing wrong with having sex outside marriage. He bragged about his extra-marital affairs and sought constantly to impress his cronies with tales of his sexual prowess. Nothing, not even the most intimate details of his partners' anatomy, was held back.

Given Johnson's outrageous behaviour, it is curious that the only sex scandal to hit his administration was a homosexual one. On 14 October, 1964, just weeks before the election, Johnson's White House chief of staff Walter Jenkins was caught engaging in homosexual activities with a sixty-year-old man in the toilets of the YMCA. It was soon discovered that he had been arrested five years before doing the same thing in the same toilet.

At the time, security guidelines stipulated that 'homosexuals and other sex perverts' were not to be employed in government on the grounds that they were a security risk. When the story broke, Johnson's legal adviser had

Jenkins check into a hospital. Johnson then called Ho-over, who issued a report saying that Jenkins had not compromised national security. The scandal died down, but Republican wits suggested Johnson change his campaign slogan from 'All the way with LBJ' to 'Either way with LBJ'.

22

EXPLETIVES DELETED

Richard Milhous Nixon was sexually, as well as politically, enigmatic. Olga, his steady girlfriend at college, said: 'Most of the time I just couldn't figure him out.'

They had met at Whittier College when Nixon was standing in the student's presidential election. She wrote in her diary: 'Oh, how I long to hate Richard Nixon.' And she voted for his rival.

A few weeks later, they were both in a college production of *The Aeneid*. Cast as Dido and Aeneas, Nixon was supposed to declare his love for her and embrace her before they threw themselves on the funeral pyre. Sadly he was not up to exhibiting that much passion on stage. He tiptoed around her, gave her a simpering kiss, then tugged at her toga. It was more than the teenage audience could stand. His performance as a classical lover was greeted with boos and catcalls. It was, he said, 'sheer torture'.

'I was never so embarrassed in my whole life,' Olga recalled. Still they started going out together.

At Duke University, Nixon was stiff and stilted with women. 'Let's face it,' said one co-ed, 'he was stuffy.' But he could come up with a date if he was forced to.

'I don't believe that girls were as important to Dick as they were to the rest of us,' a fellow student said.

Later, when he was a partner in the law firm Wingert and Bewley in Whittier, California, he admitted that he was embarrassed when it came to handling a divorce case.

'This good-looking woman, beautiful really, began talking to me about her problem of sexual incompatibility with her husband,' Nixon confided. 'I turned fifteen colours of the rainbow.'

On 16 January, 1988, he met twenty-six-year-old school teacher Patricia Ryan. It was love at first sight. He asked her for a date. She said she was too busy and he blurted out: 'You may not believe this but I am going to marry you some day.'

Gradually, she got to like him and agreed to date him provided he 'made no declarations of love or proposals of marriage'.

One night, they went to Topsy's in East Los Angeles with another couple. It was a striptease joint, one of Nixon's enduring passions. Nixon made them dress for the occasion. He wore his mother's raccoon coat. The entrance fee was $3 that night because the famous 'blonde bombshell' Betty Roland was performing. Her act ended in a shambles when some guy in the front row touched her butt with a cigarette lighter. Despite this, Pat fell in love with Nixon and married him in 1940.

Even after they were married, Nixon could not stay away from strip shows. One night they went to Earl Carroll's nightclub in Los Angeles where, for $2.50, men competed to see who could throw the most garters on to the legs of the cancan dancers.

In office, Nixon tried to fire J. Edgar Hoover several times. Each time Nixon emerged from the meeting ashen-faced with Hoover still in place at the FBI. Then Nixon got lucky, or at least he thought he did. On 2 May

1972, Hoover died. Nixon greeted the news with characteristic expletives.

'Jesus Christ!' he said. 'That old cocksucker.'

Later, at the height of Watergate, Nixon cursed his luck. If the old cocksucker had still been alive, he could have contained the scandal and Nixon would have stayed on at the White House.

Riding high in May 1972, Nixon sent his aides scurrying over to FBI headquarters to retrieve his own file and other incriminating documents. The file was bulging. Hoover had even bugged the Oval Office.

Even before Nixon had entered the White House, Hoover had a fat file on him. Johnson had read it. He especially enjoyed one item. It was the story of Nixon's illicit affair with a modern-day Mata Hari.

In 1958, Nixon, then Vice-President, met Marianna Liu, a Hong Kong tour guide in her twenties. Nixon was forty-five and eighteen years married. They met again in 1964, 1965 and 1966 when Nixon travelled to Hong Kong as a private citizen. Liu was working as a hostess in the Den, the cocktail bar of the Hong Kong Hilton. Hoover had photographs of the two of them together.

Their meetings were not limited to the cocktail lounge. Liu and a waitress friend visited Nixon in the suite of his friend Bebe Rebozo at the Mandarin Hotel. He also sent her flowers and a bottle of her favourite perfume when she was ill in hospital.

The FBI took a particular interest because there were suspicions that Liu was an agent of the Communist Chinese government in Beijing. She had already been seen fraternizing with U.S. Navy officers. As Vice-President, Nixon had had a top-secret briefing on the People's Republic of China, so any contact with Liu could be classified as a security risk.

Liu was also being watched by British intelligence. At the request of the CIA, the Hong Kong Special Branch, using an infra-red camera, photographed Nixon through his bedroom window.

Despite the FBI's attempt to monitor any visa application from Liu, she turned up at the White House at Nixon's inaugural ball. Her visa application had been given top priority. She became a U.S. permanent resident and went to live in Nixon's home town of Whittier, California. The two of them reportedly met but when a newspaperman asked Liu about her relationship with Nixon, she said: 'Are you trying to get me killed?'

When Nixon had tried to sack Hoover, Hoover had taken great delight in personally showing Nixon Liu's file. This is how he kept his job, but Liu's file, good as it was, was too blunt an instrument to use to keep the White House in order day to day. Instead, Hoover leaked scurrilous rumours about White House aides. He produced a report saying that Watergate conspirators Haldeman, Ehrlichman and a third aide, Dwight Chapin, were homosexual lovers and that they had attended gay parties in the Watergate building. The source was a barman and regular FBI informant. The three men denied the charges, but it was enough to keep the White House in line.

When Nixon fell from power, he was replaced by Gerald Ford. Before he was married, he had an affair with stunningly beautiful co-ed Phyllis Brown. At college, he had fallen instantly in love with her. She became a model in New York and he and Phyllis modelled ski clothes together for *Look* magazine. After what Ford himself describes in his autobiography as a 'torrid four-year love affair', they split when Ford turned down offers to practise law in New York or Philadelphia and returned to his home town, Grand Rapids, Michigan.

He met his wife there during the 1948 election campaign. She had been born in Chicago, but brought up in Grand Rapids. She studied modern dance at Bennington

College in Vermont and joined the Martha Graham ensemble, supporting herself by working as a fashion model. She married for the first time at twenty-four, but divorced five years later. She married Gerald Ford three weeks before the election, beginning a sojourn in Washington that lasted nearly thirty years.

Although she was already ill when they entered the White House, Betty Ford rose to the challenge of becoming, unexpectedly, First Lady in 1974. Later that year she underwent radical surgery for breast cancer. Explaining her decision to discuss this openly she said: 'If I as First Lady could talk about it candidly and without embarrassment, many other people would be able to as well.'

Her autobiography, *Betty: A Glad Awakening* published in 1987, discusses publicly her drug and alcohol dependency. Asked why his wife's life story, rather than his own, had been made into a TV movie, Gerald Ford replied: 'My wife is much more interesting.'

In the 1976 election campaign, Jimmy Carter took the bold step of giving an interview to *Playboy* magazine.

'Committing adultery,' he said, 'according to the Bible – which I believe in – is a sin. For us to hate one another, for us to have sexual intercourse outside marriage, for us to engage in homosexual activities, for us to steal, for us to lie – all these are sins.'

He admitted: 'I've looked on a lot of women with lust. I've committed adultery in my heart many times.'

If that is the only place he has committed adultery, it makes him very unusual among presidents.

23

SINNING CITY ON A HILL

One of Ronald Reagan's early jobs was as a lifeguard. 'He was the perfect specimen of an athlete, tall, willowy, muscular, brown, good-looking,' a friend remembered. 'Of course, the girls were always flocking around him.'

In church, he could not take his eyes off Bee Drew. She had a boyfriend, so Reagan would go out with them as a foursome with Bee's friend Margaret Cleaver. He later claimed to be in love with Margaret but 'she was grown up enough to know we weren't grown up enough to call this anything but friendship'. Members of their church thought they would wed.

They went on to college together. With other couples, they dated at the graveyard near by, where they could huddle together against the old gravestones.

After college, 'Dutch' Reagan became a radio announcer in Des Moines, while Margaret went to spend a year with her sister in France. This left him one of the most eligible bachelors in the city. He soon found himself a new girlfriend, the sleek and glamorous Mary Frances from Monmouth, Illinois. However, one was not enough. Reagan began to be a man about town, hanging out at Cy's Moonlight Inn 'with many girls'. Soon he broke up with Mary Frances and began dating the shapely Miss Schnelle and the beautiful Jeane Tesdell. Then came Joy Hodges, who accepted his invitation to go horseback riding, but found she had nothing to wear.

In Hollywood, Reagan's first publicity shots show him bare-chested among a bevy of bathing beauties. He maintained his friendship with Joy Hodges after making the move to California, but fell under the spell of the green-eyed beauty June Travis, who played alongside him in his first movie *Love Is On The Air*. When the shooting was over, so was their romance.

He escorted Lana Turner – then renowned as the 'sweater girl' for her figure-hugging sweater in *They Won't Forget* – to the premiere of *Jezebel* in 1948. He also dated Ila Rhodes, a beautiful blonde contract player who appeared with him in *Secret Service of the Air* and *Hell's Kitchen*.

It was in *Brother Rat* he met 'pretty, pert' Jane Wyman. She fell in love with him. He thought of her as 'a good scout' and 'loads of fun to be with'. They married in 1940.

Reagan's movie career peaked in 1942 when he played a small-town playboy who awakes to find his legs have been amputated by a sadistic surgeon in *King's Row*. His character's immortal waking line: 'Where's the rest of me?' became the title of Reagan's 1965 autobiography.

After World War II, Reagan found it harder to get starring roles and, in 1947, became president of the Screen Actor's Guild. He continued making B-movies though.

In 1948, Jane Wyman filed for divorce, citing 'continual arguments on his political views', and began a torrid affair with Lew Ayres, her co-star in *Johnny Belinda*. There had obviously been other failings in her marriage. Wyman once told a reporter that Reagan was 'about as good in bed as he was on screen'.

After the divorce, he reverted to the bachelor life he had led in Des Moines, but now he knew some of the most beautiful women in the world. His attempted reconciliation with Jane Wyman foundered when Reagan was cast opposite Patricia Neal in *John Loves Mary*. The passionate kissing scenes won him back to bachelorhood.

Arlene Dahl remembered his 'paternal' kindness which she compared to that of Gary Cooper. Virginia Mayo complimented him on his gallantry.

'He did have, occasionally, young ladies on the set,' Mayo recalled. 'His charm was overwhelming and I think that was the basis of his career as an actor.'

He chatted openly about sex to Viveca Lindfors, his Swedish co-star in *Night Unto Night*, maintaining it was 'best in the afternoon after coming out of the shower'. However, Eddie Bracken remembers him around that time as a lonely guy.

'He was never for the sexpots,' Bracken said. 'He was never a guy looking for the bed. He was a guy looking for companionship more than anything else.'

Four years after his divorce, Reagan married another movie actress, Nancy Davis. Nancy's stepmother had been a stage actress and Nancy majored in theatre at Smith College, Massachusetts, where, according to Kitty Kelly's outrageous unauthorized biography *Nancy Reagan*, she had a secret lesbian affair with a classmate. As a debutante, she fell in love with a young man who committed suicide. This left her scarred.

During World War II, she got engaged to a naval officer, a distinctly feminine character, but she broke the engagement off after a couple of months. After that, she started a period of sexual experimentation and became what men at that time called 'accessible'. She even came on to married men who were friends of her parents.

Escaping to New York, she began hanging out with homosexuals, taking a gay man, with some slight bisexual tendencies, as her lover. In 1946, she won a role in the Broadway musical *The Lute Song* and began an affair with one of the dancers, who had slept with only two other women in his life.

During her time on Broadway, she had three dates with Clark Gable. Her phone number was passed around and she went out with a parade of men. Spencer Tracy organized a screen test for her, which led to an offer from Hollywood.

At MGM, she had an affair with Bernard Thau the casting director and her career flourished. In an interview shortly before he died in 1983, Thau said that Nancy was renowned for giving oral sex in the movie company's offices. It was one of the reasons she got a contract, according to Thau. It also made her very popular on the MGM lot.

In *The Peter Lawford Story*, written by his wife Patricia, Lawford is quoted as saying Nancy's 'avocation was to have a good time'. The quote goes on: 'When she was single, Nancy Davis was known for giving the best head in Hollywood.'

Lawford told his wife of a drive to Phoenix with Nancy and Bob Walker. 'Nancy would visit her parents, Dr and Mrs Loyal Davis, while Peter and Walker picked up girls at Arizona State University in Tempe, a Phoenix suburb,' she wrote. 'He claimed that she entertained them orally on those trips, apparently playing with whichever man was not driving at the moment.'

Nancy appeared in eleven movies. In her last film, *Hellcats of the Navy*, she played opposite her future husband. At the time Reagan was running around with a number of women – starlets, singers, models, beauticians and some big stars – most of them around ten years younger than him.

Reagan liked big, blonde, outdoor women like Doris Lilly. They had a brief affair. Reagan would send her flowers and love letters. Later, two of the letters came up at auction. They were bought by millionaire publisher Malcolm Forbes. He gave them to Nancy Reagan, but she asked him to wait until Reagan had left office before he handed them over, so she would not have to declare them as gifts. Lilly believes that Nancy has probably destroyed the letters out of jealousy, so that no one would know that he had anyone else in his life.

Another of Reagan's women at that time, Betty Powers, a former model, complained that Reagan was so obsessed with Wyman that he could not perform sexually. He seemed to be quite capable with Nancy. For Reagan, the promiscuous life soon palled. He told a friend: 'I woke up one morning and I couldn't remember the name of the gal I was in bed with. I said, "Hey, I gotta get a grip here."'

Reagan proposed to actress Christine Larson, but she rejected him. Soon after, Nancy told him she was pregnant.

Around that time, Selene Walters, then a nineteen-year-old blonde, complained that after Reagan picked her up at a Hollywood nightclub, he forced his attentions on her. 'They call it date rape today,' she told Kitty Kelly.

A week later, Reagan announced that he was going to marry Nancy. They married in March 1952. Two months later, they announced that Nancy was expecting a baby in December. In fact, the child, Patti, was born in October. (When she grew up, her name was to be linked romantically to that of presidential hopeful John Kerry). Reagan was not present at the birth. He was with Christine Larson. Their affair ended shortly after, when Reagan arrived at her apartment one afternoon to be greeted by a French actor wearing only a bath towel. Since then, except for a brief affair in 1968, he seems to have remained monogamous.

Retiring from the movies on her marriage, Nancy said: 'A woman's real happiness and real fulfilment come from within the home with her husband and children.'

However, according to Kitty Kelly's biography, Nancy did not get on well with her own children and entertained Frank Sinatra privately to 'lunch' in the White House while her husband was away. These private 'lunches' never appear in the First Lady's schedule and the family quarters were off limits to everyone while Sinatra was there. He would stay from 12.30 to 3.30 or 4 p.m. and there were strict instructions that the couple should not be disturbed. Sinatra would also accompany the First Lady to fundraisers. At White House parties she would dance dreamily with her 'Francis Albert', annoyed if her husband cut in. She would take up so much of his evening that even his wife Barbara complained.

This is all the more ironic as, according to Peter Lawford, Sinatra hated Reagan almost as much as he hated Nixon. During Reagan's governorship of California, he would change the words of 'The Lady Is A Tramp' to: 'She hates California, it's Reagan and damp ... that's why the lady is a tramp.'

During the 1988 election, it was alleged that George Bush had had a long-term affair with Jennifer Fitzgerald, an aide on his vice-presidential staff. She was no bimbo. She was in her mid-fifties and bore a striking resemblance to matronly Barbara Bush, who many people said looked old enough to be George's mother. The allegation of an affair came from American Ambassador Louis Fields who had arranged accommodation for Bush and Fitzgerald during a trip in 1984. He claimed 'first-hand knowledge of the affair'.

In the 1992 campaign, Hillary Clinton brought up the name of Jennifer Fitzgerald when allegations of infidelity were being made against her own husband. When a CNN reporter brought it up at a press conference, Bush grew heated. He complained about 'sleazy questions' and refused to respond – 'other than to say it's a lie'.

Jennifer Fitzgerald also denied the story. However, in the hot house that is Washington, there were continual rumours of Bush's 'extra-marital dalliances' and his association with a mysterious 'Ms X'.

This sort of press enquiry into the sex lives of the presidential candidates was unprecedented. After all, newsmen had deliberately hushed up sex scandals concerning Franklin D. Roosevelt and John F. Kennedy. The reason reporters broke with tradition and began reporting on the sex lives of the candidates was Democratic hopeful Gary Hart.

A handsome young Senator from Colorado, Hart liked to think of himself as another Kennedy. He had the same effect on women voters, leading one Republican to quip 'my heart is for Bush, but my bush is for Hart'.

Hart had a reputation as a womanizer which the press kept quiet about until he made an astonishing challenge. In 1987, he told *The New York Times* that he had nothing to hide and invited journalists to follow him.

Reporters from the *Miami Herald* took him at his word. They staked out his Washington townhouse and discovered that, while his wife was away, Hart was entertaining twenty-nine-year-old model Donna Rice overnight. When the story hit the front pages, Hart's wife Lee rallied to his defence.

'I made a mistake in my personal life,' Hart admitted on the TV, 'I've also insisted, as I think I have a right to, that my mistake in my personal life be put against the mistakes of this administration – selling arms to terrorists, lying to Congress, shredding documents.'

It would not wash. The *Washington Post* came up with another unnamed young woman who claimed to have had an affair with Hart. The *National Enquirer* followed up with pictures of Hart, Rice, Hart fundraiser William Broadhurst and Rice's friend Lynn Armadt at a cosy drinks party on board a yacht called, aptly, *Monkey Business* in Bimini. In *People* magazine, Lynn Armadt claimed that Hart and Rice shared the master bedroom. The Hart campaign quickly disappeared under a landslide of fresh allegations. From then on, for the American press, like its British counterpart, nothing was off limits.

24

SLICK WILLIE PULLS IT OFF

One casualty of the American press's new attitude to sex scandal was 1992 Democratic candidate Bill Clinton; but in some ways, 'Slick Willie' has also been a beneficiary.

Born in 1946, in Hope, Arkansas, Clinton saw himself very much in the Kennedy mould, especially after a visit to the White House when he was thirteen. While a Rhodes scholar at Oxford, he was already such a fearless stud that he propositioned leading feminist Germaine Greer.

He met Hillary Rodham at Yale Law School. In 1974, she went to Arkansas to act as his campaign manager in the congressional election. While she ran his campaign, he slept with another of his campaign workers. Nevertheless, Clinton married Hillary in 1975. There is little doubt that their marriage had its difficulties. She was once overheard, complaining: 'Bill, I need to be fucked more than twice a year.' However, she stood beside him while he served six terms as Governor of Arkansas.

He was practically unknown nationally when he declared his intention to run for president in 1992. His good looks and his Kennedyesque approach soon put him ahead of the field. Charges of marital infidelity – echoing Kennedy – attracted media interest.

The first allegations came from the supermarket check-out scandal sheet *The Star*. It ran the banner headline: 'DEMS FRONT-RUNNER BILL CLINTON CHEATED WITH MISS AMERICA'. It went on to name five women who, the newspaper said, had slept with Clinton.

Then a former nightclub singer from Little Rock, Arkansas, Gennifer Flowers, broke ranks. She claimed that she had been Clinton's lover for twelve years. She was, in newspaper parlance, the smoking bimbo.

'We made love everywhere,' Flowers told *Penthouse* magazine, 'on the floor, in bed, in the kitchen, on the cabinet, the sink … I called his testicles "the boys" and he called my breasts "the girls".'

She also said that he once tried to have sex with her in the men's room of the Governor's mansion in Arkansas; even that his jogging was a cover – he simply jogged over to her apartment. 'I admired his stamina, being able to make love with such enthusiasm after running,' she said. 'I used to tease him about running back much slower.'

At press conferences during the 1992 presidential campaign, journalists abandoned serious political questions for much more riveting stuff, such as 'Did the Governor use a condom?'

With consummate skill, Clinton found a silver lining in this cloud. He managed to secure an interview on CBS's *60 Minutes* directly after the Super Bowl, guaranteeing a massive, happy and slightly inebriated TV audience. With his wife beside him, he admitted that they had had marital problems, but said that was all behind them now. Asked whether 'problems' meant adultery, Hillary answered coolly that 'people who had been married a long time know what it means.' She offended Tammy Wynette fans by insisting that she was not just there to 'stand by my man'. Later, she had to apologize to Tammy when the spin doctors realized that they were in danger of losing the Country and Western vote.

Clinton also admitted to having smoked a marijuana joint. But he had not broken U.S. law because he had done it while a student in England, besides he 'did not inhale'. None of this – not even the allegation that he dodged the draft during the Vietnam war – prevented him from winning the presidency in 1992.

However, the allegations of sexual misconduct would not go away. With Clinton in the White House, state troopers from Arkansas who had guarded him during his twelve years as Governor portrayed him as a man with no morals. They said he would entertain women in the Governor's mansion while his wife was outside on the lawn. One trooper estimated that he had been intimate with hundreds of women.

'There would hardly be an opportunity he would let slip to have sex,' he said.

Alleged lovers include the wife of a prominent judge, a local reporter, a former state employee, a sales clerk from the cosmetics counter of a Little Rock department store and a black prostitute called Bobbie Ann Williams who claims that Clinton is the father or her mixed-race child, conceived during one of their thirteen sex sessions. There were reports of Clinton flaunting girlfriends in public, of one-night stands and even of him enjoying a sexual encounter in a car park of his daughter's school.

Then Sally Perdue, a former Miss Arkansas, claimed to have had an affair with Clinton in 1983, when she was a radio-show host in Little Rock. She told of how the then Governor of Arkansas would cavort around in her nightie. After the affair was over, she claimed she was offered a $40,000 job to keep quiet. A Democratic Party official told her 'to behave like a good girl' – with the implication that, if she didn't, she might get her legs broken, she said.

Around the same time, rock 'n' roll groupie Connie Hamzy claims that she was approached by a Clinton aide, who arranged a sexual encounter as she lay sunbathing by a swimming pool in a scanty bikini. In an interview with *Penthouse* magazine, she boasted that she had fondled the future president.

Blond power-company executive Jo Jenkins denied having an affair with Clinton, but his phone records show that he telephoned her eleven times in one day. One of the calls, at night, lasted ninety-four minutes. According to Gennifer Flowers, Clinton liked to indulge in mutual masturbation sessions on the phone, though she claimed she faked it because his voice on the phone did not turn her on.

Then Paula Jones came forward and accused Clinton of sexual harassment while she was Governor. She claims that she was invited to his hotel room, where he got out his penis and asked her to perform oral sex on him. She declined and is suing him for 'severe emotional distress'. She claims that she can substantiate her allegations by describing distinguishing characteristics of Clinton's genitals.

The White House responded to Paula Jones's oral allegations by trying to trash her. The Republicans gave her a make-over to make her look a little less like a moose and she pressed on. She did not want money, she said, she wanted an apology. But an apology would mean an admission. That was not a chance Puffin' Billy was prepared to take.

Billy Goat Gruff tried to keep the lid on things by claiming that, as President, he could not be taken to court in a civil matter while in office. That squeezed him by the 1996 election as his Republican opponent, Bob Dole, could hardly play mister clean. He was a twice-married divorcee, who was guilty of a little intra-marital shenanigans. Besides, he was as old as Father Time and dared not risk playing the sex card against a younger, demonstrably more virile man. Clinton may not be able to keep it in his pants, but at least he could get it up.

In the polling booths in November 1996, the American people gave another overwhelming endorsement to adultery. Well, the economy was booming, stupid. Clinton's wandering willy may have been a pain in the back passage, but it did not hurt in the pocket one bit. Besides, Clinton had that little-boy smile. And when he turned on the charm, the country – like Hillary – would forgive him anything.

It did not work on the Supreme Court, though. Justice delayed is justice denied, the justices maintained. Clearly the old men were jealous of all the action the president was getting – except for Clarence Thomas, that is. Apparently, Clinton reminded him of Long Dong Silver, star of a porn movie that played a large part in Thomas's Senate confirmation hearings in 1991. In a majority decision, the Supreme Court ruled that there was nothing in the Constitution that permitted the Chief Executive to whip his dick out any time he fancied. The Founding Fathers had not envisaged such a situation. Their affairs had been handled more discreetly, usually for money or with slave girls who had little opportunity to complain. A hearing in the Paula Jones case was set for May 1998.

The President's lawyer came close to stopping the lawsuit with an eleventh-hour compromise. Slick Willie, it seemed, was about to slide again. But hubris intervened. A White House aide told CNN that Paula Jones was pulling back because she knew her case was hopeless.

This riled Paula. She put her foot back on the gas and, for the first time, she got her mouth around the details of the presidential genital deformity. When he dropped his trousers and asked her to kiss his dick back in Little Rock, she said it was erect – and bent. Now, like a boomerang, she came back, this time with a bill for $2 million for 'emotional distress'. That is a bit steep for not giving the Governor a blow job. Hugh Grant only paid $100, satisfaction guaranteed. And he got to unclip Liz Hurley's safety pins for several years afterwards.

To limit the damage, Bill and Hillary took another honeymoon in, of all places, the Virgin Islands, along with half the world's press. The happy, if slightly overweight, couple were pictured dancing on the beach in their cozzies. This seemingly spontaneous act of affection was a carefully rehearsed photo opportunity.

There has long been talk inside the Beltway that Bill and Hillary had made a pre-presidential pact long ago. She would stand by him and cover up for his womanising, if she got a big job in government. That's why, when they got into the White House, she got to do to health care what he had been doing to Gennifer Flowers.

Some commentators were taken in by the Caribbean idyll. It was said that Hillary was no longer faking it. She had actually fallen in love with the big lug again. There was talk that Bubba would settle with Paula Jones, humiliatingly if necessary, because he did not want to risk disrupting his new-found marital bliss. Dream on. The giant slurry truck of fate was already hurtling towards the wind farm of destiny.

First, Tricky Dick had to testify under oath in a six-hour, closed-door hearing as part of the discovery phase of the Paula Jones case, while Paula sat only feet away. Under tough cross-questioning by Jones's lawyer, Clinton was asked whether he had been in, er, 'close proximity' to Paula.

Billy the Kid came out shooting from the hip. He said he could not recall meeting her. There had been so many.

He denied dropping his trousers and asking her to 'kiss it'. His attorney added: 'In terms of size, shape, and direction the President is a normal man.' Though the attorney did not say how he knew this.

The President was cross-examined generally about his sex life. Wild Willie admitted, humbly, that he was as pure as the driven snow.

Also called to give a deposition was a young woman named Monica Lewinsky. She had been an intern in the White House. She was asked whether she had had sexual relations with the President. This was relevant because, if Clinton had asked her for sex, it would show that he made a practice of importuning employees. Monica stoutly denied any such sexual relations had taken place.

But the appearance of Monica was a bimbo eruption like no other. This time there were pros waiting in the wings. Forty-eight-year-old Linda Tripp was not one of the women that Clinton bedded, though her ample and alluring bosom is vital to the story. Bill must have noticed those bazookas. Perhaps he made a grab for them and was denied. Or maybe she thrust them his way and he declined.

The tantalising Tripp was no Slick Willie fan. She was a Bush aide, one of the transitional team that smoothed the hand-over of power when Clinton entered the White House. Her other claim to fame was that she served Hillary's partner Vince Foster his last hamburger before he committed suicide – or was ruthlessly gunned down by the Clinton's hired assassins if you believe the right-wing conspiracy theorists. She also knew that Monica's denial was false.

Tell-tale Tripp was on hand in the White House to witness another staffer, Kathleen Willey, leaving the Oval Office 'flustered, happy and joyful...dishevelled, her face was red, her lipstick was off'. Willey refused to comment publicly and Tripp was denounced as a liar by the President's lawyers. Reluctantly, Willey was forced to make a deposition in the Paula Jones case. She later told all on TV. The President, she said, had taken her hand and placed it on his member. Was the Chief Executive aroused? she was asked. Yes, she said.

Tripp's blood was up too. At the Pentagon, she had befriended a young graduate named Monica Lewinsky, freshly transferred from the White House. In the powder room, Lewinsky revealed that she had pleasured the President in a small room off the Oval Office – surely not the same one where Warren Harding was caught *in flagrante* with Nan Britton. She had also give him a blow job under the desk while he talked on the phone to the president of Mexico.

La Tripp consulted New York literary agent and long-time Clinton-baiter Lucienne Goldberg. Goldberg had been a $1,000-a-week Republican spy in the McGovern camp in the 1972 Nixon 'dirty tricks' campaign. She went on to represent Mark Fuhrman, the racist cop caught lying in the O. J. Simpson trial. Nice girl.

Goldberg lapped up Tripp's salacious White House tittle-tattle. But they needed evidence. Lewinsky had turned to Trip as a shoulder to cry on and Tripp began taping Lewinsky's phone calls, pumping her for erotic detail. Everything she said directly contradicted what both Clinton and Lewinsky had said in their depositions in the Paula Jones case. Clinton had even denied their affair publicly, famously appearing on the television, wagging his finger at the press and saying: 'I did not have sex with that woman, Miss Lewinsky.' That must have hurt, but he was standing next to Hillary. What's a man to do? Surely no gentleman could admit to shafting a younger model in front of his trouble and strife. It would be humiliating.

But their public denials were contradicted by Tripp's tapes. Lewinsky, the daughter of a wealthy Californian physician, had said that the affair had begun soon after she had arrived in the White House. She was just twenty-one, still fresh from school in Beverly Hills. The video of her high school prom shows her in clinches with a string of boys. At college in Portland, Oregon, she was considered 'a bit flash' at the raucous barbecues the students held. There were even rumours of an affair with the professor. Monica professor. Monica was a young woman with a taste for older men. After graduating in 1995, her mother arranged for her to be an unpaid intern, or trainee, in the White House.

'There goes trouble,' said the White House staffer who interviewed her.

She was given a desk that lay between the Oval Office and the President's private apartment. Every time he walked by, it was plain that the President noticed her. She wore dresses or blouses with at least the top three buttons undone. But what particularly attracted Bill's attention was the thong that, on occasion, was known to rise suggestively above her waistband.

At first, White House wags put his attentions down to innocent flirtation. No one suspected that there was anything going on between them. But tongues started wagging when she turned up one night with a private visitors pass, something extremely difficult to get hold of. She said she was visiting a close personal friend in the Chief of Staff's office, but the person whose name she wrote in the security log had already gone home.

Gifts were exchanged. She bought him a tie that he wore when he gave his State of the Union address in 1997. He sent her flowers, and gave her a book of erotic verse and a dress, which she kept, unwashed, because, she boasted, it was stained with presidential semen. It was a *memento amori.* And famously she was filmed in a crowd eagerly awaiting the President's attention.

Secret service men were overheard saying that she should not be visiting the President's apartment so often – especially not when Hillary and Chelsea were away. She also appeared on the guest list at Camp David. Soon gossip spread throughout the White House. So Monica was transferred to a paid job in the Pentagon, where she developed a crush on another older man. But she continued to see the President, arriving late at night in figure-hugging dresses.

She began to get disillusioned though, when she discovered that she was not the only filly in Bill's stable. She began to record her own phone calls with the President. Some of the conversations were very explicit indeed. There were hot telephone sex sessions. Memorably, the Chief Executive expressed a desire to 'coat you with my baby gravy'. Not an appetising image, perhaps, but hardly a federal offence.

However, Lewinsky told Tripp that she would continue to deny any affair, so as not to screw the President. On the other hand, she said, she would not be screwed by him. It was a bit late for that. Giving a deposition in the Paula Jones case under oath, Monica had indeed denied fooling around with the Commander in Chief. This was perjury, which was indeed a federal offence.

Tripp went to Kenneth Starr, the special prosecutor on the Whitewater affair who was investigating irregularities in various property deals that took place in Arkansas when Clinton was Governor. Starr had already spent $25 million and three years getting nowhere. Tripp convinced Starr that Clinton, the country's chief law enforcement officer, had asked Monica to lie under oath, via his attorney and close friend Vernon Jordan. Suborning a witness and obstructing justice were federal offences, stiff charges worth ten years in the slammer. Here, at last, was something Starr could get his teeth into.

Starr ordered the FBI to wire Tripp's capacious cleavage. She then invited Lewinsky for cocktails at the Ritz Carlton in Crystal City where the G-men taped their girl talk.

Lewinsky began complaining to Tripp that the President was cheating on her with four other women – three of whom worked in the White House. It seemed he was running a state-sponsored seraglio. She called him 'The Creep' and 'El Sicko'. A woman scorned. And on one of

Tripp's tapes, Lewinsky gets down to nibbling on Billy's banana. All the time, the G-men's bugs were on the G-spot.

Monica said she had asked Bill Clinton why he did not settle the Paula Jones case out of court. He apparently replied: 'I can't – because then they would all come out of the woodwork.'

'Were there that many?' Lewinsky asked.

'Hundreds,' said Billy the Goat.

The Feds moved in. They seized a copy of Walt Whitman's *Leaves of Grass* – which contains the line 'Copulation is no more rank to me than death' – inscribed by the President's own fair hand, from Lewinsky's Watergate flat. They also seized jewellery that Clinton had bought for her while on holiday in Martha's Vineyard with Hillary and tore the place apart looking for that soiled frock with FBI labs in a state of high alert. Meanwhile, Starr gave twenty-four-year-old Monica an eight-hour grilling. Clearly, she was a major criminal.

News of Clinton's claim of other conquests leaked to the media. Soon the bimbo hunt was in full swing. Who were these four other lovelies the President was currently fooling around with? Who were the hundreds he had bedded during his political career? There were plenty of candidates.

Step forward former Miss America and *Playboy* centrefold Elizabeth Ward Gracen, who was said to have had an affair with the Unabanger when she was twenty-one. By this time she was a prominent TV star, who had left the country rather than be subpoenaed in the Paula Jones case. Then there was forty-eight-year-old Dolly Kyle Browning, who said her high school affair with Clinton lasted into his White House days. She claimed to have made love to him three times in a senator's hotel room. And, while he was Governor, they had sex in the basement of the gubernatorial mansion, frolicked in houses borrowed from friends and made love in a neighbour's back yard.

Leggy Susan McDougal went down for eighteen months for refusing to testify against Clinton. Her husband, Jim, said that he had intercepted an 'intimate' phone call between his wife and her President, and that she later admitted the affair.

'I'm a small town girl,' she told the press, 'a Southern Baptist, I wouldn't do that.'

Sheila Lawrence was then accused of making love to President Clinton while her millionaire husband turned a blind eye. In return, he was made US Ambassador to Switzerland. When he died, Clinton rewarded Sheila's discretion by having her husband's remains interred in Arlington National Cemetery, where John F. Kennedy is buried. He was later moved when it was discovered that he had lied about his military service.

Fearing they were being upstaged, old slappers came out of the woodwork too. Gennifer Flowers told CNN chatshow host Larry King: 'He's chance taker and he will make you take chances. He wanted to make love with Hillary nearby.' Clinton, she said, had made her pregnant and she had had to have an abortion. Meanwhile, Bill had been caught on tape saying Flowers could 'suck a tennis ball though a garden hose'.

Back in Little Rock, Sally Perdue reminded the nation that Bad Boy Billy liked nothing better than cavorting around her bedroom dressed in her black nightie. And thirty-three-year-old Bobbie Ann Williams took a lie detector test in an attempt to get child support for her seven-year-old son and Clinton-lookalike, Danny. Strapped to the polygraph, she claimed that her first paid encounter with the Governor took place behind a hedge in Little Rock. Later, she said, she organised three-in-a-bed sessions for him with another prostitute. The polygraph operator was sweating. She was not. The needles remained as steady as her accusations. She passed the lie detector test. White House security camera footage even revealed Clinton disappearing with a young blonde as he went to take a post-jogging shower.

But Clinton's affair with Monica Lewinsky was different. If it had really happened, the President, at the very least, had lied under oath during his deposition in the Paula Jones case. He was guilty of perjury. The press were soon asking if a young intern could really bring the most world's powerful man to his knees – as he had once brought her to hers. And the 'I' word – 'impeachment' – was mentioned.

It was then that the whole thing descended into farce. Consider the prospects. According to the Constitution, a President can only be impeached for 'high crimes and misdemeanors'. This was surely a low crime if ever there was one. However, by a curious legal quirk, adultery is a misdemeanour in the District of Columbia. But Slick Willie had that one covered too. He maintained that there is no mention of oral sex in the Bible. It is not condemned and, consequently, does not constitute adultery. So if the FBI labs were going to look for copious quantities of Clinton's DNA on Lewinsky's dress, they had better look for traces of her saliva as well.

Manfully, Bill fessed up to being 'emotionally close' to Monica. How close? As close as two of Marlene Dietrich's lovers – General James Gavin and French actor Jean Gabin – were said to be? Separated only by a French letter?

Politically, there were still problems. To impeach a President, the House of Representatives has to pass the Bill of Impeachment. But House Majority Leader, right-wing Republican Newt Gingrich, was hardly in a position to throw the first stone as he had used the Clinton defence himself. In a bitterly contended divorce case, he had denied 'sleeping with a lover' on the grounds that he had only had oral sex with her. I defy any man to sleep through that.

Once a Bill of Impeachment was passed, the President then had to be tried by the Senate. And the Senate was not looking forward to this one. It was packed with old roués. Where would Ted Kennedy stand on this one? After all, he had gone down with, if not on, an intern at Chappaquiddick in 1969. Surely he had been rooting for Bill all along.

Then there was the legendary Dixiecrat Strom Thrumond, a nonagenarian and still in the Senate. He was famed for his sexual antics. When he was judge he picked up a woman, who he had recently been condemned to death, from the county jail and drove her to the death house, making love to her on the way. He was twenty-three years older than his first wife and forty-four years older than his second. He was sixty-eight when he married a twenty-four-year-old former South Carolina beauty queen and gave her four children. Well known for groping women in the elevator in the Senate building, he kept a baseball bat in his office so that, when he died, the undertaker could use it to beat down his dick so they could close the lid of the coffin. How was he going to condemn a little rumpy-pumpy in the Oval Office?

Even old Republican fuddy-duddies like Jesse Helms could hardly condemn young Billy boy's youthful indiscretions without appearing jealous. Which one of them would not want a nubile, if overweight, nymphet sucking on their seal of office?

And as to lying about it? The old Southern gentlemen would understand that. There is such a thing as discretion. It was part of their code of behaviour. What sort of Yankee carpetbagger would sleep with a young lady, then brag about it on TV? No sir. You would lie about it in court, if necessary, to keep a young lady's honour intact.

The Republicans did not even want Clinton out. They would prefer to keep him on as a lame duck. If they kicked him out, the mantle would pass to Vice President Al Gore, who was considered by one and all to be a safe pair of trousers. He is so naïve about the workings of love that he thought it was sexy to claim that the 1970s' kitsch classic *Love Story* was based on his varsity wooing of his wife Tipper. The author and schmaltzmeister-general Eric Segal said it was not so. Al fled red-faced.

Later Al tried to charge up his act with a little testosterone, snogging Tipper at the 2000 Democratic Convention for what seemed like hours – and he still lost the election by a dangling chad.

As the pre-impeachment proceedings ground relentlessly on, the redoubtable Hillary was brought in to hold the line. She went on the chat shows and said she still loved and trusted her husband! – and was promptly dubbed 'the world's most powerful doormat'. There was a right-wing conspiracy to bring her husband down, she said. That's politics.

In the midst of the crisis, Bill delivered a barnstorming State of Union address. And there was no point in speculating about the state of the Clinton's union, not with Hillary glaring from the balcony like Cardinal Richelieu in a frock.

President Clinton may not have been on the best of form. There were bags under his eyes. Too many late nights. But with the economy booming, the budget was unexpectedly balanced and he had money to spray around. The assembled throng was up and down like a jack in the box. Even Newt Gingrich creaked to his feet, though he looked like he had sucked on a lemon. Al Gore was clapping so excitedly that he looked like he was going to rush out and hug a tree. But under the circumstances, he had to contain himself.

There was even a little sabre rattling in the direction of Saddam Hussein, threatening what the Arab press were already calling 'the war of Clinton's penis'. This got both Democrats and Republicans up again. In his speech, Bill gave them oral sex at its very best. They gave them their heart and he gave them his head. He had congress with Congress. Half of them looked like they wanted to follow him out to the parking lot and exchange bodily fluids.

Bill had kept his nerve and things began to turn in his favour. The Federal judge in charge of the Paula Jones case quashed her suit. Even if the incident in the hotel room she described had occurred, she had no civil case because she could not prove that she had been materially damaged by Clinton's behaviour. Indeed, after the incident, she had been promoted. And she could not show any emotional damage as she had gone on to get married.

But Ken Starr was not so easily seduced. Even though the Paula Jones case had gone down, if Clinton had lied under oath in his deposition, he was still guilty of perjury. And if he had put pressure on Monica Lewinsky to lie too, he was guilty of suborning a witness. And if he had had some gifts he had given Monica Lewinsky removed from her apartment – as was now being alleged – he was guilty of obstructing justice. As President, Clinton was the chief law officer of the United States. Maybe he could pervert young interns, but he was not allowed to do that to the course of justice.

Starr managed to make a deal with Monica Lewinsky. If she testified in graphic detail to the Grand Jury, holding nothing back, he would guarantee her immunity from prosecution. If she did not testify, he would charge her with perjury over her testimony in the Paula Jones case. At her trial, Clinton would be called as a witness, so he would be exposed anyway.

Monica had no choice. She took the deal. She told the Grand Jury that she had both given and received oral sex with the President on numerous occasions. She said that she had entertained him by dancing around naked and performing sexual acts with a cigar. Did no one spot the tell-

tale aroma when he lit up? She also said that he had penetrated her, but he had not 'finished off' inside her. This was
enough of a loophole for Clinton to continue to argue that
he had not had sex with her. Within the narrowest Biblical
definition, a sexual act means one that could result in
reproduction. This was a whisper away.

She also handed over the semen-stained dress that she
had kept. The semen proved to match a sample of DNA
provided by the President.

President Clinton then consented to testify to the Grand
Jury. But he would do so, not in person, but by a closed
circuit TV from the White House. Again, he stuck to his
guns. Although he admitted an 'inappropriate relationship' with Monica Lewinsky, he denied having sex with her
under the tight definition he had extracted from his
painfully close reading of the Bible. He denied lying under
oath and he denied asking anyone else to do so, arguing his
case with such brass neck that, at one point, he said
famously: 'It depends on what the meaning of "is" is.'

He went on television and admitted that he had deceived
the country and brought pain to his family, and he asked
for forgiveness. The press screamed that if he had only
admitted that he had had sex with Monica Lewinsky in the
first place, he would have been forgiven and the whole
thing would have been forgotten. But that was the one
thing he could not do. If he admitted that he had had sex
with Monica Lewinsky, he would be admitting that he had
committed perjury, both in his deposition in the Paula
Jones case and in his testimony to the Grand Jury, and that
he had lied to the American people. Besides, he was rising
in the polls.

Although almost every detail of the evidence presented
to the Grand Jury had already been leaked, the House of
Representatives voted to publish the Starr report both as
hard copy and on the internet. Clinton's televised testi-

mony was released too. The Republicans in the House hoped that this would do maximum damage to the Democrats before the mid-term congressional elections in November 1998.

It did the Republicans no good. The tide of gains in the House of Representatives that had been flowing with them since Bill Clinton had first entered the White House now ebbed, though they retained a majority. And in the Senate, they failed to gain the two-thirds majority they would need to remove him from office in an impeachment. Despite this, the House of Representatives voted to impeach him anyway.

According to the *National Enquirer*, the impeachment rattled Hillary and she lashed out at Bill. His Secret Service guards had to protect the President from his own wife. Courtesy of *The Star*, Bobbie Ann Williams has now had her son's DNA compared with that provided to the Starr Committee by Bill Clinton, but it was found that the President was not his father.

Meanwhile, the Senate duly sat and tried the President, with the Republicans dragging out the proceedings in the forlorn hope that some new and even more scandalous evidence against the President would be unearthed. As author of *Sex Lives of the U.S. Presidents*, I offered to appear for the defence as an expert witness. I felt it was my duty. But my testimony was not needed. Bill Clinton continued to soar in the polls. After a twenty-one day trial, he was acquitted on all charges. Slick Willie had pulled it off.

Clinton finished the second term with Hillary by his side. While Bill went globetrotting with a number of beauties, including Naomi Campbell – lucky man – Hillary got herself elected to the Senate. Still claiming that she was last person to know about the presidential hanky-panky, she is being groomed to run for President. So at some future date we face the prospect of Bill Clinton returning to the White

House, this time as 'First Lady'. And in that roll, he is going to have time on his hands.

And there is still the unanswered question: Is Hillary a lesbian? When she first entered the White House, she admitted going up to the roof to commune with Eleanor Roosevelt. 'Nough said.

25

MORE BUSH

'When I was young and irresponsible, I behaved young and irresponsible,' said George W. Bush. You can say that again. Oh, you did.

But you can't blame him for wanting to kick over the traces. He went to an all-male prep school called Kinkaid, which must have surely been known locally as 'kink aid'. Then he was sent east to Phillips Academy in Andover, Massachusetts, which modelled itself on British public schools and prided itself on turning out 'homogeneous boys' – known in America as 'cookie cutters' as that is what they are supposed to be a product of. A popular boy who liked to party, he was elected 'chief cheerleader'.

'Texans have a hard time relating to a male cheerleader,' he would say. His nickname was 'The Lip'.

He played baseball too. Each dorm fielded a team with names such as the Crotch Rots and Stimson Steams, after the former Secretary of War, Henry Stimson, and the way a fresh dog's turd steams in the snow.

At Yale – still an all-male institution while George Junior was there. He was known as a hard drinker. The life of the party, he was elected president of the Delta Kappa Epsilon fraternity by acclamation.

'The DKE frat house was the site of soul bands and dancing and dates. There was a lot of alcohol,' recalled a friend of Junior's. Another denizen said: 'If he didn't use marijuana at that point, he wasn't alive.' This was Yale's *Animal House*

As frat pack leader, George Junior got into trouble when he stole a Christmas wreath to hang on the door of the frat house. More publicised trouble came when *The New York Times* accused DKE of a 'sadistic and obscene' initiation process and Junior only escaped being arrested for stealing Princeton's goal post before a varsity match because his father had just been elected to Congress. He was run out of town and has not returned to Princeton, New Jersey since. George Junior was merely 'making up for lost time,' it was said. But it could not have helped having a father who had been nicknamed 'Rubbers' in Congress because of his stance on family planning.

While George Junior was at Yale, he got engaged to Cathryn Lee Wolfman. She had been at Smith College in nearby Northampton, then transferred to Rice University in Houston – not to get away from the drunken lout, I trust. Maybe it was because Rice was mixed sex. The *Houston Chronicle* announced: 'Congressman's Son To Marry Rice Co-Ed.' And, as the engagement had been announced at Christmas, the gossip columnist claimed: 'Cupid Hitched A Ride On Santa's Sleigh'. They planned to marry in the summer of 1967. But they had split by then.

'I was crazy about her for a year,' said Bush later, 'but we decided not to get married in between my junior and senior year in college.'

Wolfman married a Harvard MBA two years later, but did not forget her entanglement with Bush.

'I loved him,' she said. 'But I have no thoughts of "what if" – no regrets. I was engaged to him. I was glad I was engaged to him. The relationship died and that was that.'

However, friends say that among the old-money social circle that the Bushes moved in there were some 'nasty, snobbish whispers' about Wolfman's 'merchant' family background.

'Given her last name and her stepfather's prominence in the garment industry, the Bush family pressured their son to call off the wedding because the prospective bride had a Jewish background,' said a friend. The Bushes are Episcopalians, as was Wolfman. 'They both took it hard, especially George. He was always a wild and crazy guy, but losing the women he loved, combined with the fear of going to Vietnam, kind of pushed him over the edge.'

George Junior consoled himself by dating Tina Cassini, daughter of veteran movie actress Gene Tierney and fashion designer Oleg Cassini.

'She was a real sweet, pretty girl and when she was in town we were all rushing to take her out,' recalled another friend who dated her.

It is thought that George Dubya's father pushed them together.

'Mr Bush knew exactly what he was doing,' said a friend. 'He would set up guys and girls that he thought belonged together.'

For George Dubya himself it was 'a real salvation to have a woman that everyone wanted to be with'.

'There was that kind of thrill there,' said a fellow Yale alumnus. 'She was a real show pony, and George latched on to her. They paraded for a summer. Tina was spectacular... It was a good fling.'

However, Tina was a good deal younger than Dubya and had to go back to school at the end of the summer.

After graduation, he was liable for the draft. Instead he joined the Texas National Guard and somehow found himself fast-tracked to become a fighter pilot like his dear old dad. Although he would theoretically be on active service, he stood little chance of being sent to Vietnam. However, it must be said that not one square inch of Texas was conceded to the Viet Cong while George Junior was defending it.

In the National Guard, Dubya made it his business to 'fly-hard, play-hard, drink-hard' and generally continued 'being the wild Bush son'.

'He basically continued the partying tradition post-college,' recalled one Yale classmate. 'He graduated one day, enlisted in the National Guard the next, went to basic training in San Antonio for a few weeks, and then never let his foot off the accelerator of life.' But there was a new sexual element to his reckless behaviour: 'He flew jets, drove fast cars and screwed more women than Hugh Hefner.'

In 1968, he packed up his sporty, blue Triumph TR-6 and drove to flight training school at Moody Air Force Base near Valdosta, Georgia. There he was known as a good pilot and 'a guy who could hold his own at the bar'. In fact, there was only one bar in town, and one whorehouse, both reputed to be owned by the local sheriff.

'Friday night at the officers club was a big deal,' said Valdosta graduate Colonel Ralph Anderson. 'There was draft beer, and all the girls from town came in.'

And it was not just local girls. They were bussed in from all over the state.

'There were the aviation groupies that would come to the club a lot,' said fellow trainee Roger Dahlbeerg. 'Some were very nice girls, and some you just knew what they were there for. It wasn't a bad place to spend a Friday night.'

'Everybody got crazy,' said Anderson. Especially George Dubya. On more than one occasion, he stripped off and danced on the bar naked, lip synching to the tune on the jukebox. He was one tight little Bush.

George Dubya admitted that he 'worked hard and

played hard' during flight training in Georgia. But, presumably, he kept his clothes on when a government jet picked him up from the air base to ferry him to Washington for a date with President Nixon's oldest daughter Tricia. Apparently the President's matchmaking was part of a deal to persuade George Bush Senior to give up his congressional seat and run for the Senate.

Later Junior gave up his career as an exotic dancer in the Officers' Club on a Friday night to date a 'Georgia peach' who some thought would become Mrs Dubya. Years later, Bush conceded that there had been such a woman, but he could only remember her first name, which was Judy.

Others say that he never had any intention of marrying her, and was just stringing her along, although he repeatedly promised to take her back to Texas as his wife.

'He was very much in love back then,' said a flight-school drinking buddy, 'but Junior wasn't about to settle down and raise a family, which was exactly what she wanted. He'd get drunk and promise her a big church wedding with all the trimmings, but when he sobered up he'd say, "I must've been out my goddamn mind when I told her that."'

Certainly family life held no appeal. He was more at home in seedy nightclubs. There was talk of marijuana and cocaine use too. But that did not stop him making speeches on his father's behalf in the 1970 Senate race when he returned to Texas. Bush Senior lost. But George Junior gained a reputation of being a 'Winston-bumming preppy with a disarming smile and an eye for young women and a taste for beer, Jack Daniels and martinis' in his home state. Later he said: 'I choose not to inventory my sins because I don't want anybody to be able to say, "Well, the governor of Texas did it, why shouldn't I?"'

'We all experimented back then,' recalled one of his

many girlfriends from that period. 'But you have to remember that George was just living for the moment. He never
dreamed or schemed of running for governor, let alone
president.'

By this time he had moved into a one-bedroom bachelor flat in a singles-orientated apartment complex
called Chateau Dijon on Beverly Hills Street in Houston.
It was inhabited by girls from Rice University and small-
town Texan women who had come in to the city to work
as secretaries for the downtown oil companies. Co-ed
volleyball games, impromptu water polo matches and
poolside beer-blast parties were the order of the day. And
he liked the company of young women. Spying an older
woman, a friend of the family, one night in the nearby
Milieu Club, he asked drunkenly: "So – what's sex like
after fifty anyway."

Despite his frank talking, he was never without a date.
Friends said he spent 'enormous amounts of time courting
women'. One of them was the sister of his tennis partner
Peter Knudtzon, who was negotiating the purchase of horti-
cultural interests in the US and Central America.

Already known universally as 'Dudya', he worked on
another failed senate race, this time for a friend of his
father's in Alabama. He criss-crossed the state as an unmarried man and was remembered as a 'party boy who couldn't
keep is hands off the girls'. It was said that he was 'addicted
to strong drink and women'.

Then he went to Harvard Business School, where he
boasted: 'I've got my daddy's eyes and my mother's mouth.'

'We all had steady girlfriends,' said a classmate, 'one
week at a time. Drinking and womanising – what else is
there to do in your spare time? George was no different
than anyone else.'

After that he went into the oil business in Texas at a time
when OPEC had hiked up the oil price and there were lines

at gas stations. A speed limit of 55 m.p.h. was applied to the freeways to cut oil consumption and a jovial Texan bumper sticker read: 'DRIVE 95, FREEZE A YANKEE.' But Dubya did not get cold. A friend in the oil industry recalled his 'constant bed-hopping with West Texas bimbos'. It seemed that he had to hop around other people's beds because his own bed was broken, possibly by too much hopping. Its frame was lashed together with neckties.

George Junior was not successful in the oil business – despite the favourable conditions – and often let his date pick up the bar bill. It didn't matter.

'All the ladies were going crazy over him,' recalled Julia Reed, who met him at a wedding and later became a writer for *Vogue*. Even 1970s fashion did not put them off.

'When coupled with the young George's bad-boy good looks, the total package was enough to send the many eligible twenty-somethings into a collective swoon,' she said.

Moving the centre of his operations to the Midland Country Club, he spend nights in the sweaty honky-tonks of Odessa, twenty minutes to the west.

'Wherever he went, he would have a date,' recalled an admiring friend, 'and she would be a pretty good-looking one too.' And when he did not – or even when he did – friends would furnish him with fresh phone numbers.

Dubya turned thirty in 1976. By that time both his father and grandfather had been war heroes, academic over-achievers and self-made millionaires. When asked what he had done with his life up to that point, Dubya said: 'Drinking and carousing and fumbling around.'

Then at a back-yard barbecue he met public school librarian Laura Welch, who was also a resident of Chateau Dijon. They were engaged within days. Then, without telling anyone, he introduced her to his family. Not knowing the situation, brother Jeb went down on one knee, as if making a mock proposal. Dubya flushed.

'Did you pop the question to her, George, old boy?' asked Jeb, equally embarrassed.

'Yes, as a matter of fact he has,' said Laura, 'and I accepted.'

'We didn't even know he wanted to get married until he showed up at the door with this beautiful creature, Laura, and announced that she was going to be his wife,' said his mother Barbara.

The Welches feared he would blow it by being too eager.

'I was afraid George was going to ruin the whole thing because he was rushing it,' said her mother. 'In the past, when Laura brought home these nice young men from SMU [Southern Methodist University], that had turned her off.'

But this time she was not turned off. Three months later they were married. There was no time even for a honeymoon. He was running for Congress.

At Laura's behest, he sobered up, became a born-again Christian and got boring. However, his new-found faith did not stop him smearing televangelist Pat Robertson who was contesting the 1988 primaries against Bush Senior. Dubya dished the dirt on another televangelist and Robertson supporter, Jimmy Swaggart, who had been caught, several times, watching pornography in sleazy motels with prostitutes. He also stuck up for his father, when Bush Senior was accused of bonking his secretary, Jennifer Fitzgerald. Then he bought the baseball club, the Texas Rangers. And what red-blooded Texan does not fantasize about cheerleaders – even if he had been one himself?

When George Dubya ran for President in 2000 against incumbent Al Gore, sex never raised its lovely head. All sorts of other corruption surfaced, though, with brother Jeb's state delivering its decisive electoral-college votes for Junior despite, it seemed, the wishes of the majority of its voters. In his first terms in office, at least, Dubya failed to deliver a sex scandal of Clintonesque proportions. But with a background as colourful as George Dubya's he was never going to have an easy ride and there was already movement under the covers.

According to the Russian news agency Pravda, people who knew George Bush very well in his pre-presidential life were not really surprised when Margie Schoedinger, a resident of Missouri City, Texas, filed a lawsuit against Bush, alleging sexual abuse and harassment. She said that she had been strongly recommended to keep her mouth shut and, when she did not, three unknown men attempted to kidnap her. The kidnap was thwarted, but she claims neither the Sugar Land police nor the FBI took any action against the perpetrators.

Schoedinger maintains that she and her husband were drugged and she was raped by the then governor of Texas George Dubya. Her husband may have been raped too. She does not know. As a result of her ordeal she miscarried. Her husband was fired from his job. He has been unable to find work and has been denied federal unemployment benefit. Pravda says that a background investigation revealed Margie Schoedinger has no criminal record and had dated George W. Bush as a minor. But Sugar Land police say they have no record of any investigation.

Working as her own counsel, Margie Schoedinger is looking for a mere $49 million dollars compensation for emotional distress, loss of freedom and ability to pursue her own dreams, alienation of affection from her spouse, loss of privacy, being disparaged on the internet, and loss of her ability to be a Christian writer'.

'It is hard to say if this woman's story is true or not,' says Pravda. 'Who knows, probably, she is one of thousands of American women who perform sexual favours to high-ranking politicians of America.'

The case, it says, is comparable to Bush's actions in Iraq and Clinton's fumblings as governor of Arkansas. And here was me thinking the Cold War was over.

CHRONOLOGY

George Washington (1732–1799), President 1789–1797
John Adams (1735–1826), President 1797–1801
Thomas Jefferson (1743–1826), President 1801–1809
James Madison (1751–1836), President 1809–1817
James Monroe (1758–1831), President 1817–1825
John Quincy Adams (1767–1848), President 1825–1829
Andrew Jackson (1767–1845), President 1829–1837
Martin Van Buren (1782–1862), President 1837–1841
William Henry Harrison (1773–1841), President 1841
John Tyler (1790–1862), President 1841–1845
James K. Polk (1795–1849), President 1845–1849
Zachary Taylor (1784–1850), President 1849–1850
Millard Fillmore (1800–1874), President 1850–1853
Franklin Pierce (1804–1869), President 1853–1857
James Buchanan (1791–1868), President 1857–1861
Abraham Lincoln (1809–1865), President 1861–1865
Andrew Johnson (1808–1875), President 1865–1869
Ulysses S. Grant (1822–1885), President 1869–1877
Rutherford Hayes (1822–1893), President 1877–1881
James Garfield (1831–1881), President 1881
Chester Arthur (1829–1886), President 1881–1885
Grover Cleveland (1837–1908), President 1885–1889 and
    1893–1897

SEX LIVES OF THE U.S PRESIDENTS

Benjamin Harrison (1833–1901), President 1889–1893
William McKinley (1843–1901), President 1897–1901
Theodore Roosevelt (1858–1919), President 1901–1909
William H. Taft (1857–1930), President 1909–1913
Woodrow Wilson (1856–1924), President 1913–1921
Warren G. Harding (1865–1923), President 1921–1923
Calvin Coolidge (1872–1933), President 1923–1929
Herbert Hoover (1874–1964), President 1929–1933
Franklin Delano Roosevelt (1882-1945), President
 1933–1945
Harry S. Truman (1884–1972), President 1945–1953
Dwight D. Eisenhower (1890-1969), President 1953–1961
John F. Kennedy (1917–1963), President 1961–1963
Lyndon Baines Johnson (1908–1973), President
 1963–1969
Richard Milhous Nixon (1913-1993), President
 1969–1974
Gerald R. Ford (1913–), President 1974–1977
James Earl (Jimmy) Carter (1924-), President 1977–1981
Ronald Reagan (1911–), President 1981–1989
George Bush (1924–), President 1989–1993
Bill Clinton (1946–), President 1993–2000
George W. Bush (1946), President 2000–

INDEX

INDEX